extravagant

extravagant

DISCOVERING
A LIFE OF
DANGEROUS
GENEROSITY

brady boyd

HOWARD BOOKS

ATRIA

New York · London · Toronto · Sydney · New Delhi

An Imprint of Simon & Schuster, Inc.
1230 Avenue of the Americas
New York, NY 10020

Published in association with The Bindery Agency, www.TheBinderyAgency.com

First Howard Books/Atria Paperback edition October 2022

HOWARD BOOKS / ATRIA PAPERBACK and colophon are trademarks of Simon & Schuster, Inc.

For information about special discounts for bulk purchases, please contact Simon & Schuster Special Sales at 1-866-506-1949 or business@simonandschuster.com.

The Simon & Schuster Speakers Bureau can bring authors to your live event. For more information or to book an event, contact the Simon & Schuster Speakers Bureau at 1-866-248-3049 or visit our website at www.simonspeakers.com.

Interior design by Dana Sloan

Manufactured in the United States of America

1 3 5 7 9 10 8 6 4 2

Library of Congress Cataloging-in-Publication Data is available.

ISBN 978-1-9821-0140-4
ISBN 978-1-9821-0141-1 (pbk)
ISBN 978-1-9821-0142-8 (ebook)

For Pam, my best friend and the most generous person I know

Let us hold unswervingly to the hope we profess, for he who promised is faithful. And let us consider how we may spur one another on toward love and good deeds, not giving up meeting together, as some are in the habit of doing, but encouraging one another—and all the more as you see the Day approaching.[1]

—Author of the Book of Hebrews

We owe something to extravagance, for thrift and adventure seldom go hand in hand.

—Jennie Jerome Churchill,
mother of Sir Winston Churchill

Contents

Contents

Author's Note

W HEN I RECEIVED THE typeset pages of this book from my publisher, along with a request to provide my final input on its content, like 90 percent of people the world over, my family and I were under stay-at-home orders from our local officials, self-quarantining to subdue the spread of the novel coronavirus that showed up in late 2019. As I reviewed the chapters you're about to read, I shook my head in awe over how fast everything has changed. What was considered "ordinary life" a few weeks ago I now consider outright dreams: holding staff meetings, going out to dinner with my wife, taking my kids to see a movie, getting on an airplane to go somewhere just for fun . . . let alone worshipping with my brothers and sisters at New Life—in person, on a Sunday morning, all in one room. In a flash, life was upended, and as of this writing, it remains upside down.

There was another thought that kept occurring to me, though, as I reviewed this book you hold: regardless of these wild, unforeseen circumstances, the message remains steadfastly true. Maybe more than ever, it is during times of crisis when those of us who have devoted ourselves to God's will and ways get to pray up and show up and shine. We get to trust God in new and perhaps deeper ways. We get to come alongside those who are suffering—in this case from the loss of loved ones, the loss of businesses they started with their own two hands, the loss of key events on their spring schedule, the loss of their dreams—

to bring them food, and funding, and hope. We get to work through the challenges that something like a pandemic introduces, while knowing with *absolute certainty* that God is not caught off guard, that God remains on his throne, and that God has the victory in the end. In a word, we get to live *extravagantly*, believing that all we have comes from God, and that the best way to invest the resources he has given us is to let him preside over it all.

Introduction

Give and Take

ONE OF THE REAL PERKS of pastoring the same church for a dozen years (and counting) is that I get to see what people are like not just for a few minutes here and there, but over the long haul—across months and years and, if all goes well, decades. And while spiritual maturity has dictated that I learn to appreciate all sorts of people, there is one type of person I'm drawn to more than any other, and unapologetically so. People in this category have "yes" faces. They are calm but energetic, present but still purposeful with their time. They are curious. They ask questions. They draw you out, genuine in their desire to know how you're doing, what you're up to, what you're learning, how you feel. They are tuned in to their surroundings, aware of hurts, of gaps, of need. They have a knack for always making sure that people are being tended to: the overwhelmed single mom, the local shop owner who had to go out of business, the worship leader whose wife just suffered a stroke.

These are women and men who have full-to-the-brim lives and are

1

running their own firms, hitting their own corporate objectives, raising their own families, paying their own bills, and making their own lives work—yet, somehow, they still have bandwidth to *inquire about someone else*. Not occasionally. Not even frequently. But rather all the time.

These are the givers. They are the fighters. The supporters. The advocates. The ones who love and serve and care. They step forward and offer to help; they stay until the work is done. They are generous with their resources, sometimes lavishly so. Their "time, talent, and treasure"—they give of these things reflexively without expecting anything in return.

Astoundingly, despite these characteristics being exceptional, we have not a few or a handful of these people around New Life Church in Colorado Springs, Colorado, but rather scores upon scores of them. I've been watching them. I've been studying them. I've been culling lessons from their lives. This book? It's a manual for this kind of exceptional living, for becoming the *extravagant people* we're intended to be.

WHAT IS EXTRAVAGANCE?

In these times of hyper-consumerism, the mere mention of the word "extravagant" may make you wince. Extravagance in our day doesn't exactly conjure images of anything compassionate, admirable, or wise. There's the pro sports team owner who drops eighty grand on a single bottle of champagne after his team nabs the title. There's the preening, posing red-carpet people whose getups run them upward of $200,000 each. There's rapper Jay-Z with his nice, new $8 million Maybach Exelero, the most expensive car on the road today. *That* stuff is extravagant. And that ain't us.

In a world where 815 million of its 7.6 billion people (roughly 10 percent) go to bed hungry every night,[1] is extravagance what we want to be known for? Is *excessive* what we want to become?

We're more . . . measured than that, aren't we? More responsible, more restrained. For most sober-minded Christ followers, the subtlest whiff of extravagance makes us sort of cringe. Like Judas Iscariot at Jesus' pre-Passover dinner party, we take in lavish displays with a critical spirit, wondering why anyone would waste an entire pint of high-priced perfume on mopping up the floor.

And yet.

We do well to remember that between that pour of perfume and the floor were the feet of the Messiah, and he had a far different take. When Judas objected to Mary's anointing of Jesus—"Why wasn't this perfume sold and the money given to the poor? It was worth a year's wages," John 12:5 reports—Jesus told Judas to get a life. "Leave her alone," he said. "It was intended that she should save this perfume for the day of my burial. You will always have the poor among you, but you will not always have me" (v. 7–8).

Such an extravagant gesture, the pouring out of that perfume. And yet far from criticizing or merely condoning Mary's behavior, Jesus *commends* it. To which we might ask, "What is *that* about?"

THE POWER OF A CAUTIONARY TALE

When our kids were young, Pam and I noticed that while many of the (very light, if I do say so myself) disciplinary measures that our kids were made to suffer were met with whining, complaining, defensiveness, huffs and puffs, and sometimes outright defiance, there was one response to their misbehavior that actually *reeled them in* rather than pushed them away: empathy.

Once they were out of the tantrum-prone toddler years and had achieved a measure of interpersonal savvy, Pam and I learned that the easiest way to hold their attention—and the surest way to drive home our point regarding why their wrongdoing was so very, very *wrong—*

was not to preach or teach or rant or rave but rather to whisper six simple but powerful words: "I did that one time too ..."

In the face of such a sentiment, Abram's and Callie's eyes would widen. They would lean in. The tears of shame and contrition would stop flowing as rapt attention took control. "Really?" they'd say. "*You?*"

They'd nearly be salivating by this point. "Tell us more, Dad! Tell! Us! More!"

We love hearing of others' wrongdoing, don't we? I'm a student of journalism, and these days that entire industry is pretty much riding on the premise "If it bleeds, it leads"—and for good reason: it's *true*. We can't get enough of the scandalous, the salacious, the spicy. Good Christian folk cloak such interest by elevating their quest for information to the category of "prayer requests," but we all know it's a sham. Even the holiest people I've met are still dying to know what really went down.

This insatiable appetite for the sensational is probably why as a culture we have always loved fables and fairy tales and teaching stories that come with a moral in tow. You remember the one about the shepherd boy who contrives multiple wolf attacks on the town's prized herd of sheep, causing the villagers to rush to his aid. Once there, they realize that the boy was blowing smoke—that is, until a wolf showed up and really *did* attack the sheep. The boy cries out for help, but this time nobody shows.

We can read or listen to this story and learn secondhand the valuable lesson that those who lie tend not to be believed. We can feel righteous as we take in the boy's misbehavior because of course *we* would never lie like that. Or at least we'd never get caught.

How about the fabled emperor and his fancy new clothes? Those stupid and incompetent villagers, as the story calls them, are too insecure to call a spade a spade when their fearless leader parades past them in his customary and also invisible attire.

We would never be that stupid, right?

Such is the power of these tales. If we have ears to hear, we can spare ourselves a boatload of pain. Or, at a minimum, on the heels of an idiotic misstep, we can rest assured that we're not the only ones who were dumb enough to do *that*.

HOW TO BE WISE

When searching for a way to convey a whole new way of living to a people who weren't sure they wanted to change, even Jesus himself reached for simple teaching stories—for parables, short fictitious stories that are long on instruction and advice. "The parables are nothing more than extended similes ('the kingdom of God is like . . .') and therefore far removed from the mysterious world of allegory," wrote New Testament scholar Craig Blomberg.[2]

Jesus' disciples' eyes might have glazed over if he had come at the kingdom-of-God ideals head-on, but a story about weeds and wheat or a mustard seed or a little leaven or a fishing net? These were things that the first-century mind could get behind. And so Jesus reached for those. Again from Blomberg: "As for Jesus' purpose in speaking in parables, since he wanted to win his audiences over to his point of view, he had to be intelligible to them."[3]

Just as in the cultural fables that have stood the test of time, Jesus' stories served to help his audience avoid idiocy. Tomfoolery, some might call it. Being Joe Sixpack, as I'm known to say. But they did something else as well. Not only did they explain how to avoid being foolish; they demonstrated how to be wise.

As a matter of course, Jesus' parables placed both a wise person and a miscreant in a given setting, introduced some sort of event or challenge, and then showed what each did as a result. Inherent in these stories was a question: Which action would you yourself take? Would you do as the foolhardy chose to do? Or would you emerge as one who was wise?

No surprise here; the character Wisdom is always a reflection of God. In the Parable of the Sower (Mark 4:1–20), we see in the rich soil God's sturdiness and faithfulness and depth. In the Parable of the Weeds (Matthew 13:24–30), we see in the weeds that are fit only to burn God's certainty that evil has already been defeated, that it stands no chance of winning in the end. In the Parable of the Persistent Friend (Luke 11:5–8), we see in the man who eventually provided the beggar bread God's plea that we would come to him with our every need and that we should trust him to rise, to concede, to open the door and feed our souls.

Down through the myriad parables we could go, collecting character traits of our heavenly Father at every turn. And while we'd never come up lacking, there is one parable that, on this topic of generosity, of *extravagance*, is head and shoulders above the rest. Any guesses as to which one it is?

I've done a little straw polling on this topic, and the parable that rises to the surface with great frequency is the Parable of the Prodigal Son, which happens to be my all-time favorite one. The boy coming to his senses, the father's warm embrace, the elaborate party that ensues—what's not to love?

But despite my fondness for this tale, there is one parable that trumps even that one: the Parable of the Good Samaritan. If you're looking for the clearest possible picture of the heart of your heavenly Father, look no further than the tenth chapter of the book of Luke.

THE EXTRAVAGANT HEART OF GOD

In case it's been a while since you've read the parable, I'll recount it for you here. You might grab a pen (or have a fingertip ready, if you're reading digitally), so that each time you find a reference to the Good Samaritan—either that actual phrase or else a pronoun referring to him—you can mark it in a distinctive way. We are going to spend the balance of this book diving deep into the specific choices the Good Samaritan made, and having his words and actions fresh on your mind will prime the pump for that work.

Now, to Luke 10:25–37.

On one occasion an expert in the law stood up to test Jesus. "Teacher," he asked, "what must I do to inherit eternal life?"

"What is written in the Law?" he replied. "How do you read it?"

He answered, "Love the Lord your God with all your heart and with all your soul and with all your strength and with all your mind'; and, 'Love your neighbor as yourself.'"

"You have answered correctly," Jesus replied. "Do this and you will live."

But he wanted to justify himself, so he asked Jesus, "And who is my neighbor?"

In reply Jesus said: "A man was going down from Jerusalem to Jericho, when he was attacked by robbers. They stripped him of his clothes, beat him and went away, leaving him half dead. A priest happened to be going down the same road, and when he saw the man, he passed by on the other side. So too, a Levite, when he came to the place and saw him, passed by on the other side. But a Samaritan, as he traveled, came where the man was and when he saw him, he took pity on him. He went to him and bandaged his wounds, pouring on oil and wine. Then he put the man on his own donkey, brought him to an inn, and took care of him. The next day he took out two denarii and gave them to the innkeeper. 'Look after him,' he said, 'and when I return, I will reimburse you for any extra expense you may have.'

"Which of these three do you think was a neighbor to the man who fell into the hands of robbers?"

The expert in the law replied, "The one who had mercy on him."

Jesus told him, "Go and do likewise."

Love God.

Love *like* God.

That's what the Samaritan did.

He saw a need and held nothing back in meeting it. He was *extravagant* in his care. Jesus' affirmation of Mary, upon her pouring priceless perfume all over his feet, had its origins here, in the wildly generous heart of God. But more than recognize that fact or even respect such lavishness, we are to *replicate* it in daily life.

"Go," Jesus said, "and do likewise."

Those words weren't intended for the teachers of the law only; that injunction was meant for us too.

THE TROUBLE WITH PASSING BY

In this parable, we find two general responses to the unfortunate guy in the ditch. I'll add nuance to my assessment as we journey together here, but as a setup for the ensuing chapters, allow me to paint with an absurdly broad brush.

Three people happened by the ditch that day, clearly aware that the man was in need. The man, the text says, was "half dead": there was no question that he was distressed. Verse 31 tells us that the priest saw the man and then passed him on the other side. Likewise, the Levite saw the man and passed by on the other side. It was only the third man, the Samaritan, who chose a different tack. He saw, just as the others had seen. But then he refused to just pass by. He allowed himself to be interrupted. He allowed for a break in his forward progress. He allowed for an unforeseen *pause*.

I was taught that the reason the priest and the Levite avoided the man in the ditch was because they were headed to worship at the temple and didn't want to render themselves unclean. But scholars on the subject are careful to point out that the passersby in this tale are going "down" from the temple, not "up." If they'd already worshipped, then there was no reason to fear becoming unclean. Which means some other motivation must have driven their negligence that day. The inconvenience of it all, maybe? Or the fear of the unknown? A judgmental spirit toward "one of them"? Something else, perhaps?

I've been around my fair share of "passersby," and one trend tends to hold true. The approach just can't sustain them; they're left unfulfilled in the end. Sure, for a time—years or decades or even the majority of their lives—they're able to stay on track with their will, their plans, their desires. But then life happens, as it invariably does, and they're left needing a thing called a *friend.*

They get the call from the doc: "The cancer's returned . . ."

Their teenage son overdoses and nearly dies.

The contract isn't renewed.

The relationship falls through.

Spending habits catch up with them.

Whatever the situation, now the tables have turned. And all those people in need they just sauntered right past aren't exactly eager to help.

A former CEO of a massive corporation fell ill not long ago. In fact, he was hospitalized for weeks on end, and there was no medical hope in sight. A strange infection had gone rogue throughout his system, leaving doctors perplexed and dismayed. Eventually he would recover and be discharged, but not before some truly harrowing days unfolded, when both hospital staff and family members thought they'd be wise to say their goodbyes.

During week three of this wild ordeal, a pastor the man was acquainted with stopped by the hospital for a visit. After the two had talked for a few minutes, the businessman looked at the pastor and said, "You know, during the years that I was a chief executive, I made scores of people millionaires. But given that not one of them has reached out to me these last three weeks, let alone come to visit, I guess I failed to make any friends."

It's not mine to judge that businessman's heart. Who knows: maybe he was secretly incredibly philanthropic and service-oriented and others-focused. But, based on the interviews he gave, the books he wrote, and the vibe he projected, most of his key "earning years," as they're crassly called, were spent chasing the almighty dollar. He was known for his ruthlessness in the boardroom, his savage negotiation style, and his negligence when it came to interpersonal loyalty. If those things were even mostly true, then he didn't exactly fit the profile of our Good Samaritan—one who not only notices the people around him in need but then actually pauses to see how he might help.

WHAT THE DANGEROUSLY GENEROUS DO

I've seen this dynamic play out dozens of times: people who have come to the end of what the world can provide them have an epiphany. Some finally cede control of their lives to God. They add action to the faith they've espoused for years, and from there things begin to change. They no longer consider their lives their own. Their resources are no longer "theirs." They start noticing the plentiful needs all around, the needs they chose to look past for *years*.

The filter these people used for decision-making gets a radical overhaul. While their chief concern once was getting all they could for themselves, they're now more interested in how much they can give away. "Wealth is not determined by what you have; it is predicated on what you give away," wrote Kris Vallotton.[4]

The friends of these "wealthy" people think they've utterly lost their minds:

"You're leaving a six-figure salary to go into . . . *ministry*?"

"You're buying a *pre-owned* car?"

"You're selling your house and *downsizing*?"

"You're giving that much money *away*?"

Why would anyone of any means do something like that? Why would a passerby choose to *pause*?

"Every choice we make is an investment in a future we cannot see,"[5] says author Alicia Britt Chole, in her fantastic book *Anonymous: Jesus' Hidden Years . . . and Yours*. That title is a fitting explanation for what's happened for these women and men: rather than flaunting their wild abundance, they've tasted the delicious satisfaction of hiding themselves in Christ, trusting *him* to protect them, provide for them, and promote them. This type of generosity is dangerous; historically, it has changed the world.

These people begin to understand that we're all in this thing together, and that when one who has much refuses to share, one who has little aches. But when those who have time and money and skill come alongside those who need those things, both groups experience strength and success. *Both* groups win in the end.

WE TEACH WHAT WE NEED TO LEARN

My first goal in putting this material together is to both describe and demonstrate what it looks like to live *a life of pause*. In our hurried, harried world, why is it important to pause and take in the people around us? When "fast" is the name of our culture's game, why is it wise to learn to go "slow"? What happens when we practice that magical *pause*, that moment of recognition of another's true need? What does that acknowledgment do in our hearts and souls? How are we changed by what we've seen? I'd like to answer these questions and more.

In the second half of the book, we'll explore the different ways people perceive money in relation to generosity. I'll also give you some practical advice on how to handle your money so that you will have the resources to be generous.

Shifting from being a passerby to becoming a pauser is a process, not a flip of the switch. Because of this reality, I'll conclude each chapter with an invitation to practice "pushing 'Pause'" on life as you've known it, so that you can experiment with a new approach. True, I've seen people miraculously freed from the grip of alcoholism or drug addiction or sexual deviance. By the Holy Spirit's power, in an *instant*, they've been released, and the change they experienced stuck. I believe in the immediate, redemptive work of God in people's lives. But, more often, real transformation has necessitated real work—methodically, intentionally, over time. So I want to give you actionable steps you can take in these sections.

I want to detail for you the blessings of choosing a pause-filled life. My contention is not only that God affirmed extravagance during Jesus' earthly ministry but that he affirms it still today. Whenever you and I pour out the best that we have—our best energies, our best ideas, our best efforts, our best service, our best financial backing, our best *lives*—for the purpose of glorifying God, that offering is both welcomed and praised. When we practice this sort of *dangerous generosity*—not to look good but rather to make God look good—we enter into a sort of extravagance that people can't help but notice . . . and admire. We become those people I talked about earlier, the ones with open hands, open hearts, a ready yes. We become the very reflection of God. And I defy you to find a more satisfying use for your life than to rightly reflect the heart of God. You can achieve nothing else but that one simple thing and have gained all there is to gain.

I consider myself a "pauser" these days, but things haven't always been that way. I've endured two or three devastating seasons as a "passerby," someone who was so laser-focused on making money, making a name for myself, making my mark, that I breezed by scores of what I'm sure were divinely placed opportunities to be the hands and feet of Jesus in the lives of those I passed. The worst part of those experiences was that I was a Christian. Years prior to any of those seasons, I'd "faithfully surrendered my life to the Lord." True—that's what I said I was doing. But had I really surrendered anything at all?

"It is not coincidence that the word 'miser' is etymologically related to the word 'miserable,'" one author wisely noted.[6] Misers never feel fulfilled.

Suffice it to say, I'm not interested in spending even one more minute as a self-centered, negligent guy. And yet, evidently, I'm vulnerable to doing just that—for two simple reasons, I've learned. First, I'm a pastor. And if I'm correct about what 1 Peter 5:2 is getting at, I'd better be on my guard. There, we read, "Be shepherds of God's flock that is under your care, watching over them—not because you must, but because you are willing, as God wants you to be; not pursuing dishonest gain, but eager to serve . . ." Taking a step back, look at how Eugene H. Peterson renders the surrounding passage in *The Message*: "I have a special concern for you church leaders. I know what it's like to be a leader, in on Christ's sufferings as well as the coming glory. Here's my concern: that you care for God's flock with all the diligence of a shepherd. Not because you have to, but because you want to please God. Not calculating what you can get out of it, but acting spontaneously. Not bossily telling others what to do, but tenderly showing them the way" (1 Peter 5:1–3).

Pastors are to care for the people they pastor with the "diligence of a shepherd."

Pastors are to live from a place of joyful and spontaneous service, not as one under compulsion.

Pastors are to be tender, not bossy, not demanding. They are to *guide*—and gently so.

Notice that the top priority for pastors—in Peter's mind, anyway— was not watching out for sexual deviance or angry outbursts or heresy or streaks of pride. The number one caution on Peter's list? "Pastors, watch out for *greed*."

Watch out for opportunities for dishonest gain.

Watch out for the tendency to calculate what you can get out of a situation.

Watch out for the insatiable desire for power and prominence, two bullies that kick tenderness right to the curb.

Truly, there's no greater privilege in my life than being called "Pastor." That name is *meaningful* to me. So passages like this one from 1 Peter carry weight with me. I am committed to doing all that the Scriptures tell me to do, so that I don't royally screw this thing up. The first reason I'm susceptible to self-focused stinginess is that I'm a pastor; it's as simple as that. So many needs! So few resources! It can cause a guy to want to conserve. But there's another reality stacked against me, which brings me to reason two.

Put plainly, I'm a fifty-three-year-old man.

Last month, prolific writer, onetime pastor of Moody Church in Chicago, and *fifty-year* radio ministry veteran Warren Wiersbe passed away. As I often do to honor the lives of the greats once they're gone, I went back and reread some of Wiersbe's work, including an article he once wrote about middle age. Known for being a bridge builder who served congregations between the tenures of highly prominent pastors, Wiersbe here spoke of a different sort of bridge: a bridge between two halves of life.

Recounting a line by the English poet Lord Byron, Wiersbe wrote that it's generally in our middle years that we "hover between fool and sage."[7] We all choose one of these paths, a point driven home for me a few nights ago, when I attended a dinner party and observed firsthand the difference between these two. At the gathering, I encountered two men, both in their early sixties, who had opted for different paths. The first was quick-witted, encouraging, and measured with his words and tone. The second was pretty much the opposite: sarcastic, crude, lacking in self-control. I thought about Wiersbe's assertion. I thought about how both of these men had just completed the decade of their fifties. And I reupped my desire to choose well.

I had opportunity to connect on several occasions with the late Eugene Peterson, and one time at his home outside Kalispell, Montana—which he and his father had built by hand, I should mention. He and I were reflecting on the role of pastor . . . the ups, the downs, the in-betweens. I asked who had been the toughest people for him to pastor along the way, and with barely a hesitation, he said, "Men who have reached their fifties and have not amounted to much."

I found that incredibly profound.

And painfully true.

For me, it is the men of New Life who are middle-aged and only midway successful in life who give me the most trouble too. Or maybe it's that they have been *wildly* successfully—but in the wrong things. They climbed and climbed and climbed, only to find that their ladder was propped against a structure that couldn't hold them in the end, and the tumble that ensued was significant, leaving them bitter and angry and cold. They are unteachable. They are un-moldable. They find themselves in a pit of unfulfillment, and even though there is a path out available to them, they lack courage to give that way a try.

So there they sit.

In the muck and mire of their foolishness, having no clue that *they* are to blame. I think it was A. W. Tozer who wrote, "A hard man will never be a wise man."[8]

Yep. I believe that is true.

I really don't want to be foolish. I want to do the decade of my fifties well. Not to mention my sixties and beyond. I tell New Life all the time that I want to get old with them and someday be the wrinkly guy who asks ridiculous questions, who repeats the same stories over and over again, and who has long ago lost touch with what's cool. But to do that

I have to finish well. I have to stay the course and not run this thing into the ditch. I have to *avoid becoming a fool.*

STINGINESS COMES FOR US ALL

There is a pretty sizable distribution problem between the needs that exist in our world today and the resources available to meet them. A handful of stats, if I may:

- Three out of four Americans never volunteer an hour of their time.[9]
- Only a tenth of any congregation gives to the work of its church,[10] which is at least in part why upward of 10,000 churches are closing their doors—permanently—each year.[11]
- Americans in 2016 spent more than $60 billion—that's *billion* with a *b*—on their pets, with a third of those dollars going to food alone.[12]
- More than 14 million children in America go to bed hungry every night.[13] Globally, nearly 51 million boys and girls under five years of age are literally "wasting" away, the name for having chronic low weight for one's height.
- From 2015 to 2016, Americans spent nearly $51 billion on eating out.[14]
- More than half a million people in this country alone are experiencing homelessness, and a third of those people have kids.[15]
- Nearly one in two Americans describes themselves as "frequently lonely."[16]

The issue, in a word, is *greed.* We've got our eyes on a prize, all right, but it's not the prize the Bible suggests. First John 3:17 comes to mind: "If anyone has material possessions and sees a brother or sister in need but has no pity on them, how can the love of God be in that person?"

And 1 Timothy 6:17–18: "Command those who are rich in this present world not to be arrogant nor to put their hope in wealth, which is so uncertain, but to put their hope in God, who richly provides us with everything for our enjoyment. Command them to do good, to be rich in good deeds, and to be generous and willing to share."

And Paul's promise to the believers gathered at Corinth—and to us: "You will be enriched in every way so that you can be generous on every occasion, and through us your generosity will result in thanksgiving to God" (2 Corinthians 9:11).

Again, from Alicia Britt Chole: "In small undocumented choices throughout hidden and public years, Satan continues to offer us the world in exchange for our souls. Occasionally he still uses mountaintops, but more often he shows us the view from laptops, checkbooks, boardrooms, corner offices; he takes us behind closed doors, onto trading floors, up on stages, and in front of microphones."[17] All of which is to say, evidently I'm not the only one who could benefit from a refresher on extravagant living as the Bible endorses. Stinginess comes for us all. And yet, for all the disheartening statistics out there, we know that the generous are alive and well. Really, that's the point of this book . . . to showcase what's working for these "pausers" so that we can learn from them and follow suit.

WHY ALL THE FUSS ABOUT MONEY?

It's impossible to talk about extravagant generosity without talking about money, and the Scriptures have plenty to say on the subject. Between one-third and half of the forty parables[18] that Jesus told have to do with the prevalence of money, the importance of money, and the role that money plays in our lives. There are parables about moneylenders and forgiveness of debt, about a rich man foolishly building a big house, about wise and foolish servants, about hidden treasure, about a valuable pearl—a "pearl of great price"—about a lost coin, about a Pharisee and a tax collector, and more. Depending on how you parse the parables of Jesus, in fact, every one of them could be bent to speak of money, of possessions, of the deeper longings of our fallen hearts.

Further, if we were to expand our little research project beyond Jesus' explicit words on the subject to also include what his *followers* said, we'd be swimming in pertinent texts. You may have heard pastors report that there are more words on money in the Bible than on love, which is a pretty important topic to people who believe in God—and they're right. There are upward of two thousand verses of Scripture that speak of money, verses reminding us that where our treasure is, there our heart will be also (see Matthew 6:21); that when embarking on a journey, it's completely acceptable to take nothing with us, instead relying on the kindness and compassion of generous people we encounter along the way (see Luke 9:3); that we simply cannot serve both God and money (see Luke 16); and more.

We meet the widow who makes an offering at church, even though she is destitute and frail. We meet Zacchaeus the tax collector, who is prompted to give half of all his possessions to the poor, as well as another rich young soul who is prompted to give it all. We learn Jesus' perspective on paying taxes (see Matthew 22:15–22). And still we've barely scratched the surface, let alone flipped back to Old Testament financial ideals.

We could debate the finer points of each of these verses, splitting hairs over what Jesus meant and how each applies to our lives, but can I ask you to suspend detailed judgment for a moment and just take in this theme overall? My question for our Master is this: *Why all the fuss about money, Jesus? Why is how we handle money such a big deal?*

I'm going to make a statement that you may or may not agree with but that I'd like you to consider, at least. This singular belief has come to shape how I view finances, which in turn has altered a sizable amount of my life. The statement is this: The way that we regard money reflects the way that we regard people.

The way that you and I handle our money *perfectly reflects* the way we treat human beings.

This is why Jesus made such a fuss about money. His entire purpose in coming to earth, dying on a cross, and redeeming sinful ones from their sin centered on his passion for people. And if our treatment of those people he died for is influenced by our treatment of the money in our hands, then you'd better believe he's going to have something to say about how we regard those dollars and cents.

PAUSERS IN ACTION

Jessica was living with her boyfriend in Washington State, trying to find work while enduring what was a horribly abusive relationship. She was consistently ridiculed and shamed and also slapped and slashed and punched. To make matters worse, she battled mental health challenges and had no familial support. The low point came when, at seven months pregnant, Jessica found herself locked in a closet, bloodied and scared out of her mind. She was hungry. She was thirsty. She was cold. She was alone. She had no idea when she'd get out of the cramped space or if her boyfriend was even still around.

There in the dark closet she fantasized about making an escape. If her unborn baby somehow survived this ordeal, she told herself, she vowed never to put the child in harm's way again.

From the floor of the closet Jessica traced the baseboards with her frail fingers until her hand happened upon a finishing tack. She worked that tack loose and then jimmied the door lock until she was free. Opening the door as quietly as she could, she slipped through the shadows, grabbed her purse from the kitchen counter, and silently left the dingy apartment through the front door. If her boyfriend was home, he must have been sleeping. Based on the stale air and the stench of uneaten food mixed with marijuana and alcohol, she guessed he'd passed out. Again. She didn't stick around to find out.

I've got to get to Colorado, Jessica told herself from behind the wheel of her car. She'd always dreamed of living in Colorado, and now she had her chance.

She'd left so quickly, so urgently, that she'd failed to consider how she'd make it there. She had no money. She had almost no gas. She had no clothes but the ones she was wearing. But she had left behind the terrible life she'd known. Her baby would be safe now.

Along the way, she decided, when she felt safe in a given area, she'd pull into a gas station parking lot, situate herself near the exit, and beg for gas money and food. She was stunned by how many people took a genuine interest in her, wanting to know where she was headed and why. "One woman paid to fill my car's tank all the way full," she said, "and then bought me dinner too. Two separate families brought me an entire bag of groceries. A guy and his son handed me a card for the Subway sandwich shop that wound up paying for, like, five straight meals. A man gave me a pack of cookies with a card taped on that had the name and number of a shelter in town."

Twice en route to Colorado, Jessica stumbled upon local churches that outfitted her with donated clothing free of charge. "What else can we help you with before you head off?" a staff member at one of the churches had asked her, even as she filled a sack with a Bible and snacks for Jessica's next leg of the trip.

Eventually, Jessica made it to Colorado Springs, where she pieced together the money from so many strangers and rented a storage unit. "I'm not sure it was legal for me to live out of my storage unit," Jessica later explained, "but that's the only thing I could afford." Leveraging the portable restrooms at a nearby campground, as well as a creek that ran behind her "house," Jessica decorated her space from the dumpsters that were positioned all over the storage facility's campus. "People throw away the *most* amazing things," she said.

For the month leading up to her child's birth, Jessica collected enough odds and ends to begin something of a resale business. She'd find beat-up dressers or chairs that were missing a leg and restore them with dumpster supplies. Then she'd drive to the local library, where she had computer access, and post her custom pieces on sites like Craigslist. She was starting to turn a profit when her baby decided to come.

Once her contractions started, Jessica drove herself to the nearest hospital she could find. She feared the worst: when hospital staff discovered that she had no place of residence, no job, no bank account, no insurance, and an out-of-state driver's license, they would surely take her baby from her. Her child would become a ward of the state. By the time she reached the emergency entrance, Jessica was an absolute wreck. She was crying so hysterically that triage nurses had trouble understanding why she was there. Clearly this woman was very pregnant, but there was obviously more to the story than that.

One of the nurses tending to Jessica knew of Mary's Home, the supportive-housing community that New Life and other churches run on the south side of town for mothers and their children who are homeless, and excused herself to place a call. She learned that we had a rare opening just then. The following day Jessica completed her application to Mary's Home, scheduled her in-person interview with our team, and was holding a healthy baby girl. "Everything changed in an instant," she said. "It felt like I got a do-over in life . . ."

"Welcome home, Jessica," the card on the coffee table read. That was the truth of the matter: Jessica and her baby were finally home. They were safe. They had shelter. They had food. At last, they had *a way out*. She was determined not to squander this gift she'd been given. She was ready to begin anew.

As Jessica made her way through the residence's various on-site training programs—learning to care for a baby, learning to cook nutritious food, dealing with the aftermath of trauma and abuse, managing a household budget, and more—she was introduced to an entrepreneurial coach who worked with the residents too. "I think I'm meant to be an entrepreneur," she told him. "I have a furniture business going already, and I'd like to make it grow . . ."

Fast-forward two years, and Jessica had graduated from the Mary's Home program, relocated to northern Colorado, rented a one-bedroom apartment, and officially launched her online furniture shop. Today, she clears nearly $60,000 a year in income. She pays for her own insurance. She has money for food and gas. And she is involved in a local church, holding babies the same age as her own little girl each week while those babies' parents serve on the worship team.

The first night she spent in her self-funded apartment, Jessica remembers opening the Bible she'd received at the little church in Oregon, back when she was fearing for her life. On the front page was an inscription: "To Jessica and her baby," it read. "May grace and peace be yours."

"Grace and peace."

She lay in her bed, her baby in the crook of her right arm, the Bible in the hand of the other, and she thought about those words. *Grace and peace.*

Grace. And peace.

With that, she fell asleep.

GRACE ALWAYS LEADS TO PEACE

I first heard of Jessica's harrowing experience from Pastor Matthew Ayers, CEO of the Dream Centers organization, which oversees Mary's Home. The more he talked, the more I was moved, not just by the eventual relief Jessica found, but by the generosity of the people she'd met each step of the way, for their extravagant kindness and care.

For days after I heard her story, I found myself looking at the people around me differently, the ones who were clearly in need. I saw "Jessicas" everywhere I looked: people who needed a break, some food. I began wondering how many of the people sitting on street corners and lying on downtown benches and crouching underneath city park trees were living out of storage sheds. Then I wondered how many couldn't afford even that . . . those who were truly at the end of their rope.

I thought about the people at the gas stations Jessica had stopped at, how they'd paused, and probed, and cared. And about the church staff who had welcomed her in, clothing her not just with shirts and jeans but also with Christlike love.

I thought about that nurse who'd reached out to Mary's Home. Such a simple act that phone call was, and yet look where it ultimately led. I thought about the thousands of donors who had made Mary's Home possible in the first place, and of the staff there who always work hard to make new residents feel at home. I thought about how each of us is a scene in every stranger's story, and how we get to decide whether that scene will be marked by compassion or if apathy will have its way.

So many grace-drenched scenes in Jessica's story that couldn't help but lead a person to peace. So many people who opted not to pass by but to *pause*. So much extravagance saving the day.

The "extravagance," you'll notice, doesn't seem very extravagant at all. A kind word here, a warm embrace there, a bag of snacks for a famished one's trip. But we bring in the kingdom by small gestures like these; it is here where we change the whole world.

God is a God of great blessing, and he has reserved those blessings for us. What's more, we can find the secret of those blessings even now. God has called us to be salt. He has called us to be light. I love Dietrich Bonhoeffer on this subject. He once wrote, "Jesus does not say, 'You *must* be the salt.' He says, 'You are the salt.' We are this way, whether we like it or not."[19]

I think he's got a point.

We *are* salt.

We *are* light.

And when we behave as salt and light—preserving God's glory in a world that has nearly no use for it, shining bright as stars in the midst of some admittedly dark, dark days—those blessings we've been hunting for in all the wrong places will overwhelm us and leave us undone.

A life of extravagance is ours for the taking—if only we'll define it on the same terms as God. In the words of one ancient writer, "Our whole life is to become a Liturgy, an Anaphora, a constant offering up of our talents, our time, our hearts, and our world to Christ."[20]

A constant offering up . . . of all that we have and all that we are.

This is what it means to be extravagant.

This is what Jesus is like.

Part One

YOUR MISSION

1

Life, and Where It's Found

Where we choose to store our treasures depends largely
on where we think our home is.[1]

RANDY ALCORN

TO MEET A NEED, we must first see that need. Where, then, should we look?

I was in college before I realized that spending almost every summer day during my early childhood years riding alone through the backwoods of Louisiana, armed with both a hatchet and my very own gun, wasn't how every kid grew up. Also common in our neck of the woods: any adult who lived within spitting distance of your home carried implicit rights to corporal punishment of every kid who happened to be within that range. If you misbehaved over near neighbor Joe's property, neighbor Joe didn't waste time chasing down your parents so that he could tell them the rotten thing you'd done; he'd just whip you then and there. In our part of the country, these things were normative. In other parts of the world, not so much.

This is one of the reasons I love knowing where people are from. What I'm asking when I ask about their upbringing is, essentially: *What types of people and experiences shape how you now see life?* The answers I hear from people are endlessly fascinating, because we all see the world so differently. Where we came from, to some extent, is who we are (or at least the personification of the various dysfunctions we've worked like crazy to overcome.)

So often, the conditions of our youths inform what the adult versions of ourselves come to believe that life is all about. I've met people who were raised by professional athletes and now believe that athletic prowess is what life is all about. They are fierce weekend warriors who are as competitive as they come. I've met people who were raised by fastidious homemakers who have come to believe that life is about having a clean house. If you so much as turn a coffee-table book thirty degrees, they will put it back in its place the very next time they enter the room—and probably without even realizing they've done so.

There are people who grow up around elite institutions and believe life is about intelligence and achievement and scholarships and graduating first in your class. People who are around lots of material possessions might focus on accumulation themselves once they have the means. Adventure seekers often raise future adventure seekers. Abusers can cause those they abuse to start believing that the key to success in life is to submit, to concede, to obey. Looking back at my life, I was raised in a loving environment. My sister and brother both would echo that sentiment. None of us lacked for love. But that doesn't mean it was a perfect home. For starters, we were poor. (That's another thing I didn't realize until I went to college. By contrast, I saw plainly that my station in life had a name, and "poverty" was it. Huh.)

Money was always tight, which caused a fair amount of stress for

Mom and Dad. I wouldn't have had the vocabulary for it back then, but as I entered my adolescent years, I began to form a belief about what life was all about. Life, for my family, anyway, was one big exercise in *trying to make ends meet.*

Those ends—they never did meet.

A memory that sticks out was my parents' inability to find the twenty-five bucks I needed to go on a road trip with my Future Farmers of America group to the Houston Livestock Show and Rodeo a few hours south of us. I can still feel the ribs of that blue corduroy FFA jacket on my arms . . . I was so proud to be a member of something, but my participation in the best activity of the year was not to be.

That disappointing turn of events confirmed something that I'd been suspicious about but not yet sure of, which was that it took more than your parents' devoted love to get you where you wanted to go in life. It also took cash—cold, hard cash. And evidently we had none of that.

Around this same time, unbeknownst to me my brain was entering a new stage of development—something about "increased myelination" and something called "pruning." In this new stage, I would be able to not just observe my circumstances but also to form judgments about them, and the singular judgment I remember making was this: when I grew up, I always wanted to have the twenty-five bucks to do what I wanted to do.

Life, for me, would be about making money. Keeping my money. Being a person who *had* money. That was the vow I made.

I didn't really intend to become a selfish person the day I made my vow. It's just that, to be someone who made and kept and had money, I believed I had to stick myself at the top of my priority list. After all, who else was going to ensure a life of abundance for me?

I knew the answer to that one: nobody. This mission was mine alone.

SELFISH MAN SERVING GOD

Looking back, I see how that one vow influenced all that was to come. Soon after I went off to college, I had an encounter with Jesus. I surrendered my heart to him, but there was an asterisk beside that choice, an asterisk whose footnote read, "I'll do whatever you ask me to do as long as it doesn't compromise this mission I'm on. Really, God: I *refuse* to be poor."

For too many years I kept this deal going with God, "serving" him by teaching and preaching and ministering and volunteering while still working a full-time job, striving for more, spending money I did not have, indulging desires that were not of him. All around me, people seemed to have their own deals going with God, so I'm not sure I was all that aware of what I was doing at the time—or that it would have mattered had I known. I remember justifying my material longings by saying that once I had more to give, I would give more to God, but of course that was a lie. I didn't know the Bible back then like I do today, but I'd certainly come across the verse about God trusting with more those who have been faithful with little.

As I say, I knew I'd have to manage this mission on my own terms.

Each time I reread the parable that has inspired this book, I see myself there in its setup, in the expert in the law who stands up to challenge Jesus, insisting he knows what's best for his life. "Teacher," he'd said to Jesus, "what must I do to inherit eternal life?" (Luke 10:25).

Jesus' answer would center on love: on loving God and on loving *like* God. The one conspicuously absent direct object of the love that Jesus spoke of was the love of self—which was a bummer for that expert and for me. Like me, the expert was on a mission. Also like me: Jesus really got in his way.

My goal for this chapter is to begin to reveal how you might be standing in your own way, too, in your quest for an extravagant life. In a given day, do you spend more energy and money on self-preservation and advancement or on finding and meeting others' needs? More fundamentally still, do you know how to spot a person in need, the kind of person Jesus says needs help the most?

Wisdom is available to you and me both. We can learn to see, and care, and help.

THE WISE ONES AND THE FOOLS

You don't have to be a Bible scholar to see that the line gets drawn soon enough between people who live life wisely and people who don't. I love the verses that deal with that delineation now, but along the way those words were like swift kicks to my gut. A few that took me down:

> *Those who trust in themselves are fools, but those who walk in wisdom are kept safe (Proverbs 28:26).*

> *Be very careful, then, how you live—not as unwise but as wise, making the most of every opportunity, because the days are evil (Ephesians 5:15–16).*

> *The hearts of the wise make their mouths prudent, and their lips promote instruction (Proverbs 16:23).*

> *The law of the LORD is perfect, refreshing the soul. The statutes of the LORD are trustworthy, making wise the simple (Psalm 19:7).*

> *Blessed are those whose ways are blameless,who walk according to the law of the LORD. Blessed are those who keep his statutes and seek him with all their heart—they do no wrong but follow his ways. You have laid down precepts that are to be fully obeyed (Psalm 119:1–4).*

"But everyone who hears these words of mine and does not put them into practice is like a foolish man who built his house on sand. The rain came down, the streams rose, and the winds blew and beat against that house, and it fell with a great crash" (Matthew 7:26–27).

For some time in my twenties, I wasn't exactly living wisely and I also wasn't very open to change. At the time I had my reasons ... most of them tracing back to that vow. Now? I see them for what they were. Lame excuses, at best.

EXCUSES WE LOVE

We *all* possess the rampant propensity to justify our behavior, even if that behavior is doing us harm. Especially so, perhaps. Habits researcher Gretchen Rubin spent an entire chapter of her book *Better Than Before* enumerating the myriad "loopholes" we most love to invoke. See if you recognize any of these:

- The False Choice Loophole: "I can't do this, because I'm so busy doing that ..."
- The Moral Licensing Loophole: "I've been so good, it's okay for me to do this ..."
- The Tomorrow Loophole: "It's okay to skip today, because I'm going to do this tomorrow ..."
- The Lack of Control Loophole: "I can't help myself ..."
- The "This Doesn't Count" Loophole: "Eh, it's okay. I'm on vacation ..."
- The Fake Self-Actualization Loophole: "You only live once! Embrace the moment!"[2]

When it comes to choosing our own way instead of God's, I have noticed three specific loopholes people tend to invoke. See if any of these sound familiar:

1. "It's not like I'm breaking any laws . . ." Excusing self-centered behavior just because it is "legal" is beyond ridiculous. God doesn't call us to be law-abiding—although that's not a bad goal, I must say. He calls us to be *loving*—toward him and toward the people he made.

2. "What I do with my life is my business . . ." This popular one centers on the mantra of our day: "You do you and I'll do me. It's all good . . ." It might, in fact, all be good if it were true. Sadly, it is not. Nearly every week at New Life we end our worship service by taking Communion together, sometimes called the Lord's Supper. And in doing so, we declare to God and to each other that we are no longer our own. We belong to him. We belong to his church. Which, by definition, means we belong to each other. What I do affects you, and what you do affects me. Period.

3. "It's okay in the Bible . . ." This one has gained in popularity in my home state, perhaps because, along with Washington State, we were the first to legalize recreational-use marijuana. I have lost count of the number of times I have heard some dude say, "Doesn't matter how much I smoke, Pastor Brady . . . It's just a plant, and according to Genesis, God created all the plants." If I'm feeling especially energetic, I will come back with "Yes, and cyanide comes from a plant. Go for it."

To our plentiful justifications, I have a feeling God simply shakes his head. *Nice try.* He knows that once we get a little spiritual maturity on our side, we will see those injunctions that encourage wisdom not as prohibitions but as *gifts*.

In Galatians 5:16–18, the apostle Paul, writing to believers who were struggling to finish their faith journey well, wrote, "So I say, walk by the Spirit, and you will not gratify the desires of the flesh. For the flesh desires what is contrary to the Spirit, and the Spirit what is contrary to the flesh. They are in conflict with each other, so that you are not to do whatever you want. But if you are led by the Spirit, you are not under the law."

Here, Paul refers to a great wrestling match underway in the life of every person on planet Earth. You may not be struggling with a raging addiction to pornography, but I would be willing to bet that someone you know is. The people you hang out with might not have trouble finding the motivation to get out of bed each morning, but maybe you do. Right now, someone is fighting the urge to lash out in anger, or to have another drink, or to accept the advances of a married coworker, or to carry out suicidal thoughts to their awful end. "Be kind," author Ian Maclaren once said, "for everyone you meet is fighting a hard battle."[3]

Paul's point, at least in part, was that we should be careful not to add fuel to anyone's raging fire. We should be careful not to multiply another's struggle, and the way we get that done is by being kind. By being loving. By being *generous* with our actions and words. So, in the choices we make regarding attire and beverage and attitude and recreational activity, we should think not just of ourselves but of *those affected by us*.

This injunction to love—to love God well, to love others with the same intensity as God loves them—is a boundary that is meant not for our imprisonment but for our *delight*. What God knows that we so often neglect to see is that when we are careful to live within the boundaries he has established, we find the fulfillment we've been longing for.

BENEFITS OF BOUNDARIES

When my teenagers were toddlers, Pam and I lived on the corner of a busy neighborhood street. For that reason we drew strict boundary lines around the area where Abram and Callie could play and told them in our most serious voices that there were never to cross those lines. Why? Because if they did, the chances were high that they'd get mown down by one of the hundreds of cars that were always zooming through that intersection. We were boundary-driven parents, and they were boundary-abiding kids. Within those boundaries there was endless playtime. We had a *ball* inside those lines. But outside of them, no one was to go.

Now, would you say that Pam and I were mean parents because we enforced those boundaries so strictly?

I doubt it.

Considering the context, you'd probably say that enforcing those boundaries was the *loving* thing to do. Pam and I cared about seeing our kids set up for success. We cared about giving them every opportunity to grow and thrive. And we knew that the only way for those things to happen was by *keeping them alive.*

Likewise, our heavenly Father longs for us to grow in Christlikeness, to reach full spiritual maturity, to accomplish all that he has for us during our lives here on earth. And he knows that the only way those things will happen is if we stay healthy, holy, and whole.

Which brings me back to how that expert in the law's question got answered that day when he took Jesus on.

"Teacher, what must I do to inherit eternal life?" he had asked, and in response, as he so often did, Jesus answered a question with a question: "What is written in the Law?"

The expert had no way of escape. He knew what Jesus was after. "Love the Lord your God with all your heart and with all your soul and with all your strength and with all your mind; and, 'Love your neighbor as yourself,'" the expert in the law said (Luke 10:27).

He knew good and well where the boundaries had been laid. "You have answered correctly," Jesus said. "Do this and you will live" (v. 28).

There are plenty of topics in Scripture where there is no black-or-white ruling, but the topic of where real life is found is not one of them. Despite our differences—our varied convictions and habits and voting patterns and desires—at the end of the day we are called to but two straightforward things: loving God and loving *like* God. When we elevate our heavenly Father to his rightful place, and when we are absolutely *gripped with passion* for caring for the people he created, it is then—and only then—that we're truly alive.

God knew that we would be tempted to worship something or someone besides him. That we would be tempted to hurt each other and hold grudges against each other. That we would have bad days and engage in petty arguments and let bitterness take root in our hearts. He knew that we'd be tempted to lie and cheat and steal . . . and to cover up all we'd done wrong. He knew we'd want to play God in our own lives instead of surrendering fully to him. He knew that a thousand temptations might overtake us if we didn't have productive rails to run on, if we didn't have some sort of guiding north star. And so, the two commandments:

"Love me," God says.

"And love like me.
And then you will truly live."

THE ONE THAT GIVES US FITS

If you are anything like me, only one of those commandments presents a challenge to you day by day. In my heart of hearts, I really do love God. Deeply. Sincerely. Without any hesitation whatsoever.

It's that second commandment that gives me fits. Which I suppose means the first one is a challenge too: If I struggle to love God's people, what does that say about my love for him?

I'm not alone in having trouble loving the (very) messy, (very) complicated, (very) dramatic people that exist around me: the ones who are sometimes flighty, who sometimes talk too much, and who sometimes forget to say thanks. The more people I talk to about these subjects, the more I see that we *all* are mystified from time to time with how to love one another when all those other ones are so incredibly weird. (It was John Ortberg who wrote *Everybody's Normal Till You Get to Know Them*. That's some good theology there.)

This is at least what's behind our highly individualistic approach these days. Individualism as a concept may have emerged first in Europe, but I have to believe that no other group of people has worked as diligently to apply its principles as those of us in the grand ol' U.S. of A. My son, Abram, and I joke that while Colorado's official motto is the noble-sounding *Nil Sine Numine* ("Nothing Without the Deity"), the motto that plays out in real life here is "Leave me alone." We are quite the individualists out here. They don't call it the Wild, Wild West for nothing.

Jesus' motto of "Love God. Love people. And live" is a *tiny* bit different, and not a bad bumper sticker, come to think of it. The question is: Would any of us practice what our bumpers preached?

If our hearts are as fickle as that of the expert in the law that day, the answer, I'm afraid, is no. In response to Jesus' remark that such love would lead to true life, the man said essentially, "This love-my-neighbor thing . . . could you be a little more . . . specific?" Two thousand years later, not much has changed.

THE MOST VULNERABLE AMONG US

The verse of Scripture that captured my imagination for living beyond my self-centered whims and for following Jesus not on my terms but on his was James 1:27: "Religion that God our Father accepts as pure and faultless is this: to look after orphans and widows in their distress and to keep oneself from being polluted by the world." I first committed that verse to memory in August of 1988, but it was several years before I sat with those words in any meaningful sort of way and let their implications soak into my soul.

If you've ever looked closely into the practices and parameters involved in the establishment of ancient Israel, as I did during that era, then you know that when the nation was being organized under Mosaic law, a significant number of their guiding principles had to do with caring for those in "distress"—namely, widows, orphans, and the poor. One practice, for example, was gleaning, in which farmers would leave the corners of their ripe fields unharvested so that people in need could happen by and find grain to eat. This practice was not optional. It was required. God was serious about people helping each other out, especially those in need. And who were the neediest among the Israelites in that day?

Widows.

Orphans.

The poor.

When the nation of Israel crossed the Jordan River, which runs through the valley between the Dead Sea and the Sea of Galilee, each of its tribes was given property.[4] Inside that allotment of property, each family within the tribe was given part of the tribal land—land that was supposed to belong to that particular family forever.

Instead, after a father or both parents died, people with evil agendas would come to the widows and orphans who were left behind and redefine the boundaries of the property, essentially stealing the land from defenseless landowners. Dad was dead; what was Mom going to do about it? Or else Dad and Mom both were gone; how were their little children going to stop anything?

The laws that God had handed down were for the purpose of saying, "Don't even *think* about touching those boundary stones. I am the Defender of those women and children, and I am telling you to stop."[5]

And defend those women he did, making good on what Psalm 68:5–6 has to say. "A father to the fatherless, a defender of widows, / is God in his holy dwelling," we read there. "God sets the lonely in families, / he leads out the prisoners with singing; / but the rebellious live in a sun-scorched land."

Now jump ahead to Jesus' day and the immediate decades after, when the book of James was written. Again our attention is drawn to widows . . . to orphans . . . and to those who are distressed in our midst.

Back then, in the Greco-Roman culture, there were no "orphanages" and no "retirement homes" or "nursing homes." It wouldn't be until the third century that Christians were strongly encouraged to adopt orphans and raise them to fear the Lord. And the first-generation nursing facilities, where elderly people could come and receive dignified care, weren't established until the fifth century.

Therefore, as a key leader in the New Testament church, one of the primary issues James faced in his leadership role was how to care for the widows and orphans in town. Orphaned infants were tragically being abandoned en masse, while widows who didn't have a family member to take them in were pushed to the street and told to make do for themselves. Most had no such family member, and so homelessness among widows became a pervasive issue in those days.

Acts 6:1 says this: "In those days [the days when the apostles were preaching daily in the temple courts and from house to house, according to the end of Acts 5] when the number of disciples was increasing, the Hellenistic Jews among them complained against the Hebraic Jews because their widows were being overlooked in the daily distribution of food."

In response, James and the other leaders organized a system whereby the widows would no longer be overlooked. "It would not be right for us to neglect the ministry of the word of God in order to wait on tables," they said. "Brothers and sisters, choose seven men from among you who are known to be full of the Spirit and wisdom. We will turn this responsibility over to them and will give our attention to prayer and the ministry of the word" (v. 2–4).

It was a solution that, according to verse 5, "pleased the whole group."

You may recall an exchange from the scene involving Jesus' crucifixion, during which he made sure that, upon his passing, his mother would be cared for by his beloved disciple John. Jesus' father, Joseph, was never mentioned again after Jesus' birth, causing most historians to believe that by the time of Jesus' crucifixion, Joseph had been dead quite some time. And so, in his final moments before that agonizing and tortuous death, we find that what is top of mind for Jesus is one favored widow, his mother. He was determined to find her the care she would need after he had breathed his last breath.

Leaning into the example of Jesus, the church followed suit. "Not on our watch," the church said of the rampant neglect that women and children faced. For now, they did the only thing they could do: they had women and children come live under church protection.

WHEN OUR HEARTS BREAK IN TWO

The irony of James imploring all future generations of Christians to "look after orphans and widows in their distress" was that Jesus' mother, Mary, was James's mother too. It was James, not John, who should have stepped forward to care for her. It was James who was her son. Which means that either James was an outright hypocrite or else he grew in his convictions after Christ had died.

I believe the latter is true.

James did not surrender his life to Jesus until after the Resurrection, and it is my belief that once he had spiritual eyes to see things clearly, he experienced deep inner change. Finally, he saw how needy his mother truly was. Finally, he saw how he might help. It's the same progression any of us must go through, if we ever hope to show up meaningfully in the lives of those in need. We must see the need . . . really *see* it . . . before we can begin to be of help.

I can relate to what James might have gone through emotionally upon realizing his mother's need. For me, the aha moment happened when I learned of a nine-year-old girl who lives in a neighborhood that New Life "adopted" several years ago. By partnering with those living inside this four-square-mile neighborhood, which is positioned in an underserved part of town, we as a church agreed to come alongside the members of that community to provide food, shelter, clothing, educational tutoring, spiritual direction, and more.

The little girl I mention was an elementary school student who had lost both her mother and her father, and for quite some time, as the "system" caught up with her, she would head down to the Salvation Army every day after school to receive a meal and clothing. Eventually, staff there asked where her parents were and why she always came in alone. In response, she said, "My parents died. I don't have a home. I don't have a family anymore."

She explained that friends of hers let her stay over at their houses each night, so that at least she'd have a place to sleep.

She was an orphan in every sense of the word, bouncing from place to place a mere twenty-five minutes south of my house.

Something about the proximity of this little girl's situation got to me. I have a daughter. Imagining Callie roaming around a fairly large town as a fourth grader, having to cobble together outfits and meals, hit me at a level that's tough to explain.

That this girl's situation had somehow gone unnoticed for so long was a wake-up call. How many other desperate people in our community were we not seeing? Not only did we as a church redouble our efforts to show up in the lives of both that little girl and all the residents of that struggling community with food, clothing, community, spiritual conversation, and, in the little girl's case, connection to extended family who gladly took her in, but I personally decided to show up, driving the twelve miles south to get out of my truck, walk those city blocks, meet as many people as I could meet, and be a tangible presence in their lives.

That nine-year-old girl is my neighbor. And once I knew of her distress, I began to pray, "Father, somehow use me."

What that nine-year-old orphan must represent in our collective consciousness is *anyone* who is in distress. Still today, on a global scale, the people who are most oppressed, most marginalized, most vulnerable, and most at risk are women and their children. Perhaps because of the stubborn vestiges of the vast patriarchies that have always ruled the earth, it will always be that way. I pray not, but perhaps it will. In any case, when Scripture exhorts us to "care for orphans and widows," what it is saying is that we must keep our eyes peeled for those who have no one to help them out.

Who is being pushed aside?

Who is being kicked out?

Who has been forsaken?

Who has been left for dead in a ditch?

That person is my neighbor. That person is your neighbor too.

That is the one we are called to go help . . . the one whose load we are told to lift.

UNTIL FURTHER NOTICE, DO THIS

People around New Life sometimes meet with me to ask about finding their "purpose" or "calling" in life. They feel aimless, they explain, or confused about how to use their gifts. They fear making a misstep or winding up in the wrong spot. Almost without exception, here is what I tell them: "Devote yourself to caring for orphans and widows in their distress, and keep yourself from being polluted by the world. We have dozens of ways for you to do these things around here. Your only purpose is just to say yes."

I mean every syllable of that response.

Sure, God may have a distinct calling for an individual, but until he reveals it, *we all should be about the business of doing what his Word has already asked us to do.*

Find someone gasping under a too-heavy load and refuse to just pass on by. Pause long enough to see their plight. Tell God you're trustworthy in this. String together a few days of looking beyond your own cares, your own concerns, your own desires, your own to-dos, and see if you don't find yourself feeling fulfilled in deeper ways. See if you don't start experiencing life that is truly life.

◇◇◇

Pushing Pause: Chapter 1

Being freed from the all-consuming nature of self-centeredness can feel like cleaning up an explosion of foam packing peanuts that scoot all over the floor and stick to you as you try to throw them away. But with time and attention, every last packing peanut can be trashed.

Take the time you need here. Give this work the attention it deserves. You'll be grateful that you did.

Read

To refresh yourself on the central passage from chapter 1, read James 1:1–27.

Reflect

- How do verses 1–26 raise the stakes even higher on James's exhortation in verse 27?

- When have you seen perseverance cultivated in your own life because of a trial that you lived through?

Respond

Be intentional today about spotting someone in distress. If there is an obvious way for you to help, do so. But the real goal for now is simply learning to look beyond your own concerns to see the concerns of another. Ask yourself these questions:

- Who is in need around me?
- What is it that they need?
- If someone were to help them, what form would that help take?

2

On Interruptibility

God's gift to us is ability; our gift to God is availability.[1]

ROBBY DAWKINS

T THIS POINT, A question may be on your mind, and it's a good question, I think: If this kind of God-honoring extravagant living is so altogether satisfying, then why aren't more people living this way? I can't speak for everyone. But as I look back on the seasons of selfishness I've known, the singular reason I didn't lay down my will and pick up God's will sooner was a simple one: *It's easier to go our own way.*

Or, at least, until it's not. Maybe the better way to say it is that it *feels* easier to go our own way.

There is something magical about the illusion of control, isn't there? We like to think we're masters of our own fate, captains of our own ship, determiners of our own course in life. It's a tough pill to swallow, admitting that we aren't the center of the universe, that we make a pretty sorry god.

So there's that. But there's something else, which is that, in order to shift from self-centeredness to others-centeredness—in order to become "people of the pause"—we have to *change*.

And for me, and maybe for you, change is *hard*. Especially this kind of change, which strikes at the core of who we are: our motivations, our methods, our overall approach to managing who we are and the resources entrusted to us. "No one is a natural born giver," my friend Robert Morris likes to say. "We are all born takers."[2] If true, then no wonder it's hard.

Just as when I was a teenager and early twentysomething, we carve out an approach to life that feels pretty good. We chart a course that affords us plenty of opportunity to look out for number one. We put up some self-protective walls. We do our thing, go our own way, and never look back. All seems good. All *is* good—or that's how we see it, anyway. And then the Holy Spirit comes along and says, *You gotta change all that.*

Huh? Who put *you* in charge?

We're not too sure what to make of this exhortation to stop blowing past people in need and start practicing this thing called the pause. Pause? Who *pauses* when there are this many places to go, this many people to see, this many things to do . . . this many meetings to be late to, this many errands to check off the list, this many kids to raise?

Until and unless you've had a crisis of belief, when some internal or external force overturns the carefully balanced apple cart that is your life, this pause thing is a tough sell. Until you've seen for yourself that self-focused living is not really living at all, then you just will not believe.

WHAT WINNERS DO

I have been mentoring young men for years now, and lately I've been deeply involved with two groups of guys, one of which I'm considering disbanding. None of these men really knew each other before I invited them into these gatherings, but a few meetings in I realized that there is an important characteristic that distinguishes one group from the other: *coachability.*

Coincidentally, the guys who migrated to one of the groups all happen to be great listeners, great question askers, and great at receiving coaching. They are open to trying new things. They are willing to go to school on the lessons I've learned. They are willing to course correct when they see that the path they're on isn't getting them to where they said they wanted to be. They are candid with me, they are vulnerable with each other, and they are committed to personal growth.

Case in point: one of the members of that group just became a millionaire—many times over, in fact—through the sale of the company he built. This guy is smart. He is savvy. He's a professional in every sense of the word. Guess what he did as soon as the sale went through? He scheduled an appointment with me. I am decidedly *not* a millionaire, I probably don't have to tell you. But this man trusts my walk with God and came seeking input on how to keep his own walk productive in this new financially rich environment. He met with me. He met with several businessmen in our church. He met with a financial counselor. He sat with his parents for an extended period of time. The point is he went in search of insight to avoid making big mistakes.

Coachability.

Receptivity.

Openness. Inquisitiveness. Absolutely nothing to prove.

This is a humble learner at work.

Now, the other group, for whatever reason, is pretty much the opposite of all of that. They are stubborn. They have a know-it-all spirit. They can play the victim role with ease: "It's the economy . . ." "It's those politicians . . ." "It's my neighbors . . . my spouse . . . my kids . . ."

Whatever problems are stymieing them, you can be sure those things aren't their fault.

Guess which group is more fun to mentor?

Some of us really do have to learn the hard way in life. But equally true is that some of us do not. The purpose of this chapter is to help you see where you fall in terms of being a pauser or a passerby and to show you the path toward *increased extravagance* in life, toward others-centeredness, toward purposefulness, toward the fulfillment you and I both seek. I'll show you the practices upheld by the wisest people I know. I'll disclose the lessons some have learned from challenges they've lived through. I'll expose my own wins and losses: what I did right, what I did wrong, what I learned.

When I was a kid, one of my favorite books was James Fenimore Cooper's *The Last of the Mohicans*. In it he writes, "Every trail has its end, and every calamity brings its lesson!" My hope is that by offering you this collective input, you can avoid a little calamity firsthand.

GENEROUS AS WE GO

To set up the conversation we're about to have, I should acknowledge that this entire chapter was motivated by one tiny phrase at the beginning of the Parable of the Good Samaritan, which reads, "as he traveled . . ." (Luke 10:33).

The man going from Jerusalem to Jericho had been left for dead in the ditch. The priest passed by. The Levite passed by. "But a Samaritan, *as he traveled*, came where the man was; and when he saw him, he took pity on him . . ."

"As he traveled."

"As he journeyed," in the English Standard Version.

"Who was on his journey," in the New American Standard Bible.

"On his journey" in the Holman Christian Standard Bible.

The point: there is a kind of generosity that happens on our own terms, and then there is generosity that is called out of us when we least expect it, that unfolds *while we're on our way to somewhere else.* The generosity we will assess and grow in throughout the course of this chapter is that kind of generosity. Extravagant generosity. Dangerous generosity. Generosity that we can't contrive.

The Samaritan in our story wasn't on a mission trip, seeking out ditch-dwelling people to help. No, he was *en route somewhere else.* He had intentions. He had expectations. He had plans. But then a need arose, and those plans took a back seat to God's. And in so doing, this Samaritan man took the first step of extravagance—namely, being found interruptible before God.

THE GENEROSITY QUOTIENT

I've been studying the way of extravagant people for some time now, sorting out why they do what they do, when they do it, and how. And based on the attitudes and actions I have seen, I've detected a few ideas on how the rest of us can move from where we are to where they seem to be. To that end, I have put together something of an IQ test that measures generosity . . . a test of our "GQ"—generosity quotient.

What I have observed in my own life and in the lives of scores of people I have counseled is that we tend to pass through a series of phases, regardless of our age, as it relates to increasing or improving our generosity quotient. That quotient, I think, is determined by evaluating a person's desire to be generous with her or his *faithfulness* to act in accordance with that desire. In their book, *The Generosity Factor,* authors Ken Blanchard and S. Truett Cathy say, "There's a big difference between held values and operational values. Held values are what people *say.* Operational values are what people *do.*"[3] As it relates to generosity, then, I'm interested in where those two sets of values intersect in a given person's life.

ASSESSING GENEROSITY	
High Desire + Low Faithfulness	High Desire + High Faithfulness
Low Desire + Low Faithfulness	Low Desire + High Faithfulness

Desire to Give (y-axis)

Faithfulness to Give (x-axis)

Picture a two-dimensional matrix such as the one shown above. On the y-axis, you see "Desire to Give," and on the x-axis "Faithfulness to Give." The four possible combinations of those two variables are these:

- Low Desire + Low Faithfulness
- High Desire + Low Faithfulness
- Low Desire + High Faithfulness
- High Desire + High Faithfulness

Now, here is how those combinations play out in terms that are familiar to us:

No Desire to Give + Lack of Faithfulness in Giving =
"Generosity as Aggravation"

For these people, opportunities to be generous are seen as aggravation. They place high value on autonomy and, while they may not overtly state it, wonder why people can't just take care of themselves instead of burdening others with their challenges and woes. They feel they've worked hard for what they have—certainly their money but also their discretionary time and their skill—and aren't especially excited about just "giving it away."

Great Desire to Give + Lack of Faithfulness in Giving =
"Generosity as Aspiration"

Here, people view opportunities for generosity as aspiration. They want to give; they just don't. They want to be generous; they just aren't. The reason for this is that they keep waiting for a better set of circumstances to come along—one that will make it easier for them to give. They're waiting for their schedule to clear a little, or for the busy season at work to lighten up, or for the long-awaited check to come in. *Then* they will be generous. *Then* it will make sense to give.

No Desire to Give + Great Faithfulness in Giving =
"Generosity as Compulsion"

There's a third category we should talk about, which involves people being faithful about giving even when they don't want to. For these people, opportunities for giving are seen as compulsion, things they are somehow *obliged* to seize. Maybe they have trouble saying no. Maybe there were raised to "follow the rules." Or maybe they have a fearsome view of God. Whatever the reason, while they have caught the practice of self-sacrifice, they haven't caught the spirit of it. Their giving brings them no joy.

Great Desire to Give + Great Faithfulness in Giving =
"Generosity as Invitation"

The "magic quadrant" in our matrix contains those who view generosity as invitation. They have a *great* desire to give and they maintain *great* faithfulness in giving, mostly because they truly believe that every opportunity to give and serve is an invitation to a better life. Why do pausers pause? *To read what the invitation says.*

The opportunity might be inviting them into greater purpose, or a deeper sense of fulfillment, or significant transformation. People in this phase of generosity are considered "extravagant." They no longer really aspire to generosity but rather respond to opportunities to give *reflexively*, as a habit. "With habits, we don't make decisions, we don't use self-control, we just do the thing we want ourselves to do . . . ," says Gretchen Rubin.[4]

These people *want* to give.

GENEROSITY AND YOU

I wonder: Where do you fall on the grid? Do you see opportunities for giving of yourself—your time, your talent, your treasure—as aggravation, aspiration, or compulsion? Or do you view those opportunities as invitations to help, to grow, to live? Of the four quadrants, where do you find yourself? More important still, where do you *want* to be?

To make your profile more obvious to you, answer the five questions below based on how you're *most likely* to respond.

1. *When I encounter someone in need, I wonder . . .*
   a. why they didn't plan better.
   b. about maybe helping out next time.
   c. what bad thing might happen to me if I don't at least try to help.
   d. what I might do to help.

2. *When someone asks me for a favor, I can't help but think . . .*
   a. that this is twice in two weeks that they've asked.
   b. that next week would actually work better for me.
   c. that of course I'll say yes even though I don't really want to say yes.
   d. that if it's my power to help out, then of course I'd love to.

3. *When I learn of a need in my circle of influence, I'm glad that...*

    a. the person in need has others they can surely turn to for help.

    b. I feel concerned for them but I probably won't *volunteer* to help.

    c. if I have to jump in, maybe I'll at least score some points?

    d. I know how to get in touch with them so that I can offer to help.

4. *When I think about becoming an "extravagant" person, the one word that comes to mind is...*

    a. wasteful.

    b. someday.

    c. burdensome.

    d. honored.

5. *I'd feel more satisfied in life if I could spend more time...*

    a. tending to my responsibilities, taking care of business, getting things done.

    b. planning for tomorrow, when I'll (hopefully) be better prepared than I am today.

    c. getting freed from all of the "shoulds" of life.

    d. catalyzing someone else's growth, wholeness, sense of "all rightness" in the world.

If you selected A most often, then you are most likely an aggravated giver, who views opportunities for generosity as annoyances.

If you selected B most often, then you are most likely an aspiring giver, who views opportunities for generosity as things to be seized at some other time.

If you selected C most often, then you are most likely a compulsive giver, who views opportunities for generosity as obligations you "should" fulfill.

If you selected D most often, then you are most likely an extravagant giver, who views invitations to generosity as opportunities to seize.

Most people I meet want to be known as generous—they really do. The reasons they aren't living up to that standard can vary, but there are always legitimate reasons that are to blame. Maybe they were never taught how to rightly handle money, and so, despite their best intentions to give, there never seems to be enough on hand to spare.

Maybe they suffered scarcity at some point in their lives, as I did as a kid, and, like me, made some sort of inner vow that they'd never be poor. Such a posture can look like miserliness. It can make "generosity" a tough goal to achieve.

Or maybe they just never knew that giving could actually be fun—that "cheerfulness" is okay with God.

If you fall into this camp of longing for a deeper level of generosity, as well as the increased fulfillment that accompanies it, then the balance of this chapter is for you. Not only will we look at why it's dangerous to settle for the first three views of generosity—aggravation, aspiration, or compulsion—but we will look at how to make a beeline from those views to the fourth way of viewing generosity: *invitation*.

ERRANT POSTURES AND THEIR
LONG-TERM EFFECTS

I stand by my statement that most people want to be known as generous. Most do. But catch the phrasing of what I said: they want to be *known as* generous. This is altogether different from wanting to *be* generous, because to want *that* result seems too lofty a goal, given where they presently stand.

How did these people get where they are? How did they become so entrenched in their errant posture that they no longer even dream of softening to service, of living beyond themselves?

In each of the first three generosity quotient types, real peril can unfold. You hang out in any of those quadrants long enough, and things will invariably go south. Let's look at the eventual state of people in each group.

The Aggravated Giver

You spend fifty, fifty-five hours at the office each week, come home every night—late again—have a quick dinner with your spouse and kids, retreat to your favorite chair, where you decompress in front of the TV for hours on end before falling into bed, waking up six hours later and starting the cycle over again.

Serve? Who has time to serve?

You are utterly *fascinated* with the English language. You read books on grammar . . . for fun. You listen to podcasts on how to properly proofread text. You silently correct the incorrect pronoun usage you see on social media, including in that post inviting volunteers to help with an ESL program for non-native English speakers.

Share? Who has anything to share?

You drop off your kids at school, grab a latte from Starbucks, and then head to the gym, where you take two group fitness classes back-to-back before meeting a friend for lunch. The afternoon is full of errands: Target to get new towels for the guest bathroom with a detour through holiday decor, a stop at Barnes & Noble to pick up next month's book club pick and splurge on a few new releases, the mall to get those new running shoes your daughter has been begging for, and maybe a pair yourself. A smoothie on the way back to your kids' school, then on to a piano lesson and soccer practice and . . . wow, where did the day go? You order takeout on your phone to pick up en route so the kids can eat as soon as they get home, do homework, and get to bed at a decent hour.

Give? Who has money to give?

The risk of staying in that first quadrant too long? It's hard-heartedness toward the needs in our world. You become not merely annoyed by the plight of others but utterly oblivious to it. Your life becomes consumed by self: your wants, your needs, your plans, your will. You simply do not see yourself as connected to another's challenges or needs. You don't see what you have to offer, because your resources are all spoken for.

The Aspirational Giver

In their fascinating book on how to address global poverty, *Poor Economics*, authors Abhijit Banerjee and Esther Duflo acknowledge the gap between a person's desire to make a wise choice and the practice of actually choosing wisely: "The human brain processes the present and the future very differently. In essence, we seem to have a vision of how we should act in the future that is often inconsistent with the way we act today and will act in the future. One form that this 'time inconsistency' takes is to spend now, at the same time as we *plan* to save in the future. In other words, we hope that our 'tomorrow self' will be more patient than 'today's self' is prepared to be."[5]

For those who see generosity as "aspiration," they hope that their tomorrow self will be more giving than today's self is prepared to be.

If I were to lean into a Bible verse to describe the long-term effect of remaining "aspirational" in your view of generosity, it would be James 2:17: "So also faith by itself, if it does not have works, is dead" (ESV). We can only talk the talk for so long; at some point we will be expected to walk the walk.

I'm reminded of the anecdote of the middle-aged wife who complained to her husband that he never said "I love you," to which the husband said, "I told you I loved you on our wedding day thirty years ago. If I change my mind, I'll let you know."

If you desire to give but never act on that desire, your spiritual fervor will be about as intense as that wife's fervor for her husband probably was, which is to say not very fervent at all.

The Compulsive Giver

Those who set up shop in "compulsion" for any length of time inevitably veer toward legalism. They volunteer and give and serve despite not *wanting* to volunteer and give and serve, which can't help but lead toward a decisive lack of cheerfulness in life. "God loves a *cheerful* giver," 2 Corinthians 9:7 confirms.[6] Which means he doesn't so much love it when we give "reluctantly," or "under compulsion," as the first part of that verse attests.

To dispute the compulsively generous spirit, I've heard financial whiz Dave Ramsey on radio ask, "How generous do *you* feel on Tax Day?"

Crickets, right?

Nobody in a right mind likes to have generosity legislated. It's a bad deal for all involved.

If you're a legalist, you can come out of your prison cell. Freedom . . . and a little cheerfulness . . . await.

THE JOURNEY TO QUADRANT FOUR

I'd like to spend some time charting the course from each of these errant postures to that magical quadrant I call "extravagance," but first, let's refresh ourselves on why we're making this journey in the first place. In other words, *why generosity?* Why should this practice matter to us? What's the big deal with giving, anyway?

The most famous (and most quoted) Bible verse in history is John 3:16. You know it as well as I do: "For God so loved the world that he gave his one and only Son, that whoever believes in him shall not perish but have eternal life." The Bible League International put out an easy-to-read translation of Scripture not long ago that comes at that verse a little differently. It says, "Yes, God loved the world so much that he gave his only Son, so

that everyone who believes in him would not be lost but have eternal life"
(ERV). It's a good add, that "Yes," a grand nod to the world he'd made.

> *Yes, I see you.*
> *Yes, I love you.*
> *Yes, I'm committed to making you whole.*
> *Yes, I will send my Son.*
> *Yes, you can live with me!*

If you're serious about following Jesus, your entire existence is
predicated on that "Yes." As is mine.

God said yes to us, and then he invited us to say yes right back.

> *Yes, I see you, God.*
> *Yes, I love you.*
> *Yes, I'm committed to living whole.*
> *Yes, I receive the gift of your Son.*
> *Yes, I will live with you.*

The love God asks for, according to our central parable, is directed
at him. But it doesn't stop there, as we've seen. We are also to love
our neighbor as ourselves. (See Luke 10:27.) We are to love even the
neighbors who sin, and even the ones who vote differently from us.
The injunction to "love the sinner, hate the sin"? It may be cliché, but
it's true. We most reflect the image of Jesus in the world when we love
well, when we refuse to be stingy with our love.

Love looks like God.

Love looks like Jesus, the Son God so lovingly gave.

This is why it wasn't a waste when Mary poured perfume on Jesus'
feet. There are tithes and offerings, and then there are *painful* offerings, as a friend of mine calls them. Those painful ones are *extravagant*.
Mary's was extravagant that day. It cost her something, but that cost

was worth it. Why? Because in offering something costly, she told God, "I recognize that all I have is yours, my breath, my resources, my life."

But where did this generosity come from in Mary? Why did such feelings start to bubble up?

You'll recall that just before the scene involving Mary and her perfume, her brother, Lazarus, had been raised from the dead. Do you think Mary had a different perspective on worldly possessions once her brother, who had died, was alive? I know I would.

In fact, I know I *do*.

You probably do too. We who were once dead in our transgressions understand how valuable life can be.

Costly offerings tell God, "*Thank you* for this breath. *Thank you* for these resources. *Thank you* for this life."

Extravagance always is born in gratitude; it has no other starting point. And so those of us who have the most reason to be grateful are wise to gather up as many lessons as we possibly can regarding how to extravagantly display it to God.

We love him—we do.

Now we learn to love like him.

We learn to *give*, as he himself gave.

Back to our initial question: How does each quadrant step toward this place of extravagance? Let's answer that question now.

THE PATH TO INVITATION

	Desire to Give	
Aspiration High Desire + Low Faithfulness		**Invitation** High Desire + High Faithfulness
Aggravation Low Desire + Low Faithfulness		**Compulsion** Low Desire + High Faithfulness

Faithfulness to Give

From Aggravation to Extravagance

Many people I know who once saw themselves in the descriptions of the generosity-as-aggravation quadrant have told me that a specific pattern of thinking was at work that made it difficult to move toward others-centeredness. The pattern went like this: First, they harbored a fear that they'd never have enough. They'd never have enough time. They'd never have enough money. They'd never have enough qualifications. They'd never have enough peace.

Then, because of that fear-laden belief, they began nearly hoarding their resources under the false notion that everything they had was "theirs." Instead of offering up their lives in service to God and others, they drew their resources in tighter, certain that there was no other way to keep them safe.

Third, these people made something of a resolution, not dissimilar from the vow of my youth. "I will do whatever it takes to get more," they told themselves. More money. More power. More freedom. More sex. More recognition. More _____. (Fill in the blank.)

What helped them begin to arrest that progression and consider taking a different tack? For starters, they allowed themselves to be confronted with the question "When is enough?"

If you find yourself in this category of aggravation toward the idea of generosity, then I might ask you the very same thing: *How much is enough?* Oil magnate John D. Rockefeller was once asked how much money was enough, to which he famously replied, "Just a little bit more."

If I had just a little-bit-more money, then I'd be content.
If I had just a little-bit-bigger house, then I'd be content.
If I had just a little-bit-nicer car, then I'd be content.

You can be completely content with your five-year-old car, but then your friend picks you up in a brand-new car and you're discontented again. Whatever they spray in those cars at the factory is made of crack cocaine.

Just a little bit more . . . that's all I need. *Then* I'll be at peace.

Maybe you can relate?

Some percentage of us must nod assent at that idea, because God thought it necessary to inspire more than a few passages of Scripture on the subject. One of the most useful ones is Ecclesiastes 5:10, which says, "Whoever loves money never has enough; whoever loves wealth is never satisfied with their income."

More than a dozen years ago, when I became the pastor of New Life Church, suddenly I had a public platform unlike any I'd known before. Overnight my presence conveyed more support, my words carried more weight, and my vote more easily swayed a decision. It was surreal. I hadn't changed a bit, but people's perceptions of me had, and I wasn't altogether sure what that meant.

Around the same time I was approached by several publishers who were suddenly interested in having me write books. "You need to write," they told me. "We can help make your books a success."

Now, I should mention here that unless your last name is Grisham or Rowling or King, you probably aren't going to make any money writing books. In fact, if you want to live a life of destitution, there are few better paths than the one paved by aspiring authorship. But still, I had some friends who were what I would consider "high-profile" pastors, and I had seen a few of them take book deals and lose their way. Everything started revolving around those books and the speaking tours/increased platform/conference opportunities that came with them.

When God called me into the ministry, the calling revolved around serving people, not around writing books. I suppose you could make a case that writing books serves people, but I wasn't so sure at the time. I went to Pam and said, "Most everyone who goes into vocational ministry has a pure heart. They love God. They love people. They love to serve. Do you think I would lose these loves if I decided to start writing books?"

What I had in mind was that verse we looked at before (1 Peter 5:1–3), about ministers being eager to serve, about them not being greedy for money.

I didn't want greed to be my deal.

Pam and I talked about what to do. For a few weeks we prayed together, batted around ideas, tried to come to consensus on what I would do. Sometime during those talks, God brought to mind the words of 1 Timothy 6:6: "Godliness with contentment is great gain."

In the New International Version, the broader passage appears under the header "False Teachers and the Love of Money." Sounds ominous, doesn't it? That's because it is. The verses in that section say this: "But godliness with contentment is great gain. For we brought nothing into the world, and we can take nothing out of it. But if we have food and clothing, we will be content with that. Those who want to get rich fall into temptation and a trap and into many foolish and harmful desires that plunge people into ruin and destruction. For the love of money is a root of all kinds of evil. Some people, eager for money, have wandered from the faith and pierced themselves with many griefs" (1 Timothy 6:6–10).

I thought about those words from Paul to Timothy, his young protégé. I thought about how easy it is to be eager for the things of this world—book deals included—instead of being eager for godliness, for contentment, for what the Bible calls "great gain."

Sometime after these thoughts occurred to me, I was on the back porch one evening, enjoying the presence of God. I said to him, "Lord, I want to be sure that I stay in touch with the fact that I have enough. I have more than enough, actually. I will write books if that's what you want me to do. But if writing books will compromise my intimacy with you, or if it will shift my focus from the things of your kingdom to the things of this world, then, please, keep me from writing books."

Godliness. Contentment. I wanted the spirit of those words to be true in my life. *A godly man. A content man. A man who is not greedy. A man whose gains are in the Lord alone.*

Write the book. The prompting came to me that clearly: Write the book.

I laughed. "Okay. I'll write the book."

"The book" was my first book, which was seven books ago. And with each opportunity to write, I have that same conversation with God: "I have enough. I am grateful to you for all I have. If this deal will change that posture at all, I'm out ..."

So far, the reply has been the same: Write the book.

I hope that's always the reply.

Back to the original question: How much is enough? Do you believe you have enough?

The first step to moving from aggravation to extravagance is asking God to form that belief in you. You already have enough. Any more and you'll have *more* than enough. The time to share is now. The time to give is now. The time to loosen your grip on the things of this fleeting world is now. When Jesus ascended back to the Father—you can read Acts 1 for the full scene—he commissioned us not to satisfy our greedy hearts with the things of this earth but rather to colonize the earth with the things of heaven. The time is now to do just that.

In chapter 3 we'll look more closely at how to untangle ourselves from the fears and insecurities that keep us from moving not away from but *toward* the ditches of despair so many struggling people find themselves in. But, for now, a worthwhile starting point is this: Ask God to banish from your mind and heart anything that reeks of self-centered ways. Ask him to provide the way of escape from temptation that he promises in 1 Corinthians 10:13. Commit to memory 1 Corinthians 12:7, which reminds us that the gifts God has given us are intended not only to bless our lives but for the profit of *all*.

From Aspiration to Extravagance

Let's look at quadrant 2. The path from "aspiration" to extravagance can be summed up in a single word: "Give."

That's it: *Give.*

If your challenge is that you long to give of your time and money but never seem to *actually* give of your time and money, guess what your starting point is? Give! Of your time. And your money.

When I was growing up, my dad always told me two things. First: "Do the right thing for the right reason, even at your own hurt." And second: "Say what you mean and mean what you say."

Both support this key objective: *Give.*

Give because God says to give.[7] Give because Jesus gave.[8] Give because it's a mark of righteousness.[9] Give because you will be blessed.[10]

Furthermore, if you say you want to give, let your yes be yes[11]— meaning *follow through and give.*

People I've known who were stuck in this quadrant convinced themselves that once things "settled down" or "got a little better" or were "under control," *then* they would give; *then* they would serve. It's a line of thinking that always reminds me of the permanent special offered by the restaurant chain Joe's Crab Shack: "Free Crabs Tomorrow!"

We can promise we'll do *anything* tomorrow, because tomorrow's always a day away.

If you're an aspiring giver, the growth you're seeking happens *today*. You may start small, but certainly *start*. If you've ever been hungry— and not because it's lunchtime but because you haven't eaten a square meal in more than a week—then you know that ten bucks can go a long, long way toward filling that void in your gut.

Give something.

Give anything.

Give for real, starting today.

Someone who's starving will be grateful that your walk finally mirrored your talk.

From Compulsion to Extravagance

If the path to extravagance from the "aggravation" quadrant is mostly *spiritual* in nature, and the path from the "aspiration" quadrant is mostly *practical* in nature, the one for those stuck in "compulsion" is *relational* in nature, as they learn to trust the God they serve.

I learned this one the hard way.

Despite my under-resourced upbringing, my parents always saw fit to tithe. Truly, I'm not sure they ever missed a week. Regardless of how bare our pantry cupboard was, Mom and Dad *always* tithed. Consequently, once I was married and managing a household of my own, I saw fit to tithe. But as I mentioned, an inner vow was at work in my life, which stole much of my "giving" joy. The net effect was that I was a selfish giver. (Did you know it was possible to be such a thing?) I gave because I thought I had to give, not because giving was a noble intent of my heart. It turns out that giving from a place of compulsion is far different from being divinely *compelled* to give.

The road to extravagance for those stuck in "compulsion"? It's offering ourselves back to God. Our money. Our time. Our talents. Our yes. "Generosity is about caring about the needs of others, then acting to meet those needs," wrote Ken Blanchard and Truett Cathy. "Time meets a certain kind of need. Talent meets another. Treasure still another, and touch meets its own set of needs. Generosity is about balance—about making all of one's resources available."

Those things that we've been hanging on to so tightly? They've belonged to him all along.

THE EXTRAVAGANCE WE'RE DESTINED FOR

You've probably noticed a pattern in the last several sections, which is that all roads lead to extravagance. This is intentional; it's where we're all meant to wind up. For the balance of this chapter, I want to shift from trying to describe what this place of extravagance is like to demonstrating it with flesh and blood.

Some scholars believe that Genesis 22 is the most important chapter of the entire Old Testament, and the central character in that chapter is Abraham, the great father of our faith. I want to take us to the events in that chapter because, second to Jesus' sacrifice on the cross, there may be no better manifestation of the kind of lavish generosity I'm vying for than Abraham's willing obedience regarding the death of his son.

If you're a parent, then you agree that the most difficult loss to sustain in life would be the loss of a beloved child. It has been said that not only do we raise our children but also they raise us. And to "let them go," to lose their influence in our lives, seems a fate far worse than death. So much is wrapped up in our kids—our thoughts, our legacies, our hearts. And yet that is precisely what God went looking for one day . . . a parent's willingness to part with a child.

Abraham and his wife, Sarah, had waited more than twenty-five years to have their first baby, and then he arrives, little Isaac—the one who makes his mother laugh, the one who brings great joy. That's Genesis 21.

Then comes Genesis 22.

Let's begin with verse 1. "Some time later God tested Abraham," it reads. (God never tempts us to disobey him, but, oh, does he test our character. Abraham was about to discover that firsthand.)

"Abraham!" God said, to which Abraham replied, "Here I am."[12]

Verse 2: "Take your son, your only son, whom you love—Isaac—and go to the region of Moriah," God said. "Sacrifice him there as a burnt offering on a mountain I will show you."

A bit of context, in case like so many people in the world who read this story and decide they don't want to follow a God like this God, who asks parents to kill their kids: Abraham was living in the most pagan culture around. He was surrounded by false gods, by idols erected to those gods, and by people who chose to worship those idols instead of the one, true God. In many cases those gods demanded that people sacrifice their firstborn children to show their devotion to them. What Abraham was experiencing was a *common occurrence* in those days. The uncommon part was that Yahweh was involved. And he's not just *any* god. He was about to show himself strong—supremely strong, in fact.

Scholars think that Isaac was in his thirties when this event took place, so while Abraham is often lauded for his faithfulness, it was both father *and* son who obeyed. Isaac willingly accompanied his father, evidenced by his carrying his own wood (see Genesis 22:6) and his choosing not to overpower his elderly father when the man raised a sharp knife to him.

And yet you know how this story goes: that knife that was raised would never touch human flesh. Jehovah was on the scene.

Verses 10–12: "Then he [Abraham] reached out his hand and took the knife to slay his son. But the angel of the LORD called out to him from heaven, 'Abraham! Abraham!'

" 'Here I am,' he replied.

" 'Do not lay a hand on the boy,' he said. 'Do not do anything to him. Now I know that you fear God, because you have not withheld from me your son, your only son.' "

Crazy story, right?

The Bible is full of them.

And yet the message here is one of sanity and comfort to us: God is not like the gods of this world. He is the God of the new creation. The God of rescue and grace. The God who comes for us, time and again, to show us a new way to live.

God was not trying to take anything from Abraham; he was trying to win Abraham's heart. And the same is true for you and me. God doesn't need our stuff. He doesn't need our bankable hours. He doesn't need our skill, as though he's lacking anything in himself.

He needs nothing.

But he *desires* our hearts.

And for that allegiance, he will fight. The only question here is: Will he win us over? Will he persuade us to fully be his?

When Pam and I were a young couple living in Amarillo, Texas, I was working in the television industry, running a station for NBC. We were a ten-hour road trip away from our family and friends, who were still living in North Louisiana, and that distance often stung. We missed our parents. We missed our closest friends. We were lonely and longed for home.

One day I got a call. It was from an NBC affiliate thirty minutes from our hometown. I was twenty-eight years old, and they were offering to double my salary if I'd come. That sum equaled more than I'd ever made in my life, and at the sound of the offer my jaw literally dropped. They would cover the move, our first month's rent, and more. "We will take care of getting you and your wife settled," the exec assured me. "What do you think? . . . Are you in?"

I told the man I needed to consult with Pam and God before I gave my final answer, but that was just a formality, I knew. This deal was too good to be true.

I got off the phone, passed the details to Pam, and then broke out in laughter. "Can you believe this?" I cheered. "Babe! We're headed *home*!"

I was so overcome with emotion and gratitude that I physically needed some air. I told Pam that I was going to go for a quick walk, and as I left I said, "Call our parents! Call our friends! Call everyone we know!"

Now, I can be prone to exaggerations, but I'm not exaggerating here. The moment my feet hit the sidewalk and the screen door slammed shut behind me, I sensed the clearest prompting I've ever received from the Lord. This is what he said: No.

I stopped walking. "What?"

NO.

"God, is that you?"

No, Brady. Trust me. No.

In a haze of confusion and disappointment, I did an about-face and headed inside. I told Pam that despite all evidence to the contrary, this job opportunity wasn't for us. She replaced the phone in its cradle, sat down at the kitchen table, and wept.

I felt like weeping, too, even as I knew what I had heard.

This perfect opportunity wasn't God's perfect will for us. And so I called the executive back that night and said, "Thank you. But no, thanks."

Several months later Pam and I met a woman who asked if we would take in her newborn baby. So we adopted our son, Abram, and then we adopted our daughter, Callie, that way too. Not long after that, a little church in West Texas asked me to start preaching there. Two years later I helped Robert Morris start Gateway Church. Seven years after that, New Life Church came calling.

Let me be clear in acknowledging that the sovereignty of the Lord could have overcome my disobedience had I ignored that initial "No." But you will never convince me that disobeying his voice would have brought me more fulfillment than I've known in obedience, in laying down all for him.

God doesn't need our sacrifice. God desires only our hearts. And it's in the laying down of *all that we have*, choosing to be instantaneously and utterly interruptible when he calls, that our hearts become fully his.

If you've been aggravated by opportunities to give of yourself, will you start by acknowledging the resources you have? Then will you admit that God has blessed you richly, for a purpose that goes beyond yourself?

If you've been aspirational in your views on generosity, living as one with faith but precious few works, will you step forward in *activated* faith, returning to God what is already his?

If you've been compulsive in your approach to generosity, will you choose to start trusting the Lord?

To you and me both, God extends an invitation, to give back to him that which we love.

Take your son, whom you love, and lay him down for me.
Take your job promotion, which you love, and lay it down for me.
Take your 401(k), which you love, and lay it down for me.
Take your gym membership, which you love, and lay it down for me.
Take your detailed to-do list, which you love, and lay it down for me.
Take your every last idol, which you dearly love, and lay it down for me.

Extravagance says, "I have laid all things down, for the purpose of honoring God." It is this extravagance that we are destined for, if only we'll let God have his way.

<><><><><><><><><><><><><><><><><><><><><><><><><><><><><><><><>

Pushing Pause: Chapter 2

You and I both have a perspective on the opportunities we find day by day to practice generosity. We're either drained by those opportunities, energized by them, or find ourselves landing somewhere in between. Take a few moments to work through the sections below, taking as much time as you need to sort out where you fall.

How do you view opportunities to be generous? What is your GQ (generosity quotient) these days?

Read

In John 6:38 (MSG), we read these words: "Give away your life; you'll find life given back, but not merely given back—given back with bonus and blessing. Giving, not getting, is the way. Generosity begets generosity."

Reflect

- When have you experienced in your own life the idea of generosity begetting generosity?
- How resolute would you say that you are in your belief that practicing generosity really will yield not just returns but returns that are "bonuses" and "blessed"?

Respond

The challenge I have for you today is to assess your GQ by taking the brief quiz earlier in the chapter. Once you have determined whether you are in the "Aggravation," "Aspiration," "Compulsion," or "Invitation" category, choose *at least one* of the steps toward extravagance suggested below and act on it before you continue to the next chapter.

To Move from "Aggravation" to Extravagance:

- Acknowledge, before God, the resources you've been entrusted with. Make a list if you need to, to prove to yourself just how blessed and rich you are.
- Ask God to chip away at your self-centeredness and install others-centeredness in its place.
- Memorize 1 Corinthians 12:7, which reminds us that "to each one [of the believers] the manifestation of the Spirit [of God] is given for the common good."

To Move from "Aspiration" to Extravagance:

- Ask God to show you where you might be of help in the life of someone else today.
- Commit to God that you will not just say that you have faith in him but that you also will activate that faith today.
- Give!

To Move from "Compulsion" to Extravagance:

- Begin today to trust the Lord. Intentionally tell him that you trust him.
- Intentionally take steps of faith that demonstrate that trust. Intentionally follow up with God afterward to say thank you for providing his trustworthiness once again.
- When you say yes to an opportunity to serve, fight the urge to feel put-upon. Instead, say to God (aloud!), "Thank you, Father, for trusting me with this opportunity."
- Memorize Colossians 3:23, which says, "Whatever you do, work at it with all your heart, as working for the Lord, not for human masters."

To Deepen Extravagance in Your Life:

- Remind yourself that you are not crazy for devoting your life and your resources to God.
- Ask God to carve out greater capacity in your mind and heart for both seeing and responding to needs around you.
- Encourage one person today to lay down something for the sake of serving someone else.

3

The Five Fears

*Fear breeds hatred, and hatred has the power to
destroy everything in its path.*

KEVYN AUCOIN

DESPITE MY UNAPOLOGETIC CHAMPIONING in the last chapter of
the aim of becoming interruptible, I probably don't have to tell
you that no matter how interruptible to God you are compelled to be,
interruptibility is but the first step in living an extravagant life.

Is it the only step we should take? Hardly. How much we would
miss in this life if we stopped there and refused to move on!

The whole *point* is moving on.

Whenever people in the Bible encountered God (Hebrew testament) or Jesus (Greek testament), *action* was expected, following the
interruption they'd known. Moses was supposed to go talk to Pharaoh
so that the Israelites could be freed from slavery. Jonah was supposed

73

to go prophesy against the Ninevites. Samuel was supposed to go relay a message from God. Saul was supposed to go to Damascus, where he would receive further instruction on following Jesus the rest of his days. One hundred percent of the disciples were supposed to go and leave their businesses and families and preach to the nations the good news of Christ. We could go on, but the point would be the same: what comes after a divine interruption is action.

Go.

See.

Speak.

Ask.

Move.

Give.

Help.

In short: Be the hands and feet of Jesus. *Minister to those in need.*

Which is when, for most people—you and me among them—things get a little . . . complex.

THE FIVE FEARS

Almost without exception, the thing that keeps you and me and every other member of humanity from being as good as the Good Samaritan—the thing that compels us to pass by instead of pause whenever we see someone in obvious need—is plain old everyday fear. We may not own up to being afraid: fear is for the weak, the insecure. But fear is always to blame. We're afraid of what might happen. We're afraid of what might *not* happen. We're afraid of the unknown. We're afraid of being known. We're afraid of what lies beyond our comfort zone, of standing up, of *showing up*, of venturing out.

I've been talking to people about the fears that keep them planted in place or passing on by, and I think I've distilled them all into five key fears. See if you see yourself in any of these categories. As you'll soon see, I sure do.

Fear #1: The Fear of Being Interrupted

We just spent an entire chapter looking at this fear and diagnosing how deeply we experience it. I bring it up again here because this fear of having our plans hijacked by someone or something else tends to be the most obvious symptom of a self-focused life. Sounds harsh, I know. By the end of this chapter, maybe that harshness will seem well-placed.

For now, let me say this as plainly as I can: in the same way that a stuffed nose and difficulty swallowing signal that a full-on head cold is about to level you flat, the presence of this fear—the fear of being interrupted—signals that spiritual disease has taken hold and is having its way.

Fear #2: The Fear of Being Inconvenienced

Look beneath the fear of being interrupted, and you'll find a second fear there: the fear of being inconvenienced. Proverbs 14:12 reminds us that there is always "a way that appears to be right" to us, "but in the end it leads to death." This verse carries salvific credibility—no other way but the path that leads through belief in Jesus' existence, incarnation, redemptive death, burial, and resurrection will get us to eternity with God—but it doesn't stop there. It also is significant in lesser matters of our lives. Day by day, you and I have "a way that seems right": stuff we intend on doing, people we plan to see, ideas we hope to activate, agendas we'll move ahead. And yet, apart from the empowerment of the Holy Spirit, the divine nod on those plans and ways, something will die a little bit. Our faith, for starters. Our trust in God's abundant provision. Our belief that we're not alone in this great big world.

And also: our ability to be of use, in redeeming all that sits in need of redemption.

The Samaritan—the one Jesus called "good"—was *on his way*, you'll recall, when he allowed himself to be interrupted. Which is noteworthy, because interruptions invariably lead to inconvenience; they are two sides of the very same coin. What arrests us inevitably troubles us, and trouble is nobody's friend. And yet at least part of what made the Samaritan good was this very allowance: trouble. He welcomed trouble with open arms.

In March 2018, the Forbes Finance Council posted an article with the title "The Age of Convenience: It's More Than We Can Afford." In it they noted that while "over the course of the nearly two decades, incomes have remained largely stagnant," in every facet of our existence, costs of living have gone through the roof. The result? "For the first time in our country's history," they wrote, citing recent Federal Reserve findings, "outstanding credit card debt has crossed over the one trillion dollar mark . . ."[1]

If I were to sum up the reason behind this out-of-proportion debt load we've collectively entered, I'd need only one word: "convenience." Retailers have made things so terribly convenient that we are helpless to avoid their snares.

Think of it: there was a time in North America when if you wanted to eat food, you'd have to grow food. You'd fatten up an animal. You'd feed it, and wait, and slaughter it, and only *then* be able to eat it. You'd cultivate a crop. You'd plant it, and wait, and plow it, and wait, and harvest, and only *then* be able to eat it.

Agriculturists would combine forces eventually, creating thriving rural economies, but the approach was still the same: You want food? You make it—an admittedly inconvenient approach.

Once towns were established, farmers came in from their farms to sell the fruits of their labor in open-air marketplaces and bazaars, located in the centers of those towns. The seasonal marketplaces soon became permanent stalls where goods were traded or sold, and by the 1600s country stores emerged, trailing development to the West. Now, if you needed flour or salt, you could happen by the "country store." Someone standing behind a counter would dole out your desired portion from the bulk supply and then would put it on your tab. Once you were able to sell your own crops or livestock for some money, you'd come back to pay your bill. More convenient, you might say, but nothing like what we know today.

In the blink of an eye, it seems, we went from country stores to self-serve chain retailers to stores delivering right to your home. Today, you can have your usual groceries automatically delivered through a subscription so you don't even have to think about placing an order, and there will probably come a day when we find even *that* an inconvenient approach.

Take any industry or service and apply this same little "convenience" exercise, and you'll see that while, yes, we can accomplish nearly every task in life these days with a couple of clicks and a credit card, it *has* cost us something in the end. We no longer have to put our hands in the earth. We no longer have to till the soil. We no longer have to work a field. We no longer have to travel a short distance, coming upon people and situations as we go. We no longer have to interact with another human being. We no longer have to be trusted to pay our bill. For a quick 5 percent delivery fee, we don't even have to *move*.

Which is a good thing, because *who has time to move?*

Is now the right time to mention that the most current data reveals that we spend upward of four hours a day on our devices, with half that total spent on social media?[2] (My trusty iPhone tells me my totals were more like five hours a day last week, but before you judge me, you should know that I *read* on my phone. So there.)

The wild propagation of peddlers of convenience have told us that we simply can't be bothered to lift a finger, that we don't have *time* for the fine points of life. But what are we doing with the minutes they save us? We're scrolling Instagram and playing the latest hot game on our smartphones—that's what. Fun? For sure. Worthwhile excuse for not living beyond ourselves? Um . . . the B-I-B-L-E seems to have a strong opinion on that.

"A Samaritan traveling the road came on him [the man who had been attacked by robbers and left for dead in the ditch]. When he saw the man's condition, his heart went out to him. He gave him first aid"— *inconvenient*—"disinfecting and bandaging his wounds." *Inconvenient!*

"Then he lifted him onto his donkey, led him to an inn, and made him comfortable." *Inconvenient, inconvenient, inconvenient!* "In the morning he took out two silver coins and gave them to the innkeeper, saying, 'Take good care of him. If it costs any more, put it on my bill— I'll pay you on my way back.'"[3] *Inconvenient times a multiple of ten!*

"What do you think?" Jesus asked the teacher of the law. "Which of the three"—the priest, who'd passed the man by; the Levite, who'd also passed by; or the Samaritan, who'd chosen to pause—"became a neighbor to the man attacked by robbers?"[4]

Well, what do you think?

What do *I* think?

What do our *lives* say about what we think?

It is absurdly inconvenient to care for others, and yet. still, Jesus had the gall to say of the Samaritan's behavior:

"Go . . ."

He said "Go . . ." to me.

He said "Go . . ." to you.

Go, you people who say you love me and want to be like me.

"Go, and do the same."[5]

Fear #3: The Fear of Inadequacy

Dig deeper underneath the fear of inconvenience, and yet a third fear shows its face: the fear of inadequacy. Upon encountering someone who is clearly distressed, the fear of inadequacy asks: What if I don't have what they need?

Equally haunting is this question: Then again, what if I *do*?

There's a name for this you may have heard: "imposter syndrome." You probably even suffer imposter syndrome from time to time. I came across a cartoon online once titled, "Number of People Who Get Imposter Syndrome." In the center of the cartoon was a pie chart divided into three pieces. The medium-size piece—representing about 40 percent of the pie—was labeled, "People who get imposter syndrome." A smaller piece—about 10 percent of the pie—was labeled, "Other people who get imposter syndrome." And the third piece—the other roughly 50 percent of the pie—was labeled, "Literally everyone else, all of whom also get imposter syndrome."

At some point in life, we're *all* going to feel ill-equipped for the task at hand, regardless of what that task specifically involves. We wonder if we have what it takes to accomplish a mission. We fear we'll be found lacking in some important skill. Worse still, we are terrified that we *do* have what is needed and we'll be called on to show up and prove ourselves. These feelings all fall under the fear of inadequacy, the concern that we're not capable, that we're less-than—that we're *duds*.

Looking back on my upbringing, I am astounded by my mom's refusal to give way to this particular fear. As I've noted, we were not very well-off. We *really* were not well-off, and yet I strain to remember a time when a young man in need wasn't calling our house his home. My mom was forever welcoming in "strays," as she lovingly called them, boys from our church who had no place to go, no food to eat, no dream to chase. Even when we were hardly making ends meet ourselves, Mom extended our resources to them. My brother and sister and I always thought it was great having a "third brother" around, and Mom loved helping those aimless souls find a little steadiness and certainty and love.

Now that I have the benefit of hindsight, I see how she could have said, "Take in another child? I can't even care for the ones I've got!" Everyone would have given her a pass . . . perhaps even God himself.

She *did* have her hands full. We *were* scraping to get by. But, equally true, she knew that even a little faith in God's provision could produce bigger-than-life results.

My mom taught me dozens of lessons, but one of the most poignant is this: having compassion for someone doesn't require you to give of yourself as much as it requires that you desire to see God do for someone in need what *only God can do*. In his book *You Can't Go Wrong Doing Right*, Robert J. Brown, the great-grandson of a slave, who has served on the boards of several massive corporations and influenced leaders in the White House, tells of his mother forever feeding hungry neighbors even as his own family had little to eat. "Son," his mother would always tell him, "you don't have to be rich to give. We aren't rich, but we had food in the pot today. The Lord provided that food, and he provided it to me so I could share it with others. He gave us enough to share."[6]

Likewise, my own mom always put the responsibility of provision at God's feet, not her own. And because of that singular decision, miracles tended to unfold. Hands got held. Bellies got fed. Hope got restored. And Mom lived to serve another day.

All of this leads me to an awareness these days, which is that there is no need to fear inadequacy when we're pausing to assess another's need. Our heavenly Father has everything that person needs. Maybe he'll use us to help provide some of those things, or maybe he'll tap the shoulder of someone else. Either way, it is *his* work to accomplish, *his* mission to complete.

When Jesus' disciples, humbled by his call to forgive those who wrong us, asked him to please increase their faith, he replied, "If you have faith as small as a mustard seed, you can say to this mulberry tree, 'Be uprooted and planted in the sea,' and it will obey you" (Luke 17:6). Next time you're in a grocery store, stop by the spice aisle and take a look at a jar of mustard seeds. Those suckers are *tiny*. Such tiny faith! Such massive results.

How is this possible? we wonder.

It's possible because of God. He is the one working. He is the one solving. He is the one moving. He is the one who redeems.

In my experience, people who most easily understand this concept are those in recovery for addiction. You know of the Twelve Steps of Alcoholics Anonymous. The reason those steps work is because they break down a *massive* effort—getting unhitched from addiction—into manageable, digestible bites. Further, those steps begin with admitting powerlessness (step 1), believing in a greater power (step 2), and turning one's life over to the care of God (step 3). A full 50 percent of the steps reference God overtly, as if to say, *If anything positive is going to happen here, it'll be because of him . . .*

A little bit of faith, God asks of us. The rest? He'll take care of that.

And yet we're never quite sure about this plan of his, are we? We insist on believing it's up to us.

Recently, I was sitting in our church's "First Wednesday" service, a monthly gathering of about a thousand people where we sing worship songs, read Scripture together, and pray. It's an unrushed time I always look forward to, and I had come eager to hear from God.

Five minutes into the service, there in my front-row seat, I heard clearly, "Take up an offering for those deputies . . ."

I knew the prompting was from God.

A few weeks prior I'd had a conversation with our sheriff, during which he informed me that 155 of our city's deputies do not possess adequate tactical gear for managing hostile situations. Whenever those women and men responded to a situation in which shots were being fired, they went in knowing they were ill-prepared. They needed bulletproof vests, and yet there was no money to fund that need.

God wanted us to help with those vests.

My wife is always a voice of reason in my life, so before I took any action, I leaned over, whispered to her about the deputies and what I'd heard, and studied her expression to know what to do.

We never collect an offering at First Wednesday. But Pam didn't mention that.

The ushers had no clue I was considering calling an audible. But Pam didn't mention that.

Bulletproof vests and requisite tactical gear are *expensive*. But Pam didn't mention that.

This would be a huge need to throw out to this size congregation. But Pam didn't mention that.

Here is what she said: "Do it. Make the request. Do what God has asked you to do."

Translation: "God is at work; let him do his thing. Do not be afraid."

But still: For real? Did Pam (or God!) have a clue how much each set cost? Fourteen hundred bucks a pop. Fourteen hundred times *155*.

My brain whirred to make sense of this. Upward of *$200,000*.

Here.

Tonight.

On a *whim*.

The fact was, God hadn't asked me to "fund" anything. He'd asked me, and I quote him verbatim, to "take up an offering for those deputies."

Okay, I reasoned, *what if I just keep the ask really low . . .*

I knew what I was doing even as I was doing it. I wanted to keep the expectation low so that I'd be set up for success either way. If we raised the smaller amount I wanted to ask for, we'd feel good about our contribution and move on. If we raised *more* than that smaller amount, we'd be veritable heroes in our town. And if we happened to fall short of our less-than-big goal, then, oh, well . . . big deal. Who cared?

That was the first whiff of fear for me: that I, on behalf of New Life, wouldn't have what it took to help our deputies out.

Here was the second whiff: *What if we do have what it takes to help, and I'm punished, as a result?*

I get plenty of hate mail in my role at the church, and I just knew the emails this offering would spawn. "You always stick up for the po-

lice, Brady! Even when they're wrong." "Raising money for law enforcement? You're on your way to being owned by them!" "Giving money for
tactical gear? What are we going to be funding next? *Guns?*"

The fact is that our local law enforcement is teeming with good, hon-
orable people. But that didn't stop fear from having its vicious way with
me. Fear of inadequacy says, *I can't help! I don't have what they need!*

And also: *I can't help, because I do.*

I knew it was time to help.

More than $100,000—that's what came in that one night.

And scores of officers felt a level of safety and protection they had
never, ever felt.

Fear #4: The Fear of "Issues"

Let me be quick to move into the fourth-level fear, because it relates
intimately to the third. You see, the real reason we fear our inadequacy
is because of what that perceived inadequacy might expose. What's
underneath the fear of inadequacy? The fear of "issues"—others' issues, specifically, and how those issues might present issues for us.

What keeps us from pausing instead of passing by? We're afraid
of the issues that the people we're helping are dealing with. And we're
afraid that the sheer act of offering aid will create complex issues in
our lives as well. Sure, the sizable sticker price was an obstacle to
my reflexively, willingly, and joyfully collecting the offering for tactical gear that Wednesday night. But the bigger stumbling block, if I'm
being honest, was the *issues* that offering might raise. Would the move
be seen as a political one? Would it seem like I could be "bought"? Was
funding body armor ever the right step for a church? What backlash
would I receive?

We're afraid to help because we're afraid of *issues*. We have enough
issues of our own.

Tribalism has been part of the human experience since humans
were around to have experiences, and yet despite our no longer need-

ing actual tribes to protect us from warring intruders or wild animals, we are still a tribal society in some respects even today. But instead of organizing ourselves according to familial lineage—in what the Pew Research Center calls a "restless, rootless population," a full 63 percent of us do not reside in the town of our birth[7]—we now come together according to *issues*. We band together over a political stance—pro-choicers here, pro-lifers there. Or because of socioeconomic status—those with first-world problems on one team, those who can't make ends meet on the other. Or skin color, or religious beliefs, or mental health, or along a thousand other categorical lines. We "tribe up" with those who share our convictions, believing that our issues are somehow tolerable, while *other* people's issues are simply insufferable. We can't hang around *them* because "they have *issues*, man."

And it is *those* issues that we fear.

I wrote extensively in my last book, *Remarkable: Living a Faith Worth Talking About*, about our decision as a church a few years ago to merge with the largest Spanish-speaking church in the region, Nueva Vida, and about the unfavorable input I received from a small percentage of our congregation as a result. I won't recount the details of that merger here, but I would like to cast fresh light on what I believe was motivating such an unhospitable response. To be crass, the people of Nueva Vida have issues. Owing to incessant media coverage regarding our country's immigration crisis, the people of Nueva Vida *are* issues. More than half of our Nueva Vida congregants happen to be living in this country illegally, and the portion of New Life that was irate over our decision to merge didn't want illegality to be an issue for them. Granted, the people who were threatening to leave our church over the merger had issues of their own. (Don't we all.) But *this* issue— embracing a group of immigrants living here illegally—was an issue they couldn't allow. To quote the title of that 1970s World War II film, it was simply "a bridge too far."

So people with issues decided to disparage other people with different issues, emboldened by the belief that those different issues were somehow worse than the issues they themselves faced.

We disparage them.

We distance ourselves.

We otherize, and then we move on.

Except it's never as clean-cut as that.

"Otherizing contains within it the potential for cruelty, because establishing some group as different all too readily becomes a justification for conceiving of that group as less than us in some way— less intelligent, less patriotic, less hardworking, less victimized," writes author Sally Kohn.[8] In my experience, this potential is *almost always* realized. Which is why Jesus' parable spoke out against the practice: a Samaritan was somehow ... good?

In those days, Samaritans were dogs. Outcasts. Less-than. Feared. Having been written off as of no social value to Israel, which was a poor nation suffering high taxation under vicious Roman rule, they were a fringe group in a fringe society, quite literally "the least of these." Samaria was positioned directly between Galilee and Judea, the most convenient route between the two, and yet travelers took pains to go around the region to avoid encountering "that kind." That kind had *issues*, man.

How does Jesus refer someone of that kind?

Not as a dog.

Not as an outcast.

Not as a loser.

But as *neighbor*.

A neighbor who's good.

Earlier this year our church funded the construction of a community center next door to Mary's Home, the transitional housing development we established in the heart of our city to get single moms and their kids off the streets. Within about three weeks of these women moving into their new apartments, invariably their sense of connectedness emerges. They start sharing meals in each other's apartments, playing games in the evenings with each other's kids, and so forth. We knew that by providing them a larger space, a shared space, where they could cook together and celebrate birthdays together and do life together, an even deeper sense of community would take hold. We knew we wanted this community center built. We just didn't know we wanted it built quite so fast.

Our pastor in charge of the build thought it would be engaging and exciting for the community if we accomplished the project not in ten months or even ten weeks but rather ten *days*. A "speed build," just for grins. After securing the requisite permits and the enthusiastic buy-in of engineers, builders, and contractors—all of whom were donating at least a portion of their time and supplies—our entire congregation was blitzed with info on how they could be involved. Late on the third day I went down to check on the progress that had already been made, and as I was walking the property and surrounding streets, I noticed a preponderance of Spanish-speaking volunteers.

Later, when I was catching up with the general contractor on the build, I asked about those workers I'd seen. He told me that every single one of them was there as an undocumented worker, and that they'd all donated their time with great joy. "So they're working contract construction jobs all day," I said, "and then volunteering their time here after hours?"

The contractor nodded his head with a smile. "They love what this effort is all about, Brady. They want to be part of this thing."

"Illegal immigrants" can be . . . good?

Barbarians, this same group of people has been called. And, in fact, some from that group have come to this country plotting evil. But need I remind us that some living here legally are known to plot evil too?

All groups have issues, even though those issues may differ. All groups have evildoers, too, but all groups also have people who seek opportunities to be extravagant.

The Islamist who helps the fundamentalist Christian snowplow driver dislodge his vehicle from the snowbank he's stuck in.

The lesbian who helps the anti-gay protestor who slipped on the curb back to her feet.

The Samaritan who happens by a man left for dead and cares for him as though they were friends.

Jesus knew what he was doing here.

Unity, this parable begs of us. *Please: Live as one.*

Back in April, Yahoo! ran an article about four diners at a restaurant in Alabama. Three of the diners were men in their twenties; the other a woman perhaps eighty-five. After the three friends had been seated and ordered, one of them noticed the woman sitting at a nearby table, alone. *Dang,* he thought, *I'd hate to have to eat alone.*

Then inspiration struck.

He was waiting for his food to arrive and had a few minutes to kill, so he approached the woman, asked if he could sit down, and chatted with her awhile. Which is when he learned that she was a widower and that the following day would have been her husband's and her sixtieth wedding anniversary. "I offered her my condolences," he said, "and asked her to come sit with us."

The woman accepted his offer and together, they shared a meal. More importantly, they shared their stories, something that left the men undone. "She changed my outlook on life," the man later reflected with a smile, "and how I look at other people."[9]

Candidly, how could she *not*?

When you're a strong, virile twentysomething, an eightysomething *will* change your life.

When your skin is one color, someone of a different color *will* change your life.

When you're enjoying the fruit of healthy community, someone wrestling with painful loneliness *will* change your life.

And—according to Jesus, anyway—this is *exactly* how it should be.

Sure, there probably do exist the immature exceptions, the people who swear that they would rather *die* than to have their lives saved by . . . the gun-toting Republican . . . the flaming liberal . . . the gender-fluid person . . . the Bible-beating Southerner . . . the socialist Northerner . . . the (pick any other stereotype and place it here).

But I remain steadfast in my belief that those folks *are* the exception and that the norm is vast in size. We want to be loved. We want to love well. We want to "all get along." The challenge is this fear of the other, this fear of their issues, this fear of our own. Which is why I've written this book, I must say. We'll dismantle these fears as we go.

For now, a dose of inspiration, a taste of what's to come: we can do better than live in fear. We can do better than push people away. We can live as Jesus lived. Remember: "We are not a self-authoring community," as my colleague Matthew Ayers says. "We're a community being transformed by Jesus *in the face of other people.*"

In the face of other people.

In the *faces* of other people.

In the *issues* of other people, because who among us doesn't have those?

If the goal of the passerby is abdication, the goal of the pauser is association. We can choose to associate with *all people at all times.* We can live as ones who understand that the edges, as Lidia Yuknavitch writes, are what "hold the center together."[10]

So a starting point, if you wrestle with this fear: Consider that the others you tend to otherize hold a key to the transformation you seek. Have you ever read the Parable of the Ten Virgins, found in Matthew 25? Jesus is explaining to his followers what the kingdom of heaven will be like, how quickly its full arrival might unfold across the earth. Here is what he then says: "At that time the kingdom of heaven will be like ten virgins who took their lamps and went out to meet the bridegroom. Five of them were foolish and five were wise. The foolish ones took their lamps but did not take any oil with them. The wise ones, however, took oil in jars along with their lamps. The bridegroom was a long time coming, and they all became drowsy and fell asleep" (v. 1–5).

Jesus went on to say that at midnight the bridegroom arrived, much to everyone's surprise. All ten virgins woke and trimmed their lamps. But only half had any oil to use. The foolish ones begged the wise ones for help, but there wasn't enough to go around. "Go to those who sell oil and buy some for yourselves," the wise ones said to the fools (v. 9), but this plan would fail in the end. "While they [the foolish virgins in search of oil] were on their way to buy the oil, the bridegroom arrived," verse 10 says. "The virgins who were ready went in with him to the wedding banquet. And the door was shut."

Later, the foolish virgins would beg the bridegroom to open the door for them, but it was too late. Their lamps had gone out in full.

Now, what this parable usually represents is the fact that we know neither the time nor date of Jesus' return, and we should be diligent about keeping our "lamps" trimmed and our "oil" in plentiful supply—enjoying intimacy with our Savior, practicing spiritual disciplines that fuel our growth, making disciples of all nations, as he asked us to do—so that we're prepared for his arrival, so that he'll find us faithful in the end. But over the past couple of years this parable has taken on new meaning for me.

As I have come to know and love and worship with our Nueva Vida congregation, I have begun to see myself not as the wise in that story Jesus told but rather as the foolish. Who are the wise ones, then? These "undocumented" lovers of God. But here's the beautiful thing: instead of turning me away as my lamp goes dark, *they share all they have with me.* Far from withholding the depth of worship they know, they extend it, graciously, to me, to us, to anyone who cares to receive.

In his book *The Twenty-Piece Shuffle: Why the Poor and Rich Need Each Other*, author Greg Paul wrote of his coming to a similar conclusion along the way, regarding how he viewed not necessarily immigrants but rather people who were poor. "I could see that there were

a lot of people over 'there' somewhere who were caught in unfortunate circumstances, circumstances they had done nothing to deserve
and about which they could do very little. But like most wealthy first
worlders, I really thought that the poor people in my own patch must
be lazy, rebellious, wrongheaded, willfully ignorant, or more sinful
than most. In short, I thought they must be the architects of their own
misfortune.[11]

"The reality, of course," Paul continued, "is that the rich are usually,
because of their riches, barely conscious of their deep poverty and the
consequent invitation to embrace their true identity in relationship
with their Maker that can be found only in those depths."[12] His conclusion is a beautiful summary of what can happen in your life and mine,
when we refuse to let this fear of others' issues run its course. "I believe
that God urges the rich and powerful to care for the poor and vulnerable throughout Scripture because we have what the other needs . . . ,"
he writes. "We are guiding each other on the way home."[13]

After one especially powerful worship service at Nueva Vida,
during which the presence of the Holy Spirit was nearly palpable, I
pulled aside several of their pastors and leaders and said, "In case
you've forgotten, let me remind you that this merger we entered into
wasn't an effort to colonize you. Listen, I know we had some things
you needed: resources, some leadership direction, a little help. But you
have *so much* that we need. Vibrant faith. Unwavering belief. Unfettered worship. *Total* devotion to God. You're carrying oil that churches
in this country need. We need your presence. We need your hearts. We
need your oil."

I meant every word that I said. If the trend holds, and if immigrants
in this country ever choose to organize themselves, the United States
will soon be brown. Fearmongers will claim that this is a terrifying
prospect, but I humbly disagree. The fastest-growing, most spiritually
directed groups are all presently living south of the equator. One hundred percent of them. Jesus followership and church growth is simply

exploding in places such as Brazil and Argentina, Guatemala and Peru. (We'll have to tackle Africa another time, but the growth there is staggering as well.) And this much I know: as members of those groups make their way north and into this country, they will be looking for churches whose arms are open to them. New Life will be one of those churches standing tall, arms extended, no fear of "issues" to be found.

When those who have been relegated to the margins of society find a home in your midst, you are beginning to taste fear-free living. I'm telling you, *great good* happens on the margins, the seam that holds all things in place.

Yes, we need strong borders.

Yes, we need wise immigration policies.

Yes, those tasked with protecting our citizenship have a ton of work to do.

But while those efforts are underway, we can love the people we find in our midst.

If I were to lay out the opposite of the "fear of people's issues" in a single action item, that's it: *Love the ones you find.*

Fear #5: The Fear of Injury

I was twenty-eight years old when I first encountered the fifth and final fear we'll talk about—the fear that underlies *every other fear* related to engaging with people in need. The fear of personal injury. In short, we don't engage with people in ditches because we're afraid that we, too, will get stuck in a ditch. Underneath all the other fears is the primal fear of being harmed somehow. For starters, we're afraid of being *physically* hurt. Women, especially, have told me how troubling it can be to know how to be helpful when encountering people in need because they fear actual bodily harm. "We have been steeped from the youngest of ages," one woman said to me, "in the whole stranger-danger mentality. That posture is tough to override . . ."

Listen, I have a nineteen-year-old daughter. The last thing I want to encourage young, single women (or anyone!) to do is to put themselves in harm's way. "Employ your 'helpfulness' in the context of the work of our church," I often tell Callie. "There's logic to Jesus sending people out two by two to minister in the world. Don't go it alone." True, she might forego a few in-the-moment opportunities to be helpful, but she'll also dramatically minimize risk of personal harm.

Added to this fear is the fear of being taken advantage of in other ways: emotionally or financially, spiritually or relationally. Which is what makes "passing by" such an appealing option upon encountering someone in need. *If pain can't get to us,* we think, *it can't harm us.* And so we keep moving, head down, heart closed.

I get it. Really, I do.

Back to me, age twenty-eight.

I was working in radio and television, managing several stations in Amarillo, Texas, when I met a young woman named Jenny who needed a job. Jenny had recently graduated from college, her husband had just been hired at a local John Deere dealership, and she was looking for something in sales. I hired her and began the training regimen I ran all new salespeople through. We'd drive from one client to the next, talking to them about their overall marketing plans, and about ads they wanted to run. I quickly noticed that Jenny had a magnetic presence and would likely be a superstar in sales. She was smart, witty, engaging, and attentive to clients' needs. I was impressed, even as storm clouds started to form amid those bright rays of sophistication and savvy.

The first sign of trouble showed up when Jenny told me that her marriage was in trouble. She and her husband hadn't been married long, and yet they were constantly embroiled in fights. The stress of that situation had pushed her into clinical depression, which made daily life a chore. I was concerned about her, but I was also aware that there was only so much I could do. I was a married man, and she was a married woman. What was my "loyal friendship" supposed to include?

Pam and I talked often during those months about how I could support Jenny while still maintaining appropriate boundaries, both as a husband and as a lover of God. I did my best to listen carefully to her, to encourage her, and to set her up for success in sales. Pam and I prayed fervently for her and invited her to church on several occasions, although she never agreed to go. I know that her success at work was a bright spot for her while things were crumbling around her back at home.

"My husband moved out," Jenny said plainly one Monday morning, after I'd asked how her weekend had been. He'd found an apartment, packed his things, and left. She was wrought with deep despair. Tuesday and Wednesday were a slog for her, and Thursday and Friday she didn't show. This was during prehistoric times, technologically speaking, and despite my concern over her absence from work, I had no way to reach out to her. There was no email. There were no cell phones. The number she'd noted on her employment application had been disconnected. I had half a mind to drive to the street address listed but figured I'd give things another day.

Saturday afternoon my phone rang. It was Jenny's mother, who had driven to Amarillo from Houston, where she lived. Not exactly a quick, easy trip. "I came into town to find my daughter," she said, explaining that she hadn't been able to reach her in three days. "I found your number in the phone book and originally was calling to ask you to help me find her, because I knew that in addition to being my daughter's boss, you'd also been a good friend to her. She told me as much, and I'm grateful for that . . . which makes the reason for this call all the more difficult . . ."

The mom began to cry. "I found my daughter," she said. "She's dead."

I inhaled sharply. "What?" I asked. "What on earth happened to her?"

Jenny had driven over to her estranged husband's apartment complex, parked her car, walked up to her husband's door, knocked on the door, and then, upon seeing the whites of his eyes, raised a pistol to the side of her head and pulled the trigger.

I wracked my brain for clues. Had she ever even *hinted* at suicide? Had she been crying out for more significant help all along, and had I neglected to see how bad things really were? How could this happen to someone I saw—and supervised—five days a week? How could I not have known?

It sucked the air out of my entire system, the thought of her having taken her own life. The loss her family had just suffered. The pain she must have been in. I felt like a failure. I felt like a horrible friend. I was distraught. Just deeply, completely *sad*.

So much potential . . . gone.

The funeral would be held back in Houston, the mom told me through tears. Then, hurriedly, she said, "I have to go." She hung up the phone, and there I sat, the line dead, the receiver still pressed to my ear.

In the wake of losing that employee and friend, I experienced an odd juxtaposition inside. I've always been a high-energy/high-optimism kind of person, and while that was definitely true of me in my twenties, news of Jenny's suicide deflated my high-flying balloon. I became guarded. More circumspect. Less eager to invest in the people around me. Suspicious that their pain might leak onto me and harm me from every side. If this was what could happen when you tried to help someone in need, then maybe helping wasn't the best approach for me.

Can you relate at all to what I'm saying?

You loan your colleague money to help get him out of a bind, and he uses it to fund his addiction to booze.

You invite your twentysomething niece to come stay with your family while she gets on her feet in the world, and then you catch her silently pulling cash from your wallet.

You give your friend a shining recommendation for a job at your employer, and then he is fired for cutting corners and padding his expense account.

Over the past ten years I have watched six close friends and colleagues of mine walk away from a friendship I thought was secure. I was deeply invested in each of those relationships, and yet they're essentially nonexistent today. I tried my best to love each of them well, but my best clearly wasn't enough.

The effect of these and a thousand other flubbed "opportunities to help" is that we get a bad taste in our mouths. If left unchecked, that momentary bad taste turns into a permanent film that no amount of brushing can get off our tongues.

Fearing injury at every turn, we develop a cynical edge. We stop looking, stop feeling, stop engaging, stop *being helpful*, no matter the need.

It's just not worth it, we tell ourselves. *It always costs me way . . . too . . . much.*

And so, regardless of how compelled we are to pause here and there, we start letting seven words direct our steps: "I think I'll just pass on by."

STABILITY AND HOW IT'S REGAINED

It has long been held that we arrive in this world with only two fears, the fear of loud noises and the fear of falling. But if you stop to consider why these fears exist, you'll see that even they don't spur long-term dread. Picture a baby crawling along the top of a picnic table. The fear of falling will keep that baby from toppling over the edge of a surface, but once that baby redirects, the fear can dissipate.

Or think of a sleeping baby who is awakened by a crash of thunder. The child may cry out in acknowledgment that something unfamiliar has disrupted her peaceful slumber, but once the thunder rumbles away, she can fall back to sleep.

Both fears are intended to protect the child. But only until stability is regained. At that point, boldness resurfaces. The urge to explore takes hold once more.

For several months after my friend committed suicide, admittedly I crawled around like a baby about to go over the edge. I was so afraid of being injured again that I simply refused to engage. *Can't hurt me if you can't catch me*—that was my mantra back then. But then, through a series of events, I saw that my stability was being regained. I had backed away from that drop-off. Danger no longer lurked, which meant I had no good reason to be afraid.

The first thing that happened was that, during an uneventful time of Bible reading, I was drawn to Psalm 46, which is a psalm I'd read on hundreds of occasions before. But with the suicide fresh in mind, I came to those words as if for the very first time. It says this:

> *God is our refuge and strength,*
> *   an ever-present help in trouble.*
> *Therefore we will not fear, though the earth give way*
> *   and the mountains fall into the heart of the sea,*
> *though its waters roar and foam*
> *   and the mountains quake with their surging.*

> *There is a river whose streams make glad the city of God,*
> *   the holy place where the Most High dwells.*
> *God is within her, she will not fall;*
> *   God will help her at break of day.*
> *Nations are in uproar, kingdoms fall;*
> *   he lifts his voice, the earth melts.*

> *The Lord Almighty is with us;*
> *   the God of Jacob is our fortress.*
> *Come and see what the Lord has done,*
> *   the desolations he has brought on the earth.*

He makes wars cease
  to the ends of the earth.
He breaks the bow and shatters the spear;
  he burns the shields with fire.
He says, "Be still, and know that I am God;
  I will be exalted among the nations,
I will be exalted in the earth."

The Lord Almighty is with us;
  the God of Jacob is our fortress.

The part that arrested me was a straightforward trio of phrases: "Be still, and know that I am God; / I will be exalted among the nations, / I will be exalted in the earth" (v. 10). In those verses God was reminding me of a very important thing, which is that regardless of whether I cooperated with his plan, he *would* be exalted in the earth. But based on the front end of the psalm, I saw another truth hiding there: God's desire, his unchanging desire, is that I would cooperate with him. And the same is true for you. Yes, he can accomplish his purposes without us, but that's not at all his desire.

He is our refuge. He is our strength. He is the reason we can live without fear. He is the giver of fresh stability, again and again and again.

It was eighteen months after Jenny's death that Pam and I adopted Abram. We had fought through serious infertility challenges until that point, and the moment we held Abram in our arms, something awakened in me. Around the same time I was invited to become the pastor of a tiny church in Hereford, Texas, and again it was as if God was saying, *Brady, I'm still at work down there.*

I didn't see it so plainly at the time, but I was regaining my stability. My sense of hope was being renewed. It may have only been the size of a mustard seed, but my faith was coming back. God *was* at work in the world around me, and I didn't want to miss out. I wanted to be part of his redemptive plan, showing compassion to people who needed his care.

Slowly but certainly I began to reach out again. As I came upon needs in the lives of those in our congregation, I stopped what I was doing and took note. I put a hand on their shoulders. I listened without having an agenda. I nodded in understanding. I offered up resources that were mine to give. On my birthday in 2001, January 11, I remember sitting with kind Wesley "Hap" Hagar, a member of our church, as he passed away, holding his hand as he stepped from one reality to another, and then, hours later, in the very same hospital, sitting beside a beaming couple in our church as they welcomed their first child into the world.

It was like having emotional whiplash, but the contrast heartened me some. It was God's reminder that, despite our losses, gains still get made, and that he holds agency over it all.

I am your refuge.
I am your strength.
You do not need to live in fear.

That passage as I paraphrase it above from Psalm 46 reminds us that the worst fear imaginable is nothing more than a bluff. If "the earth [can] give way and the mountains [can] fall into the heart of the sea" (v. 2) and we still can trust in God, then our fear has zero hold on us.

In this world filled with troubles and needs galore, how are we able to pause and care instead of callously pass on by? By remembering that it is in the pausing and caring that we are divinely fortified. It is in cooperating with God that his strength shines. It is in the stopping and stooping and offering a hand that we bear witness to an extravagant King.

◇◇

Pushing Pause: Chapter 3

What keeps us from living the lives of extravagance we long for? *Fear—* plain, old fear. We may not be able to evict fear from our lives altogether, but working diligently to move *past* our fears into the effectiveness God has in store for us is work that is never in vain. Take whatever time you need to rightly assess the fear that is holding you back, and then work through this chapter's challenge to practice moving past it.

Read

Remind yourself of the opening words of Psalm 46, which say this: "God is our refuge and strength, an ever-present help in trouble. Therefore we will not fear, though the earth give way and the mountains fall into the heart of the sea, though its waters roar and foam and the mountains quake with their surging. There is a river whose streams make glad the city of God, the holy place where the Most High dwells. God is within her, she will not fall; God will help her at break of day" (v. 1–5).

Reflect

- How might the assurance of God's ever-present help when the mountains quake and surge and the earth is literally falling apart comfort you regarding God's willingness to be present with you as you help meet the need of one of his beloved daughters or sons?

- When have you experienced God's nearness, his strength, his care, during an especially fear-inducing situation? What did that support sound like or feel like? How did it change the order of things for the better?

Respond

This chapter's challenge is a straightforward one. Simply name the fear that most often holds you back from helping others in need, and then ask God to help you move past it—just once—today.

Again, the five fears we looked at include:

- The fear of interruption
- The fear of inconvenience
- The fear of inadequacy
- The fear of issues
- The fear of injury

Place a checkmark beside the fear above that most resonates with your experience. Then craft a prayer of petition in the space below.

_____

_____

_____

_____

_____

_____

4

Unclenching the Fist

*Jesus came to announce to us that an identity based on
success, popularity and power is a false identity—an
illusion! Loudly and clearly he says: "You are not what
the world makes you; but you are children of God.*[1]

HENRI J. M. NOUWEN

I F YOU HAVE SPENT any time in a remote village of Asia, then you
know what I'm about to tell you: there are monkeys. Not an anecdotal monkey here or there, mind you. Not a sweet, well-trained,
perfectly behaved monkey that everyone thinks is cute. No, no:
monkeys—plural—and mischievous ones at that. They are everywhere, climbing, falling, scratching, screeching, wreaking havoc wherever they go. As you might guess, their presence elicits something less
than joy. They are considered roach-like pests. And what do we do
with roach-like pests? We launch all-out *wars* to get them gone.

101

Over time, the villagers tried all sorts of maneuvers to kick those monkeys out of town. They tried sweeping them away with their brooms. They tried luring them with bananas. They tried hollering at them until their voices were hoarse. But the monkeys stayed. Just when the people were at their wits' end, a bright idea emerged.

First, a group of villagers rigged empty coconuts by piercing the bottom of each one with a small hole, just enough to thread through it a thin rope, which they knotted on the other side. Then they cut in the top of the coconut a hole a few inches in diameter, wide enough for a monkey to work its hand through but no wider. Finally, they dropped a piece of candy into the main hole, left the coconut on the ground, and waited nearby.

Within minutes the plan worked. The curious monkeys made their way to the coconuts, sat with them on their laps, and shoved their hands into the holes. They just *knew* those candies were in there, and they were overjoyed when they found the loot. As soon as a monkey wrapped its hand around a candy, a villager at the other end of the rope would pull the coconut to him. And along came the monkey. Why? Because it refused to unclench its fist.

Now, you're probably aware that monkeys can be fast when they want to be. If those monkeys would have simply released the candies, they could have pulled their hands out of the coconuts and darted off to freedom. Out of all the monkeys that investigated those coconuts, guess how many opted to release the candies and run . . .

That would be a big, fat goose egg. Not a single monkey did.

TO COOPERATE IS TO UNCLENCH

I put this picture of annoying Asian monkeys in your mind to give you something to think about each time you're arrested by fear. When we allow our fear of being inconvenienced, or our fear of inadequacy, or our fear of personal injury to dictate our response to someone in need, we are behaving like impetuous monkeys, forfeiting the long-term assurance of fulfillment on a selfish, short-term whim. And if we accept this trade-off, we cannot cooperate with God.

As we begin to take steps toward the extravagance God intends for us, we simply have to abandon the fears we are so accustomed to clinging to. Fear and faith are incompatible; there's no balance to be struck between the two. You and I will either hold fast to one or hold fast to the other, but we can't grasp both at the same time.

When I counsel an engaged couple in the months leading up to their wedding day, I remind them that once they're married they will always be doing one of two things: moving toward each other or moving away from each other. There is no middle ground. The husband will choose to lean into his marriage, prizing his wife, serving his wife, daydreaming about his wife, loving his wife . . . or he will subtly lean away.

He will criticize his wife.

He will stir up strife with his wife.

He will be demanding of his wife.

He will daydream of someone else.

Likewise, the wife will either lean into the union, *actively seeking* to honor and respect and love and serve her husband, or else she will allow their relationship to drift. A frustration here. A pet peeve there. A *Why can't he get this right?*

She'll move ever so slightly away from her mate as she indulges in a fantasy life. *This house would be so* clean*! Our bills would be paid* on time*! Nothing would smell like* sweat*! I could watch something on TV besides* golf*!*

He may think, *Eh, it's no big deal. I still love her—of course I do . . .*

She may think, *Well, sure, I* entertain *certain thoughts, but I'd never actually* leave . . .

At that point, however, as I tell those starry-eyed near newlyweds, "you've opened up the door."

The "door" I'm referring to is infidelity—literally, a lack of faithfulness to one's spouse.

With that analogy in mind, let's return to faith and fear. If your rationale for not being utterly extravagant in your response to the needs you see in the world around you is *even a little bit* of trepidation— "I don't have time"; "I'm sure someone more familiar with these things will help"; "I don't have any cash on me"; "I'd be biting off more than I can chew"—then your heart has fallen into a state of faithlessness. You've begun to be governed by fear.

The freedom and fulfillment you long for? They can be achieved only by abandoning that fear.

WHO CAN LIVE FREE FROM FEAR?

If, because of some weird neural glitch, my voice got stuck on repeat, and I could convey only one message every hour of every day for the rest of my days on this earth, this is what I'd say: "Because of what Jesus has done for us, we can live as beloved children of God."

I'd shout it from the tops of these beautiful Rocky Mountains: "Because of what Jesus has done for us, we can live as beloved children of God!"

I'd sing it in the shower: "Because of what Jesus has done for us, we can live as beloved children of Gah-ah-ahd."

I'd whisper it beside the ocean: "Because of what Jesus has done for us, we can live as beloved children of God . . ."

I'd remind the believer and I'd regale the one whose spiritual light is dim: "Because of what Jesus has done for us, we can live as beloved children of God."

I'd tell the guy next to me on the airplane: "Because of what Jesus has done for us, we can live as beloved children of God."

I'd tell the teenagers crossing the street: "Because of what Jesus has done for us, we can live as beloved children of God."

I'd tell the congregation at New Life: "Because of what Jesus has done for us, we can live as beloved children of God."

To which they'd probably say: "We got it! You told us last week!"

I'd tell everyone in every setting on every day of my life: "Because of what Jesus has done for us, we can live as beloved children of God."

And even *then*, as I was taking my last breaths, I wouldn't tire of speaking those words. We need to be reminded of this message. We need to start living what we say we believe.

Because of what Jesus has done for us, we can live as children of God.

But if we aren't living as though we're children of God, you may ask, then what *are* we living as?

Picture a continuum where on one end is faith and on the other sits fear. Remember, I said that at all times, in all situations, you and I are moving in one direction or the other, either closer and closer toward faith or else closer and closer toward fear. We could be meandering, running, or baby stepping, but whatever our pace, we're getting closer to one end or the other.

Let's build on that idea. In my experience, for the follower of Jesus, there are but three approaches to life. I showed you my cards already regarding the first one, which is that we choose to live as children of God. We'll go deeper into that idea in a moment, but, for now, let's tackle the other two.

If you have not owned your identity as a beloved child of God, then you're living either as a spiritual *orphan* or a spiritual *slave*. The trouble with choosing these identities is that they have their origins in fear. Whether you believe you're a spiritual orphan or you believe you're a spiritual slave, you're inching closer and closer to fear, which means you're *going the wrong way*. You can say you have faith in Jesus, and you can desperately want that faith to bloom, but until you do an about-face and accept God's free gift of grace—in effect, matching your talk with your walk—that faith will never be realized. It will stay eternally dead to fear.

The Orphan

In John 1:12, we read that to those who believe in the name of Jesus, "he gave the right to become children of God . . ."

In 1 Peter 2:9, we read that we who believe in Jesus are "a chosen people, a royal priesthood, a holy nation, God's special possession, that you may declare the praises of him who called you out of darkness into his wonderful light."

In John 15:15, we read that Jesus no longer calls us "servants, because a servant does not know his master's business. Instead," he says, "I have called you friends, for everything that I learned from my Father I have made known to you."

Ephesians 2:10 says that "we are God's handiwork, created in Christ Jesus to do good works, which God prepared in advance for us to do."

Philippians 3:20 confirms that "our citizenship is in heaven" and that "we eagerly await a Savior from there, the Lord Jesus Christ . . ."

I bring up these verses by way of context; spiritual orphans may nod assent at these ideas, but they don't live as though they are true. They don't see themselves as chosen children of the King, as "handiwork," as "friends." Instead, they forever question their place in God's family, wondering if they'll ever truly belong.

Some spiritual orphans I have known had lousy experiences with their earthly fathers or other male authority figures, and now they just can't imagine a heavenly Father who sees them, who adores them, and who welcomes them with open arms. Anecdotally, Richard Rohr, who for fourteen years served as a jail chaplain in Albuquerque, New Mexico, says that despite their widely varied backgrounds, ethnicities, religious beliefs, personality traits, and more, the prisoners he met all had something in common: dysfunctional relationships with their dads. If you happen to fall into this category of not having been fathered properly, then you know that the idea of a proper heavenly Father is nearly inconceivable to you. Those I know who fit this description often wander through life disillusioned, with no sense of purpose, and find it difficult to make any long-term commitments—to a career, to a marriage, to a community, to a church.

And you don't have to live behind physical bars to experience this sort of spiritual imprisonment. In my book *Sons and Daughters: Spiritual Orphans Finding Our Way Home,* I wrote of an occasion when our church's college pastor invited more than fifty students to the group's weekly gathering. At the end of the service he called his four young sons to the stage and proceeded to speak a distinct blessing over them by highlighting each child's gifts, talents, and specific personality traits and then saying a prayer of protection and provision over his life. There were perhaps a thousand people in the room that night, and yet it was silent in that space.

Afterward, that pastor turned to the crowd and said, "In a group this size, a good number of you have never had a dad bless you or pray for you like that. You've never had a father figure say that he is proud of who you are and who you are becoming. You've never had a spiritual dad place a hand on your shoulder and smile. Tonight, if you wish, that will change."

The fifty-plus students flanked the front of the stage as every person in the audience was invited to come forward and receive prayer. Lines filled every aisle as they waited to be seen, to be touched, to be encouraged, to be loved. I found it especially telling that, after receiving their blessings, some of those young women and young men marched right back to the end of the line, where they waited for a second turn.

That night the orphan spirit—the spirit that says, "Nobody sees me. Nobody knows me. Nobody values me. Nobody cares"—was arrested in those students. Spiritual orphans can be cynical. Spiritual orphans can be skeptical. Spiritual orphans can be simply unconvinced. But they're always being driven by fear.

They tend to hurt others before they themselves get hurt, and often that hurt looks a lot like simple neglect. Nothing has been poured into them, and so they have nothing to give away. They simply pass by people in need of help, never considering that they should engage.

The Slave

One day Jesus was teaching at the Temple Mount, explaining to a curious crowd of Jewish listeners some pretty big ideas, including who he was, where he came from, where he was headed, who his Father was, and more. He must have been compelling, because, as John 8:30 attests, "even as he spoke, many believed in him."

That's how you know your talk is working, by the way: *People come to Christ.*

To those Jews who believed, Jesus said, "If you hold to my teaching, you are really my disciples. Then you will know the truth, and the truth will set you free" (v. 31–32).

And just when everything was going so well, things took a turn for the worse.

I wonder if at least some of those Jews literally puffed out their chests as they spoke their reply: "We are Abraham's descendants and have never been slaves of anyone," they answered Jesus. "How can you say that we shall be set free?" (v. 33).

In other words, "Who are *you* to peddle freedom to *us*, when—*hello?*—we're *already* free?"

If Jesus rolled his eyes and exhaled in exasperation, we don't learn of it from the passage. Here is all we know: he replied earnestly to his audience by explaining what real freedom means. "Very truly I tell you," he said, "everyone who sins is a slave to sin. Now a slave has no permanent place in the family, but a son belongs to it forever. So if the Son sets you free, you will be free indeed" (John 8:34–36).

Jesus went on to say that he was fully aware that they, the Jews, were Abraham's descendants and that that lineage did not determine their status of free or slave. It is God's lineage that guarantees freedom, which is precisely what Jesus declared. Verses 42–47:

"If God were your Father, you would love me, for I have come here from God. I have not come on my own; God sent me. Why is my language not clear to you? Because you are unable to hear what I say. You belong to your father, the devil, and you want to carry out your father's desires. He was a murderer from the beginning, not holding to the truth, for there is no truth in him. When he lies, he speaks his native language, for he is a liar and the father of lies. Yet because I tell the truth, you do not believe me! Can any of you prove me guilty of sin? If I am telling the truth, why don't you believe me? Whoever belongs to God hears what God says. The reason you do not hear is that you do not belong to God."

Jesus didn't mince words with them. Neither does he do so with us. If we're looking to anything or anyone besides Jesus to garner salvation and eternal life, we are looking to a false messiah—and we do not belong to God.

Like the spiritual orphan, the spiritual slave doubts her place in the family of God. But rather than this doubt catalyzing disillusionment and a certain proneness to wander, it prompts the slave to work—and work *hard*.

I told you earlier that, in my estimation, the best parable Jesus told is that of the prodigal son—the "Lost Son," in the NIV (Luke 15:11–32). If anyone typifies the mentality of the spiritual slave, it is the older brother from that tale. As the story goes, after the prodigal son demands an early return on his father's inheritance, flees to a distant country, blows everything on self-centered indulgences, eventually comes to his senses, determines to return, and is greeted with the outstretched arms of his grace-filled dad, a massive party is thrown. The father says to find the best robe for his son, who has returned. And to place a ring on his finger. And sandals on his dirty bare feet. And to kill the best calf for a feast in his honor. And to *seriously* celebrate.

But at least one person wasn't feeling so celebratory: the father's older son.

The prodigal's brother was out in a field when he heard the raucous party begin. There was music. There was dancing. Shouts of joy. Lavish food. What was going on? he wondered. He came close to sort things out.

The father's staff informed the older brother about the goings-on, inviting him to join in. He wanted no part of this party. Maybe the father could get him to come.

Then there was this, from the older son: "Look! All these years I've been slaving for you and never disobeyed your orders. Yet you never gave me even a young goat so I could celebrate with my friends. But when this son of yours who has squandered your property with prostitutes comes home, you kill the fattened calf for him!" (Luke 15:29–30).

The sentiment, I should mention, is precisely what *all* slaves believe. The only way to please the Father is to work hard, to *perform*. Why? Because their place at the family dinner table depends on their having showed up and served well. If they fail to produce, they forfeit their spot—or that's what they think, anyway. The well-known verse in Ephesians 2 that talks about our being saved "not by works, so that no one can boast " (v. 9)? Yeah. They don't subscribe to that. Without their works, there is nothing left; their works are *everything* to them.

And so they struggle and strive and labor and toil, hoping beyond hope that all that they've done will be counted as "good enough" someday.

Sounds totally exhausting to me.

True for you too?

Anytime I've tried to "do good" on my own power, my own strength, I've fizzled in the end. I fire up quickly, believing the sky is the limit, only to be brought back down to earth too soon. Why is this? What accounts for this gap between my desire to do good and my ability to *produce*? It's curious, don't you think? Especially given the exhortation from the apostle Paul, who was as accurate a reflection of the way of Jesus as ever walked the earth, found in Galatians 6:9: "Let us not become weary in doing good, for at the proper time we will reap a harvest if we do not give up."

Don't become weary in doing good. Yes, Paul. Yes, but . . . how?

How quickly we forget the topic Paul covered a few verses prior: living not by the flesh but by the *Spirit of God*.

And so the code gets cracked.

A refresher: Paul has just given the believers at Galatia a series of compelling injunctions regarding embracing the freedom that is theirs in Jesus. "For in Christ Jesus neither circumcision nor uncircumcision has any value," he writes. "The only thing that counts is faith expressing itself through love" (Galatians 5:6). He then spells out how to practically get that done.

"You, my brothers and sisters, were called to be free," he says. "But do not use your freedom to indulge the flesh; rather, serve one another humbly in love. For the entire law is fulfilled in keeping this one command: 'Love your neighbor as yourself.' If you bite and devour each other, watch out or you will be destroyed by each other.

"So I say, walk by the Spirit, and you will not gratify the desires of the flesh" (v. 13–16).

Then comes the famous litany of demonstrations of what those "fleshly desires," such as hatred and jealousy, sexual immorality and fits of rage—and also their counterparts, the desires of the Spirit, such as love, joy, peace, patience, gentleness, and all the rest—include. Paul's conclusion is not to be missed: "Those who belong to Christ Jesus have crucified the flesh with its passions and desires. Since we live by the Spirit, let us keep in step with the Spirit. Let us not become conceited, provoking and envying each other" (v. 24–26).

So, yes, we can do some good in our own strength, which explains how it's possible that even the various branches of the American Atheists organization offer service opportunities to their constituents.[2]

But if we want to "do good" over the long haul, and in a manner that addresses not only superficial needs but also the truest needs of the human soul, we've got to come in the power of God. We've got to live "in step with the Spirit," to quote Paul (v. 25), because it's in him that abundance is found. Try to sustain do-good efforts over the long haul on your own, through circumstances that are beyond your control, through "issues" you couldn't foresee, through the chaos that always surrounds pain, and you'll waste away. You'll burn out. You'll flame out. You'll drown. Pick any fatalistic euphemism you like, and it will be true. You'll get what's known as "compassion fatigue."

If you are suffering from compassion fatigue, you are living as a spiritual slave. You may be doing tons and tons of good, but you're doing it on your own strength. And unless you find a better approach, you're a burnout waiting to happen.

Just as we saw in the response of the older brother, spiritual slaves can become enraged by other people's apparent lack of contribution, by their lack of righteousness, by their lack of good deeds. They may give, but it's only so that they can then get; altruism isn't really their thing.

Returning to the Parable of the Good Samaritan, you get the feeling that the priest and the Levite, who passed by the man in the ditch instead of pausing to help, were sufferers of spiritual enslavement.

They were pious.

Righteous.

Faithful keepers of God's law.

And also of no use that day, save for showing you and me and the rest of humanity exactly how *not* to behave.

Jesus did not face the horrors of the Roman cross so that God could control our behavior. Or usher in a grand meritocracy. Or appoint world-renowned keepers of the law. He came and bled and died and was buried so that we could be *adopted as daughters and sons*. Regardless of how you're living today—as spiritual orphan? as spiritual slave?—you are destined to be a child of God. You are destined to live life free from pleading, free from performance. You are destined to live as one who knows without hesitation that you are accepted, that you are loved.

The Daughter, the Son

Which brings us full circle to the role of spiritual daughter, spiritual son. Again, this is the only approach to Christian living that *involves truly walking by faith*. Here, in the abiding presence of your heavenly Father, every fear is "suddenly wiped away," as the lyric of "Here in Your Presence" says.[3] You are no longer unsure of your place in the family. You're no longer begging to be seen; neither are you racking up good deeds in hopes of gold stars. You're beloved—and you *know* it. You're secure and you're at peace. From that place of divinely held confidence, you can go and see and care. You can help and serve and love. You can be Jesus to those in need. You are not only *positionally* free but you can *live practically* as though it is true. And because you're free, you can now help others who want freedom too.

Colen is a friend who used to be on our ministry staff at New Life. He is a retired Army colonel who played football at West Point, graduated from the academy just after the Vietnam War, and for thirty years led regiments as an artillery commander. He's a tough guy, what once was called "a man's man." I had lunch with him a few weeks ago, and he told me a story he'd never told me before.

He said, "Brady, seven years ago, you mentioned from the platform that New Life was heading to Guatemala to help with an orphanage there—the kind of mission trip we've done for years. For some reason I was prompted to get more information, and so my wife and I turned up at the 'interest' meeting that was held after the service."

What Colen didn't know until that meeting was underway was that (a) this was a college-age mission trip, (b) the only people who had signed up for the trip were eighteen- and nineteen-year-old girls, and (c) our mission pastor who oversees all such trips was in desperate need of a trip leader. "Would you like to lead it?" he asked Colen and his wife.

Colen told me that he just laughed and said he would.

Specifically, he and his wife would chaperone fourteen young women in a tiny village in Guatemala, where for ten days' time they would support a building project that was already in progress. "Brady," he said, "I spent every waking minute there burning trash."

At the orphanage, there was no good way to dispose of the trash that accumulated day by day, and so the people who ran the place would just let it pile up out back. As you might imagine, this practice created all sorts of health hazards, and so when Colen noticed what was going on, he decided that the first order of business was for his team to build a small-scale incinerator. They planned for the ash pit, they laid the bricks, they build the protective enclosure—the whole bit. And then for ten straight days Colen stood outside the orphanage burning every bit of that years-old trash. "The stench was almost unbearable," he said. "But as I helped them take care of this very basic need, I felt ennobled somehow in my work. Jesus would have been at that trash heap, I think. I like to think I reflected him there."

I smiled so intently over this story of Colen's that I broke into a laugh. "*That's* what I want for every follower of Jesus: to find the fulfillment that only faith brings," I told him.

Colen could have said no to leading this trip, I should point out. There was no pressured pitch. There was no guilt trip. There was no arm-twisting involved.

He could have bowed out gracefully, fearing looking like a fool. And really, who would have blamed him? He was ill-prepared. He was inexperienced. Truthfully, he was out of his league. But he had the one thing that would win the day: faith—the tiniest bit. And seven years in, he's still riding that wave—of fulfillment, of gratitude, of *joy*.

CHOOSING FAITH, NOT FEAR

Let me say here that I highly doubt that any well-meaning follower of Jesus is angling for more chances to live in fear. None of us *wants* to be afraid. And yet each time we allow our fear of interruption or our fear of inconvenience or our fear of inadequacy or any of the rest to win the moment, we *become people of fear*.

My son is a grown man now, but when he was ten, he was a huge "Peanuts" fan. Every October, a highlight of the month was watching the TV show *It's the Great Pumpkin, Charlie Brown.* The character Lucy's determination to find the biggest pumpkin in the patch always inspired Abram, who hunted until he found one for our family that was too large for him to heave. One year in early summer, Abram and I were walking through Home Depot and saw a rack with dollar packets of seeds. "Dad!" Abram said. "Can we get some pumpkin seeds? This Halloween, we can just go out and grab the pumpkins we grew and carve those!"

I was skeptical. Nothing grows on the Palmer Divide, where we lived at the time. Plus, we have approximately thirty days of warm weather a year in Colorado, and pumpkins love heat. But when I saw my kid's near-palpable enthusiasm, I caved. "Yeah," I said. "Sure, you can get the seeds." I then proceeded to give this task my all.

I was raised on a farm. I know my way around a seedbed. I prepared the soil, placed the seeds in their little black mounds, covered them with compost, watered them, and wished them well. I kid you not: ten days later, I went outside to find fourteen sprouts of flowering pumpkin plants. The place was *covered* in them.

Abram and I created a little routine in which we'd go outside every day, water the pumpkin seedbeds, and chat about the vast quantities of pumpkins that would be showing up soon, each from a seemingly insignificant seed.

The parallel I'd like to draw is this: when you and I allow fear to rule even a moment of our lives—when we assume the identity of either a spiritual orphan or a spiritual slave—we plant a little seed. And despite our disbelief that that seed will find the resources it needs to grow and develop and flourish and thrive, seeds are hearty folk. They will strain for the sustenance they need, and at some point they'll totally take over your life.

We say to ourselves, *I'm slammed today. I barely have time to breathe.* And the fear of interruption, of being deterred from working for our significance, gets dropped like a seed in the soil.

We say, "I'd give you a lift, but I'm not going that way. You'll have to find somebody else." And the fear of inconvenience, of being connected in a familial way, settles in, there under the soil.

We think, *I'm not the right person to help them . . . Surely someone better equipped will come along.* And the fear of inadequacy, of being called out and called on and called up, takes root, its flower blossoming, telling the world that the seed has stuck.

Why can't they get themselves together? we wonder. And the fear of others' issues, of their refusal to also work for grace, sprouts a giant pumpkin, seemingly overnight.

"I always get hurt when I get involved," we whisper. And the fear of personal injury, of taking the risk to engage, results in the arrival of scores of pumpkins, a *massive* pumpkin patch.

Before we move ahead, let me restate this chapter's original premise, which is that regardless of how faithful we *want* to be, we won't actually *be* faithful until we move intentionally away from fear. As we'll see in chapters to come, this will necessarily include practicing spiritual disciplines of solitude and prayer, of service and giving grace, of extending compassion and selflessness and generosity, of a little thing called *love.* Each of these things demands a choice, but the choices are ones we can make.

In their book *Radically Happy: A User's Guide to the Mind,* authors

Phakchok Rinpoche and Erric Solomon write, "Take a moment to reflect on your life. Did you make your best decisions when you were feeling really anxious or fearful or when you were feeling calm and spacious? Did your best, most creative and fruitful ideas come when you were relaxed and at ease or when you were consumed with irritation and worry?"[4]

We assume the question is rhetorical even as our life experience betrays how often we veer the other way. And so: this book. I've written it in hopes of calling us back to that calm and spacious place, the place on the other side of our choosing faith over fear, the place where the fruit of extravagance is borne.

◇◇

Pushing Pause: Chapter 4

Truly, to keep moving past our fears day after day so that we can joyfully and—extravagantly!—serve others in need, we must view ourselves as daughters and sons of God. Remember, because of what Jesus has done for us, we can live as children of God. We must let go of the notion that we have to somehow earn good standing with him. We must let go of the tendency to hold on to "our" stuff. We must let go of that "tomorrow logic" we talked about that convinces us we will somehow be better suited to help others then than we are today. And we must *hold fast* to the idea that we are accepted just as we are, that we have everything we need—today!—to be of service to God, and that generosity will not *drain us* of resources but rather multiply them in an abundant sort of way.

Read
Let's recenter ourselves on how God views us, in light of how he views his Son's role in this world, by reading John 1:1–14:

*In the beginning was the Word, and the Word was with God, and the
Word was God. He was with God in the beginning. Through him all
things were made; without him nothing was made that has been made.
In him was life, and that life was the light of all mankind.*

*The light shines in the darkness, and the darkness has not over-
come it.There was a man sent from God whose name was John. He
came as a witness to testify concerning that light, so that through him
all might believe. He himself was not the light; he came only as a witness to the light. The true light that gives light to everyone was coming
into the world. He was in the world, and though the world was made
through him, the world did not recognize him. He came to that which
was his own, but his own did not receive him. Yet to all who did receive
him, to those who believed in his name, he gave the right to become
children of God—children born not of natural descent, nor of human
decision or a husband's will, but born of God.*

*The Word became flesh and made his dwelling among us. We have
seen his glory, the glory of the one and only Son, who came from the
Father, full of grace and truth.*

Reflect

- What do you suppose it means for John to say that, as believers, we have "the right to become children of God"?
- What might change in your posture, your attitudes, or your as-
  sumptions today if you lived as a "child of God"?

Respond

This chapter's challenge is this: Just for today, choose to manifest the
confidence that is yours as a child of the one, true King. Power is yours.
Insight is yours. Peace is yours. Patience is yours. Generosity is yours.
All noble, right, and excellent things are *at your disposal today*. Lean into
these resources. Leverage them. Joyfully give them away.

5

What We Mean When We Say "All"

The very first lesson the gospel teaches believers is to despise all things for Christ. Give all away. Take up the cross and follow him. If this mind is not in us, then we are not in Christ.[1]

JOHN OWEN

VERSE FOR VERSE, I'VE always thought that the book of Acts provides some of the most stimulating reading of the entire New Testament. In the first three chapters alone, we see Jesus ascending to his Father in heaven, a cloud hiding him from his disciples' sight; we see Judas, the disciple who had betrayed Jesus and wound up committing suicide, replaced by Matthias; we see the first appearance of the Holy Spirit, which came upon believers as "tongues of fire" atop their heads;[2] we watch as the apostle Peter delivers one of the most powerful and prophetic sermons ever given; we see the early church form the key practices—devotion to teaching, consistent fellowship, the breaking of bread, prayer—that mark a group of believers still today; we see the daily adding of followers to Jesus' mission on the earth; we see the disciples accomplish bona fide healings, leaning into the divine power Jesus had told them was theirs; we see Peter and John passionately pleading for hearts to surrender and come to Christ.

Then comes chapter 4.

In Acts 4, Peter and John face intense persecution for preaching the gospel of Christ. "The priests and the captain of the temple guard and the Sadducees came up to Peter and John while they were speaking to the people," verses 1–2 say. "They were greatly disturbed because the apostles were teaching the people, proclaiming in Jesus the resurrection of the dead."

The men were jailed overnight while the officials sorted out what to do next.

The following day, Peter and John were brought before the officials and asked by what name they had healed the lame man they'd healed. Where had they gotten this power they'd shown?

Peter and John stood so firmly on the name of Jesus, declaring that "there is no other name under heaven given to mankind by which we must be saved" (v. 12), that those in charge of the grilling were left "astonished" (v. 13) and, believing they had no other option, essentially gave the men a slap on the wrist and decided to let them go.

The apostles, upon being released from jail, immediately went "back to their own people," verse 23 says, to report all that had happened to them. Those believers were thrilled. They cheered. They rejoiced. They offered praised to God. They'd been praying for this exact outcome, and now God had delivered a *yes*. Then they prayed again, this time for boldness, asking God to perform miracles through them in Jesus' name. And afterward "the place where they were meeting was shaken. And they were all filled with the Holy Spirit and spoke the word of God boldly" (v. 31).

Another longed-for yes.

Now, on the heels of this dramatic turn of events comes an interesting sidebar from Luke: "All the believers were one in heart and mind," he writes. "No one claimed that any of their possessions was their own, but they shared everything they had. With great power the apostles continued to testify to the resurrection of the Lord Jesus. And God's grace was so powerfully at work in them all that there were no needy persons among them. For from time to time those who owned land or houses sold them, brought the money from the sales and put it at the apostles' feet, and it was distributed to anyone who had need" (v. 32–35).

Those early believers prayed for one another, and we find that a reasonable thing.

Those early believers talked with one another, and we find *that* a reasonable thing.

Those early believers celebrated each other's wins, and that, too, is reasonable to us.

But passing around their possessions, such that not even one person was in need?

It's the pinnacle of unreasonableness. Who in a right mind thinks their stuff isn't *theirs*? "Wanting," as author Jen Pollack Michel puts it, "is the earliest language we learn."[3] If people's possessions weren't "their own," as verse 32 scandalously asserts, then whose were they? To whom did their belongings belong?

THE ONE WHO OWNS IT ALL

I mentioned earlier that Psalm 24 played an instrumental role in helping me unearth the spirit of cynicism that took root in me after my colleague's death. I'd like to return to that psalm now, focusing on the verse that kicks it off. It reads, "The earth is the LORD's and everything in it, / the world, and all who live in it; / for he founded it on the seas / and established it on the waters" (v. 1–2).

The psalmist David says it so plainly that we hardly notice it at all. *All* things belong to God. All things are his alone. This straightforward reminder helps us make sense of Jesus' requirement that his followers leave "all" to follow him.

In the Gospel of Luke, we find Jesus being trailed by large crowds who are curious about his teachings, eager to understand his "way." Turning to them, he said, "If anyone comes to me and does not hate father and mother, wife and children, brothers and sisters—yes, even their own life—such a person cannot be my disciple. And whoever does not carry their cross and follow me cannot be my disciple . . . [T]hose of you who do not give up everything you have cannot be my disciples" (Luke 14:26–28, 33).

This declaration seems harsh to our individualistic minds, but I think what Jesus was saying was "Demonstrate your understanding that nothing here is 'yours.' Show that you know that all comes from my Father and that *everything*—even your very life—belongs exclusively to him."

A friend of mine refers not to "her" car or "her" house, instead saying, "the car" or "the house." I'm not even sure she knows that she does it, but it's theologically sound. Nothing she has is "hers," any more than anything I have is mine. Nothing you "own" is yours, either, I should mention, if you're catching the gist of Jesus' words. English theologian John Owen caught the gist of them, which is why he could speak of despising "all things for Christ."

Are you sure you know what you're talking about, John Owen? Are you sure, Jesus, that you mean *all* the things? Can't we hold a little back for ourselves? What would be so wrong about that?

You may recall that Ananias and Sephira dared to test that assumption by trying to deceive God, and things didn't go well for them. Ananias sold a piece of property and brought part of the proceeds to the apostles, saying that it was the full amount. With Sephira's full knowledge, Ananias pocketed the rest. Peter called him on the wrongdoing, and in the next scene Ananias fell to the floor and died. Moments later Sephira, too, died, causing certain fear to grip "the whole church and all who heard about these events," says Acts 5:11. The text doesn't say that *God* killed this couple, but it does remind us in plain terms that deceit never serves us well. In short, Jesus meant what he said before; it turns out that all means *all*. God made it all. God owns it all. God can do with it whatever he wants.

POSSESSIONS THAT AREN'T MEANT TO BE PRIZED

Eighteen years ago I was part of the core team that planted Gateway Church, in Southlake, Texas. We were a tiny congregation back then, with a giant opportunity before us. A million-dollar piece of property came available for us to buy, and it was an unbelievably good deal. Our pastor, Robert Morris, looked at us and said, "I know there are only two hundred of us, but let's just pray and see what God does."

He said, "Don't give even one penny that God does not prompt you to give. But if he *does* prompt you, I hope you'll be faithful. I commit to doing the same."

My kids, Abram and Callie, were babies, still in diapers, toddling around, pint-size personifications of need. Pam and I didn't have much money, but we'd holed away some savings and were trying to be wise. I prayed to God, asking him for insight regarding what we should give. I wanted to be part of the building project, but things were a little . . . tight.

Give it all.

This was the prompting I got from God.

Wait. What? Give *what* "all"?

I want you to give it all—everything you've got.

The prompting was so clear that there was no amending or denying it. God wanted me to take 100 percent of Pam's and my money—and at the time I *absolutely* thought it was ours—and put it in the offering plate so that Gateway could purchase some land.

I wanted to ask God for reassurance: Was he certain that this was a good idea? But in my heart of hearts I was clear on the input. I knew what he'd say to that.

For several Sundays, Pastor Robert allowed for a special time during the service when offerings for the property would be received. On the appointed morning Pam and I stood from our seats and made our way to the front of the room, decision made, check in hand. I remember feeling very possessive, as though God should feel grateful for this sizable, lavish gift. But as we got to the makeshift altar, where ushers were standing with plates in hand, and I laid that check down, God did a radical work in my heart. He taught me the futility of prizing possessions and that the only thing to be prized is him.

In the story of the Good Samaritan, Jesus shows us another way to view "stuff." You'll recall that, upon seeing the man who had been left for dead lying in a ditch, the Samaritan bandaged the man's wounds, treated him with oil and wine, hoisted him on his own donkey, and took him to an inn. But there was more. "Look after him," the Samaritan told the innkeeper, "and when I return, I will reimburse you for any extra expense you may have" (Luke 10:35). Nobody had to pry anything from the Samaritan's grip—did you notice? He gave *freely* of all that he had.

Eighteen years ago I had a lot to learn, if God was to have his way in my life.

The point I'm chasing: I don't know if God will ever prompt you to give everything you have away. Perhaps he will not; perhaps his requests will be more reasonable than that. Frankly, I'm not concerned with what God may or may not choose to do. What I'm concerned with is this: Are you *prepared* to part with everything should the request ever come your way?

Step one in that preparation: Remember that nothing is "yours." Author Randy Alcorn says, "As long as I still have something, I believe I own it. But when I give it away, I relinquish control, power, and prestige. At the moment of release the light turns on. The magic spell is broken. My mind clears. I recognize God as owner, myself as servant, and others as intended beneficiaries of what God has entrusted to me."[4] In other words, it's easier to hand something back you've been handed than to give a prized possession away. All that we have has been handed to us by God, who essentially says, *Here. Hold this for me for a little while, would you? I'll be back to pick it up.*

THE POSTURE OF POSSESSIONLESSNESS

I've reflected often on what I'd yet learn about God and about me and about my wise stewardship of my not-mine things, back when that offering was taken up. Had I known then what I (hopefully) understand now, the giving of those savings would have elicited not even a moment of hesitation from me.

For the balance of this chapter, I'd like to lay out the three big takeaways that surfaced for me following that important day, ideas that will change how you live, if you let them, concepts that will stand you up in a posture of possessionlessness and free you from me/mine thoughts.

Lesson 1: Lead with Compassion

Compassion is believing that God can redeem every part of every person's life. Being "compassionate," then, means seeing people as God sees them: full of potential, well on their way. In Matthew 9:36, we read that "when [Jesus] saw the crowds, he had compassion on them, because they were harassed and helpless, like sheep without a shepherd."

He viewed people not as targets of pious judgment but as prospective recipients of his deep love. He wanted not to separate himself from them but to *join them in their pain*. And in so choosing, he led with compassion, always seeking ways to serve.

In Mark 8, the fantastic story is told of Jesus heaping compassion on those he saw. By way of context, Jesus was walking in the middle of nowhere, teaching ever-increasing crowds of people what his kingdom is like. And for the second time in Mark's retelling, those crowds come ill-prepared for lunch. It was midday, and people were hungry. It was hot, and there was no food.

Now, these people knew as they were following Jesus that they weren't out for a quick jaunt. It would have been reasonable for him to survey the crowds and find them woefully lacking in the planning department. How could you not bring food when you knew you'd be gone all day?

But that's not at all what he did. I remember when Pam and I were dating, and sometimes we'd leave for a date in the afternoon and not return until long after the sun had set. As day gave way to night, Pam would wish she'd brought a coat. Did I berate her for her lack of foresight? Did I shame her for not being prepared? Hardly! I was *glad* to care for her by slipping my jacket off and draping it over her shoulders. I was more than happy to help. Why? Because my posture toward Pam has always been one of compassion. This is the work of Christ in my life.

When Jesus saw those hungry people, he had but one thought: *Let's get them fed.*

Let's get them clothed.
Let's get them hired.
Let's get them a place to live.
Let's get them inclusion.
Let's get them into recovery.
Let's get them thriving in life.

This is the voice of compassion: "Let's get them whatever they need."

"In our choice to be with those who suffer," writes James Orbinski, "compassion leads not simply to pity but to solidarity."[5] Compassion says, "I see you. I'm *with* you. I care."

In her book *Carried: How One Mother's Trust in God Helped Her Through the Unthinkable*, author Michelle Schmidt, a devout Mormon, wrote of losing her daughter, Annie, a twentysomething hiking and climbing enthusiast, to a solo camping trip gone wrong. When Annie failed to pick up Michelle at the airport for an expected visit, Michelle knew something was terribly off. To her horror, she would soon discover that her daughter had slipped on a trail and fallen to her death, alone. But before that knowledge came to her, she met with the police investigator who was tasked with finding Annie. During that initial meeting, she wrote, she asked the officer if it would be okay for them to say a prayer. "Please help this officer," she then prayed, "and anyone else who will work with him. Please bless them to work to the best of their abilities to help us find our daughter."[6]

This is compassion at its finest, setting aside your own concerns momentarily to care for another in your midst. It is returning to God something he's asked you to hold—breath or talent, money or skill, a ride or the ability to pray—knowing that that thing you've been holding can be a gamechanger just now in the life of somebody else.

The officer was taken aback. He'd been all business when he walked into the room but following Michelle's prayer, she "noticed a definite softening and gentleness in the way the officer treated me." He said he would get an officer on the case immediately and would contact Michelle as soon as they knew more.

This can look like outright negligence, I realize, refusing to trumpet our own cares and concerns. But in fact the opposite happens: we gain strength as we lift others up. Again from Alicia Chole: "Jesus' authority flowed not from possessions or positions but from *submission*. What was the surprising source of Jesus' authority? Submission to his Father's will and Word."[7]

The same is true for us. When we lead with compassion for those God created and loves, we look a lot like Jesus to the rest of the world.

Back at Gateway eighteen years ago, had I stopped to more carefully consider the vast ministry that would be accomplished in the buildings that would be built on that land, I might have spent more energy going about God's good work than waiting for a divine pat on the back.

Lesson 2: Long for Biblical Shalom

So: Lead with compassion, remembering God's rich, redemptive plan. Here's lesson 2: *Long for biblical shalom.*

In that passage from Acts 4, we learn that there is a direct link between *our sharing* and *God's powerful work.* "No one claimed that any of their possessions was their own," we read, "but *they shared everything they had.* With great power the apostles continued to testify to the resurrection of the Lord Jesus. And *God's grace was so powerfully at work in them all that there were no needy persons among them*" (v. 32–34, emphasis mine). This, I think, is *shalom.* It is unity; it is sought-after peace. When we long for things like peace and unity more than we long for the stuff of this world, we begin living as possessionless stewards who are completely devoted to God.

Now to how this gets done . . .

Monica Diaz was a fast-food worker who also happened to be homeless. She and her husband, Pete Etheridge, along with their dog, Sassy, were among those living in tents under overpasses in Washington, D.C.—that is, until Gabriela Sevilla happened by.[8]

A twenty-five-year-old Howard University law student and intern with the Washington Clinic for the Homeless, Gabriela was attending one of the city's biweekly "encampment sweeps" as a legal observer, when she saw Monica and Pete being removed from the street. She took time to talk with Monica that afternoon and for days following the interaction couldn't shake the couple from her mind. She, too, was a Latina who'd been raised by immigrants. She, too, had been shy on resources before. "This [homelessness] could happen to anyone," she wrote in her GoFundMe post introduction. Her goal was twenty-five hundred bucks. A security deposit, maybe first month's rent—that's what she wanted for Monica and Pete. But within seven days, donations raced to nearly ten times that much: more than $22,000 came in.

Partway through that campaign, Gabriela drove to where she figured Monica and Pete now lived, easily finding them in their tent. She told them of the fund-raising she'd done and then loaded them into her car. After stops at Denny's (breakfast), T.J.Maxx (new clothes), and the Humane Society (new collar and a checkup for Sassy), she helped Monica put together a résumé. She made copies, which she dropped off for Monica later that day, and helped her find jobs with better pay. She helped them work on a housing application—ironically, for an apartment not far from her own. And she kept showing up every few days until the couple was back on their feet.

It bears mentioning that while Gabriela was tending to this couple, she maintained all her own responsibilities as well. She was a student with a full course load. She was a fully invested volunteer. She had a mother and a brother to help care for. She valued an active social life. But instead of using those obligations as excuses, she peeked around them and saw someone's need.

That someone, Monica Diaz, needed housing. To get that, she needed better income. To get that, she needed a higher-paying job. To get that, she needed an interview. To get that, she needed an updated résumé and something appropriate to wear. To get those things, she needed some errands run. To get that done, she needed a friend. And while Gabriela might not have known everything, she knew how to be a friend. When Gabriela surveyed Monica's situation, she saw holes that she could help plug. She had resources that could relieve someone's resourceless state, and so she came near, she engaged, she *shared*. And God used what was in her hand.

"Somewhere, somehow, God is asking each of us to do something so entirely common as to love someone," Jen Pollack Michel wrote in *Teach Us to Want*. "If we let the truth of this sit on our skin—that we are one in seven billion, a speck on the still point of the turning world, the present pinhead *I* in the enormous bulk of human history—it has potential for allowing us to be swept into the grand calling to be small, smaller, smallest for the kingdom."[9] As it relates to our topic at hand, so often, what this "love" looks like is our sufficiency encountering another's need, two puzzle pieces whose tabs and blanks perfectly and pleasingly match up. Our resource, however insignificant it seems, perfectly suiting another's need.

Lesson 3: Live as One Who Has Distinguished Need from Greed

Another way to get at the core of that second lesson is by saying that the only good reason for abundance is to address scarcity in all its forms. This straightforward explanation takes us right into lesson 3: If we believe that those with abundance are to share with those in need, then the onus to share is on us.

You may have seen the group exercise before where everyone stands shoulder to shoulder at the start, on the same level, in a wide line. A facilitator then poses a series of questions, and those who respond "Yes" take one step forward, while those who say "No" take one step back. The questions are abundance questions: "Extra this? . . . How 'bout extra that?"

"Have you ever traveled to another country?" Those who have take a long step forward. Those who have not, one long step back.

"Did you ever attend summer camp as a child?" Those who have take one step forward. Those who haven't, one step back.

"Did you grow up with two parents living in your home?" Yes, step forward; no, step back.

"Did your family take a vacation at least once a year?" Yes, step forward; no, step back.

"Did your family have help maintaining the house?"

"Did you get a four-year degree?"

"Do you own your own home, now that you're an adult?"

"Do you have a savings account?"

On and on the questions go, until the gap is plain to see. We have far more excess than we realize. We are more resourced than we know. And yet, for too many of us, the abundance we enjoy will never be quite enough.

Eighteen years ago, all I could see when I looked at my financial landscape was scarcity . . . insufficiency . . . lack. There was so much I wanted for Pam's and my life that our paltry bank account could not afford. And so I made it my life's work to bulk up those funds, to acquire every last thing on my list. It was a doomed endeavor from the start. "Among the slow—the apparently lifelong—lessons I seem to be catching on to," wrote Scott Cairns, "one significant discovery has to be the paradoxical, shooting-yourself-in-the-foot nature of self-interest, the self-defeating nature of self-regard."[10]

Yes, that.

Exactly that.

God knew what he was up to when he whispered that prompting back then. I had excess I wasn't even in touch with. Yes, even *I* had something to give.

Across the years to come, God would teach me the vast difference between "need" and "greed." He would show me that my needs had already been met, and that greed was getting me nowhere fast.

So many shiny things we decide to chase are just grand distractions from others' actual needs. I started seeing it then and know it with certainty now: *We can do better than this.*

Lesson 4: Let God Preside Over It All

Back to that scene in Mark 8 involving a crowd of hungry people. As I mentioned, this was the second time in a matter of weeks that Jesus faced a famished group. The first time he took the bread and the fishes and fed the masses, there were twelve large baskets of food left over. This time there were seven. What do these leftovers mean?

For two thousand years, Bible scholars have wrestled with these texts, desperate to know why they're there. Of the seven remaining baskets of food, some say they represent the seven tribes who lived on the other side of the lake from where Jesus was preaching, symbolizing God's ability to reach the unreached.

Others say that seven is the number of completion and that seven baskets reflect God's sufficiency to meet all our needs.

Perhaps.

This much we know: by telling us that not only were the crowds filled to satiety that day, *there was still more available to them.* Ephesians 3:20–21 tells us that it is God alone who is "able to do immeasurably more than all we could ask or imagine" and that "his power" is *always* at work.

Jesus' disciples needed to be reminded of this in their time because they were about to face days when their boats would capsize; and days when they would be ridiculed for their belief in Christ; and days when they would be tortured and sent on the run; and days when they would be fed to hungry lions or else crucified upside down. They needed to know that when those days dawned, God still was God. He still would *have enough* for them.

You and I need to be reminded of this in our time, because we will continue to be forced to swim upstream in a culture that has no use for God. We will increasingly be mocked for our faith. We will increasingly be called "intolerant." We will increasingly look like fools to the world. We need to know that, as we fight the good fight of faith, *God will be enough for us.* He has everything we need for life and godliness, and he has promised to give it to us. (See 2 Peter 1:3.)

Pam and I have learned what the hungry throng of thousands learned that day: God does not bless what we own; he blesses *that which we give to him.* The more we give to God, the more blessings he returns. What we offer, he multiplies.

When we hand back "our" time, God returns it to us, hours on each minute we gave.

When we hand back "our" talent, God returns it to us, expertise replacing novice attempts.

When we hand back "our" treasure, God returns it to us, dollars for those pennies we spent.

When we hand back "our" life, God returns it to us, abundance marking it now.

Whatever we hand back to the One who first handed it out comes back to us in multiplied form. It's a lesson extravagant people have already sorted out, which is why they're so faithful in gathering up every resource they can find and look heavenward with full arms and full hearts. "Here, God!" they say, their smiles wide. "I trust you. Take it *all.*"

◇◇◇

Pushing Pause: Chapter 5

Following Jesus may be simple, but it is anything but easy. As God incarnate, he demands our ultimate allegiance and refuses to share the top spot with anyone or anything else. In a manner of speaking, this should come as good news to you and me. Given all the decisions we must make in a day, here is one that is already made: if we say that we want to follow Jesus, then we must live fully devoted to him. No ifs. No ands. No buts. No question about it. No further decision to be made. We are his, and he is ours. He is our "all in all."

Read

You'll recall that in Luke's gospel, Jesus tells those who are eager to follow him that it will take their full commitment and more. "If anyone comes to me and does not hate father and mother, wife and children, brothers and sisters—yes, even their own life—such a person cannot be my disciple," he tells them. "And whoever does not carry their cross and follow me cannot be my disciple . . . [T]hose of you who do not give up everything you have cannot be my disciples" (Luke 14:26–28, 33).

Reflect

- How do you feel about your level of commitment to Jesus these days, given the gist of these verses in Luke?
- By asking his followers to forsake even intimate family members, what is Jesus telling us about himself and his ability to fulfill the deepest longings of our hearts?

Respond

The challenge for this chapter is twofold: First, consider the aspect of life that you tend to grip with viselike strength. Is it your time? Your talent? The money that comes your way? What is your "precious," that thing you hyper-manage and hyper-control?

Just for today, lay that one thing down. If you obsess over your time, then shut your day planner or close your calendar app. Open your Bible instead. Tell God, "For today, my schedule is yours."

If you obsess over your money, then, just for today, turn to God and say, "All yours. Do as you please."

If your talent or skill feels precious to you, then perhaps spend more time communing with your heavenly Father than you do creating your next brilliant thing.

Lay down your "thing." Pick up more of God instead. See if he doesn't wow you with his ability to manage your thing better than you.

6

What's Yours, and Mine, to Do

*The plea from antiquity goes out: Seek wisdom! Seek
wisdom! Seek wisdom! It is the underlying system that
provides the basis of thought, of goal setting, of finding
the courage to say no, of discerning how money might
be properly used.*[1]

GORDON MACDONALD

IF I'VE BEEN ASKED one question more than any other, regarding
living an "extravagant" life, it is, "How do I know what's mine to
do when there is just *so much wrong* in the world?" At the root of this
question is the belief that because of the pervasiveness of the problems that we as a society face, and because of the sheer weight of each
one of those problems, it is just too overwhelming to sort out where
to begin in relieving the pain they see. What's more, these people are
most always followers of Jesus, people who take seriously what he had
to say along the way, about caring for those in need.

To set the stage for this scene, Jesus is explaining to his disciples what his second coming will be like and how they should prepare. He is speaking in parables, trying to help them understand all that's about to unfold. And then he comes to this word picture, a picture of sheep and goats: "When the Son of Man comes in his glory, and all the angels with him, he will sit on his glorious throne," he says. "All the nations will be gathered before him, and he will separate the people one from another as a shepherd separates the sheep from the goats. He will put the sheep on his right and the goats on his left.

"Then the King will say to those on his right, 'Come, you who are blessed by my Father; take your inheritance, the kingdom prepared for you since the creation of the world" (Matthew 25:31–34).

Such an intro begs the question: Well, how do we know if we'll be considered sheep or goats?

Jesus continues: "For I was hungry and you gave me something to eat, I was thirsty and you gave me something to drink, I was a stranger and you invited me in, I needed clothes and you clothed me, I was sick and you looked after me, I was in prison and you came to visit me" (v. 35–36).

But Jesus' disciples hadn't done these things for him. They told him so, to which Jesus said, "Truly I tell you, whatever you did for one of the least of these brothers and sisters of mine, you did for me" (v. 40).

So far, the disciples were tracking.

Sheep equals good.

Goat equals bad.

Sheep go to his right side.

Goats go to his left.

Whatever you do, don't end up on his left.

Got it.

But just in case there was any confusion regarding the weightiness of the fates of those two groups, Jesus clarified what their destiny would be: "Then he [the Son of Man] will say to those [goats] on his

left, 'Depart from me, you who are cursed, into the eternal fire prepared for the devil and his angels'" (v. 41).

Not exactly destined for frolicking in green pastures, right? No fun
there at all. And why would they be sent to this not-fun place? According to Jesus: "For I was hungry and you gave me nothing to eat, I was
thirsty and you gave me nothing to drink, I was a stranger and you did
not invite me in, I needed clothes and you did not clothe me, I was sick
and in prison and you did not look after me" (v. 42–43).

They, Jesus said, would then go away to eternal punishment, while
the righteous—the sheep—went to eternal life.

THE BELIEVER'S BENT TOWARD WORKS

Before we dissect this list of Jesus', it's important to clarify that it was
never meant to equate to a rundown of salvation's to-dos. Ephesians
2:8–9 kicks that idea to the curb: "For it is by grace you have been saved,
through faith—and this is not from yourselves, it is the gift of God—
not by works, so that no one can boast," the apostle Paul wrote. Clearly,
we are not saved by good works. Instead, we are saved *for* them.

Let's read on. "For we are God's handiwork," verse 10 says, "created
in Christ Jesus to do good works, which God prepared in advance for
us to do." The passage in Matthew 25 regards end times, when Jesus
returns to the earth again. What he's saying here is that the reason it
will be *so incredibly easy for him to sort out who his followers are* is that
they will have *borne distinctive fruit.*

The fact is that you simply can't do enough good deeds to gain salvation.

Nor can I.

But once we have gained salvation—again, through grace alone—
we will simultaneously *gain a new bent.* Galatians 2 says it this way:
"For through the law I died to the law so that I might live for God.

I have been crucified with Christ and I no longer live, but Christ lives in me. The life I now live in the body, I live by faith in the Son of God, who loved me and gave himself for me" (v. 19–20). The bent of the believer is a bent toward Christlike things. No longer do we crave the things we once craved; now we crave the things of God.

This Godward, Christlike bent, according to Jesus' words in Matthew 25, is marked by a selfless meeting of needs. Those who follow Jesus quite naturally will want to feed people who are hungry, offer a cup of cool water to those with ravaging thirst, hand over a warm jacket to the one who is jacketless, care for the sick, and all the rest. I think what Jesus is saying in Matthew 25 is "I know this is true of who you are, which is how it will be easy to spot you upon my return! What's more, take heart: when you act on this newfound bent of yours, you're acting as if on *me*."

So far, so good, right? If you are a believer, as I am, then we're both probably nodding our heads. Yep. We see what he's saying. Yep. We *do* want to care.

The challenge for us isn't theoretical consent; it's in getting that list checked off.

WHAT JESUS ASKS US TO DO

While we may agree that the way to care for people in need is to feed them, quench their thirst, enfold them in community, clothe them, and visit them when they're sick or imprisoned, surely I'm not the only person to have a question float through my mind: Does Jesus realize how *massive* each of those objectives is?

Take hunger, for starters. Today, more than 820 million people worldwide are under-resourced when it comes to food. Across the globe, *one in nine people* is what is considered "food insecure." They can't lead a normal, active life for the simple reason that they don't have energy—the fuel that comes from food. Closer to home, more than 41 million Americans face daily hunger, 13 million of whom are kids.[2] The places where most sufferers happen to live? Mississippi. Louisiana. Alabama. New Mexico. Arkansas. Kentucky. Maine.

Or what about thirst? The latest statistics show that more than 700 million people in forty-three countries suffer from water scarcity, which means they have limited or no access to clean drinking water. The organization Water for Life estimates that by 2025 more than 1.8 billion people will be living in countries or regions with "absolute water scarcity," and two-thirds of the world's population could be living under what they call "water stressed conditions."[3]

The Water Project, a group that builds and maintains water solutions such as water wells, sand dams, and spring protections in developing countries reminds us of these sobering stats:

- Nearly one out of every five deaths under the age of five worldwide is due to a water-related disease.
- Less than one in three people in sub-Saharan Africa has access to a proper toilet.
- Half of the world's hospital beds are filled with people suffering from a water-related disease.

And in case we here in the States are entertaining the belief that this lack of clean water is "over there" in some far-off land, it's worth noting that those studying our usage rates estimate that by 2071, half of the 204 freshwater basins in this country will not be able to sustain our consumption demands.[4] Intermittent foreshocks have already occurred, including one in 2017 that took out water service to 1.4 million people living in more than a half million American households—in Detroit and Oklahoma City, in Springdale and New Orleans. The reason? "Certain climate changes are threatening the levels of major bodies of water like the Colorado River and Lake Mead, which in turn drives up water bills."[5]

When demand exceeds supply, prices get driven up. We may not be trekking a two-mile round trip to a water well south of the Sahara, but if you can't afford to pay your water bill, you'll be in an equally sorry state.

This task of quenching the thirst of those without water is closer to home than we think.

And then there's *community:* "I was a stranger," Jesus said, "and you invited me in . . ." (Matthew 25:35).

Plentiful news reports of late have confirmed that despite our highly connected state these days from a technological angle, we are less emotionally connected than perhaps we've ever been. I won't belabor the point here. But let's at least remind ourselves that, statistically, more than half of all people living in this country report feeling "alone," "left out," and like "no one knows them well."[6] Worse still, these figures hold fast in nearly every country surveyed on earth. Over the past five decades, the number of single-person households in the United States has more than doubled and now represents the most prevalent living arrangement in larger cities.[7] It may seem like a benign statistic— maybe people are just introverted; maybe they *like* living alone . . .

Maybe.

But numbers don't lie. And the numbers associated with living alone are sobering, to be sure. Living alone increases the risk of loneliness, which leads to higher reported levels of perceived stress, even when the person is exposed to the same stressors as non-lonely people. Loneliness leads to less satisfying social interactions when they *are* with other people. Loneliness increases blood pressure and undermines the circulatory system's ability to regulate itself. Loneliness compromises effective sleep. Loneliness increases the risk of suicide— for young people and old alike. In *Psychology Today*, psychologist John Cacioppo of the University of Chicago, who has been tracking the effects of loneliness for some time, said this unfortunate state of being "sets in motion a variety of 'slowly unfolding pathophysiological processes,'" resulting in "a cumulative wear and tear."[8]

Too many of us are going it alone in this life despite Scripture's injunctions to live "as one." Sheep, Jesus said, take action here, enfolding the lonely in community and care.

He also spoke of *clothing those who need clothes,* an issue closely related to homelessness. Being without shelter, and often without clothing adequate to the climate, is a reality faced by more than *half a million* Americans at night, 50 percent of whom are white adult males and 7 percent of whom are children or adolescents under age twenty-five living on their own.[9]

Clothe them! Jesus said.

Shelter them!

Provide the vital protection that they need.

Here was the last one: *Visit those who are sick or in prison . . . Go to those who can't come to you.*

Did you know that the United States of America imprisons more people than any other country in the world? I'm not talking about "per capita" here; I'm talking nonadjusted sums. More than *2 million* citizens of this country are currently behind bars, which eclipses the totals of the next three countries on the list: China (1.7 million); Russia (650,000); and Brazil, (600,000).[10] Another 6 million Americans are on parole.[11]

If our country's current trends hold, and in the same racial proportion as they exist today, writes lawyer Bryan Stevenson, then "one in every three black male babies born in this country is expected to be incarcerated."[12]

Question: Whose job is it to tend to those who find themselves in this awful situation? To visit them? To love them? To care?

Jesus' words are clear: The sheep that hear his voice, the ones who wind up on his right side—*they* are the ones who will show up here. *They* are the ones who will care.

A WORD ON DOING WHAT'S OURS TO DO

New Life Church is the largest church in our region, and as such, I often feel the weight of pastoring our city at a level that overwhelms me most days. I am keenly aware of the needs of our city, of the 400 homeless families we turn away annually from Mary's Home for lack of space, of the 290 children and teens waiting to be adopted into their forever families,[13] of the 260,000 Coloradans each year who are desperate for *real* care for the most severe mental illnesses,[14] of the families left living inside a massive question mark after our area's horrific spike in suicide of late. I know moms and dads who can't afford groceries. I know professionals who can't find a job. I know people who can't kick their addictions.

I know the needs of our firefighters.

And of our police officers.

And of the people running the rescue mission downtown.

I know the needs of our military personnel returning from combat.

And of the parents in our community raising children with special needs.

And of the 36,000 prisoners living in "Prison Valley"—Cañon City, Colorado—an hour and ten minutes from my front door.

I know of these and a thousand more needs right here in front of me, in Colorado Springs alone, and the burden of those needs is *heavy*. It's the heaviest thing I hold.

It's heavy because while New Life is well resourced, there isn't enough money in our bank account to address every one of those needs.

It's heavy because, while we are given the luxury of 168 hours in a week, *still* there isn't time enough to address every one of those needs.

It's heavy because, while there are some supersmart people hanging around our church, even collectively we don't possess the knowledge to rightly address every one of those needs.

As I see it, there are two choices: because I can't do *everything*, I can choose to do nothing at all; or, like the Good Samaritan, who didn't let his inability to assist all wounded people keep him from caring for one in need, I can sort out precisely *what's mine to do* and get busy doing only that work.

Candidly, the same is true for you. You can either survey that list of Jesus'—feeding and quenching, enfolding and clothing, visiting and tending to—and determine that, since you can't do everything, there's nothing you can do. Or else you can devote yourself to understanding what's yours to do and then commit to doing that thing.

A SCHOOL IN SKILLED LIVING

Throughout the Bible—Hebrew and Greek testaments alike—the theme is trumpeted of seeking wisdom, prioritizing wisdom, holding fast to wisdom, and letting wisdom have its full way. We learn that the Lord is the keeper of this wisdom, that "from his mouth come knowledge and understanding" (Proverbs 2:6), and that this wisdom we're after sometimes makes sense only to him. "For my thoughts are not your thoughts," Isaiah 55:8 says, "neither are your ways my ways, declares the LORD."

The world's "wisdom" may say to go with our gut, to trust ourselves, to "live your best life" and "be you!" But God says that's no wisdom at all. Worse still, it's self-deceit.

"Do not deceive yourselves," Paul wrote in 1 Corinthians 3:18. "If any of you think you are wise by the standards of this age, you should become 'fools' so that you may become wise."

"Wisdom's instruction is to fear the LORD," we read in Proverbs 15:33. "Fear-of-GOD is a school in skilled living," Eugene H. Peterson renders it in The Message (MSG).[15]

We do well to embrace this wisdom.

We are wise who choose to fear God.

But what is this wisdom like? Can we trust it with our lives?

God promises that the wisdom he offers, the wisdom that "comes from heaven," James 3:17 says, is "first of all pure; then peace-loving, considerate, submissive, full of mercy and good fruit, impartial and sincere." We can be sure, in other words, that when we receive God's wisdom, we are receiving something that is at its core *good*. It is wisdom that is *useful*. It is better than gold, even, says Proverbs 16:16, and will lead us, according to Proverbs 19:8, to prosperity in life.

Those who "find me," wisdom says in Proverbs 8:35, "find life and receive favor from the LORD."

So, how do we find this wisdom? How can we possibly get it into our lives? According to the apostle James, who was Jesus' half brother, we simply need to ask. "If any of you lacks wisdom," James 1:5 says, "you should ask God, who gives generously to all without finding fault . . ."

Put another way, if you're curious about what's "yours to do" in this world, divine direction is just one prayer away.

THE USEFULNESS OF PRAYER

I've pastored a local church for three decades now and thus have spent countless hours around pastors, talking to them, partnering with them, learning from them. And based on all that I've seen and all that I've experienced firsthand, while there are myriad talents, gifts, and skills that I would say make a person well suited for pastoral ministry, there is one capability that rises above them all.

That's a pretty good setup right there.

You're dying to know what it is.

It's this: *having a prophetic imagination.*

Brilliant Old Testament professor and scholar Walter Brueggemann says of "prophetic imagination," in his book of the same name, that by joining the two words one is led "in an artistic direction in which truth is told in a way and at an angle that assures it will not be readily coopted or domesticated by hegemonic interpretive power."[16]

In admittedly less flowery language, let me tell you what the phrase means to me. Having a *prophetic imagination* means leading with God's wisdom instead of my own. To avoid exerting "hegemonic interpretive power" at its core is simply not pushing my agenda onto God's truth. It is to not allow a spirit of dominance to manifest in place of submission before God. It is trusting his will and ways, not mine. Because this "hegemonic interpretive power" is a dangerous practice for any believer, but especially so for those who lead others. If I have learned anything across the years I've been pastoring, it's that to lead others well I must first be well led by God. And, being the gentle presence that he is, that divine direction won't occur unless I invite it, unless I actually *want* it in my life.

Some may view this process of seeking wisdom and direction from God as burdensome, thinking, *I'm a mature adult. I know myself better than anyone. I'm a good decision-maker. I'm fine just going it alone.* This is flawed thinking. I live in Colorado, where the Wild West spirit still prevails. And yet, even for the die-hard individualists, the truth is that the only trustworthy wisdom is wisdom that comes from God. I love A. W. Tozer on this subject, who wrote, "It is better for Christians to sit on their hands until the judgment than to undertake pursuits God has not willed for them. It is the wisdom of God that enables a man to be delivered from these pursuits, giving him discernment so that he will know God's truth and be delivered from false doctrine."[17]

For my part, I believe it's not a burden but a *blessing* that all wisdom is held by God. Why? Because God is already at work in people's lives, long before I show up on the scene. Just yesterday I was walking my dog, weaving through our neighborhood along familiar streets, and I caught myself fixating on each house I walked by, thinking, *I wonder what's going on inside that house* . . . Have you ever done this? You imagine the conversations that people are having, or the struggles that they are enduring, or the joys that they're celebrating.

Now, we can't go peeking through windows, or people will file an invasion-of-privacy complaint against us. But here's what we can do that isn't creepy at all: we can pray. The Holy Spirit is not deterred by things like doors and walls, and when we ask him for insight on what's happening in those homes, in people's lives, he will do the most amazing thing: *he will tell us things we can't otherwise know.*

"No one can come to me unless the Father who sent me draws them . . . ," Jesus says in John 6:44. The Father is softening hearts, wooing souls, tending to lives, in advance of our arrival. And, astoundingly, he is willing to share insights with us on this work. When we call out to him for wisdom, we read in Jeremiah 33:3, he will answer us and tell us "great and unsearchable things" we don't yet know.

This is why I begin every day with a whispered prayer even before I climb out of bed. "Come, Holy Spirit," I pray. Yes, I know that technically he's already there, living inside of me as a believer, providing direction for each step I take. What I mean by my three-word prayer is this: "I *welcome* that work today. I *invite* you to overwhelm my own thoughts, my own whims, my own wisdom, with input from on high. I am asking you to enter into my day's agenda, helping me to be as effective as I can be."

In his book *A Diary of Private Prayer*, nineteenth-century Scottish theologian John Baillie put it this way: "O God my Creator and Redeemer, I may not go forth to-day except Thou dost accompany me with Thy blessing. Let not the vigour and freshness of the morning, or the glow of good health, or the present prosperity of my undertakings, deceive me into a false reliance upon my own strength. All these good gifts have come to me from Thee."

That line about not going forth without God's accompanying presence . . . such wisdom there, for you and me both.

You might consider starting your day this way too. Invite God's work as you begin your morning. Tell him that you're eager for his direction, that you crave his insight into people's lives. If you're stuck on the specifics of what to pray, you can't go wrong opening your Bible and praying God's Word back to him. I've always loved the words of the twenty-third psalm and often pray it back to my heavenly Father, saying something like this:

> *Father, because you are my shepherd, I know I have everything in need. Thank you for the green pasture rest I find in you. Thank you for the refreshment your presence offers me when I'm feeling overwhelmed and overcome. I welcome your guidance today. I welcome peak experiences and valley experiences alike, knowing that I have nothing to fear. You are here! You are near! You offer constant comfort to me. My cup does overflow because of your rich provision in my life. Help me to manifest the goodness and love to everyone I encounter today that you have lavished on my life. I love you, and I thank you for being a good Father to me.*

Let me ask you a question: Do you think God would be interested in favorably answering the requests in this prayer? I believe that he would. Jesus happens to agree: "If you remain in me and my words remain in you," he says in John 15:7–8, "ask whatever you wish, and it will be done for you. This is to my Father's glory, that you bear much fruit, showing yourselves to be my disciples."

When we pray for help in bearing fruit in accordance with Christ-likeness, that help will come to us. When we ask in accordance with God's fruit-bearing mission in our lives, it *will* be done for us.

GOD'S HEART FOR THOSE IN NEED

In his book, *Acquiring the Mind of Christ*, Orthodox monk Archiman-drite Sergius (Bowyer) wrote that, "prayer is the only bridge over the despondency of the world with its death, sins, and passions."[18] Coming at things from an entirely different vantage point, celebrity personal trainer Alec Penix wrote of prayer being a gift we give to someone. "When most people think of giving to others, their minds move to the physical, such as gifts, donations, or monetary gestures. But prayer itself is a potent tool that we can offer others because it's a way of providing for someone spiritually."[19]

Prayer as *bridge*.

Prayer as *gift*.

I like these metaphors. I might add one to the mix: prayer as *map*. When we long to know how to help those in our midst, prayer shows us the way to go. Let me demonstrate what I mean by directing us to three passages of Scripture that constantly come to mind as I'm asking God what's mine to do. What I hope to do here is give you something to watch for as you ask for wisdom from God. These can be considered destinations on that map I mentioned, places you're sure to travel from time to time as you stay on the fruit-bearing path.

Destination 1: Listen for Their Cries

Proverbs 21:13 says, "Whoever shuts their ears to the cry of the poor will also cry out and not be answered." Child-rearing experts say that when the parent of a newborn fails to respond to that baby's cries, the baby loses trust that his caregiver actually cares. A newborn can't put words to that, of course, but the sensation is there in spades. Similarly, when someone in distress cries out for help, and we who say we love Jesus refuse to listen and respond to those cries, the one in distress surely wonders if we care. What's worse, he may begin to wonder if *Jesus himself* cares, given how tone-deaf his followers are.

This begs a question of you and me: When was the last time we sat with someone in distress and said, "Tell me what's going on in your life. What are things like for you these days?" If you have to really think that over for a few minutes, then it's been too long. *Plentiful examples* should immediately pop to mind if we're serious about bearing fruit.

Jesus said that if we open our ears to the cries of the poor, then he will hear our cries too. But if we shut our ears to the cries of the poor, our cries will go unheard. This means that if we are captivated by our own dilemmas, our own struggles, our own needs, then God has every right to respond to us by saying, "I understand that you want me to hear and respond to your cries, but you yourself aren't doing that for others."

When we are faithful in listening to others, God is faithful in listening to us. So let today be the day. Step outside of your safe zone of known community and invite someone outside that sphere to share their heart.

Destination 2: Respond to Their Pleas for Help

"Whoever is kind to the poor lends to the LORD," Proverbs 19:17 says, "and he will reward them for what they have done." You want a solid return on your financial investment? Give money to the poor! We will cover this more in depth in part 2, but often, once we take time to listen to people's cries for help, we are presented with obvious, practical needs we can meet. My encouragement to you is that as God prompts you, step forward by faith to meet those needs, knowing that you will assuredly be repaid.

From time to time, we set up tables in the foyer of New Life and load them with little packets containing pictures of children living in the developing world and information on organizations such as Compassion International and VisionTrust International. We then announce from the stage that there are kids in our world today who do not have food or clean water or clothing or the opportunity to go to school. We ask our congregation to give up their fifth or sixth gourmet coffee drink each week so that they can send the thirty or forty bucks a month over an ocean and provide these necessities for one child. We do this *without apology*, you understand, because I ask you: Is there a sounder financial investment than that? "I will repay you!" God says to us. "I will repay every dime you give to the poor . . ."

My advice on this issue: If God, by his Spirit, prompts you to give, then give. Without hesitation.

You will be blessed, as a result.

Destination 3: Choose to Give Them a Voice

A third destination God tends to lead me to, whenever I ask for wisdom in helping people in need: Give people in need a voice.

Proverbs 31:8–9 says this: "Speak up for those who cannot speak for themselves, / for the rights of all who are destitute. / Speak up and judge fairly; / defend the rights of the poor and needy." Throughout the world, whenever wars break out or plagues descend on a country or foreign armies invade a locale, the first two groups of people who suffer are women and children. They are the first to starve. They are the first to die. Positionally, they are the weakest among us, rendered powerless by a patriarchal society that continues to hand the lion's share of power to the middle-aged white man.

Scripture exhorts us to stand against this trend. When we see an injustice occur, most notably when women and/or children are involved, we are to speak up. We are to defend those who cannot defend themselves—or maybe pass the mic to them so that they can defend themselves. We are to take whatever power and privilege we've been given and *use it for good in the world.* "Power is for flourishing," author Andy Crouch reminds us. "When power is used well, people and the whole cosmos come more alive to what they were meant to be. And flourishing is the test of power."[20]

Is a neighbor being mistreated by a business?

Is someone who is homeless being dehumanized?

Is a child being bullied or abused in some other way?

Is a woman's story not being heard?

We who follow Jesus can't sit idly by and expect to appear sheep-like in the end. Psalm 68:5–6 says "a father to the fatherless, a defender of widows, / is God in his holy dwelling. / God sets the lonely in families." And he prompts us to do the same.

ON KNOWING WHICH WAY TO GO

If you long to be extravagant in your care for other people, then don't be surprised when God points you toward one of these destinations: listening to the cries of their heart, responding to those cries in practical ways, standing up for them when they are unable to stand up themselves. In my experience, he directs us in this manner not just anecdotally but *time after time after time*. He doesn't want us to be compassionate bottle rockets, which go up with great flair but then fizzle right back down to the ground. No, his vision is that this mode of leaning into his wisdom and then going where he says to go would utterly define us, that it would absolutely mark who we are.

Listen, playing to hype is easy. Committing to the Holy Spirit? Less so. And yet that is precisely what we're asked to do. Earlier I mentioned our commitment as a church to the 13,000 residents living inside a four-square-mile neighborhood in a rough part of Colorado Springs. Technically, it's not the poorest neighborhood in our city, but it's the one God directed us to. And so we went. We connected. We served. We loved. We met needs. We asked questions. We listened carefully. We kept coming, again and again. There were no T-shirts for volunteers who joined us. No balloons for the kids who served. No video montage promoting the whole deal. Just faithful service over a long period of time.

Not a bottle rocket but a candle. This is who we're called to be.

Here's the benefit of serving over the long haul: you don't need a formal "serving strategy." You simply need the voice of God. Had you asked me when we began work in that neighborhood what we were going to be doing specifically, I would have had to shoot straight with you: "We're not exactly sure."

That was the truth. The sometimes-painful truth. Why was it painful? Because I happen to *like* a plan. I love strategies. I love systems. I love surefire paths to success. And yet, what I've been telling you in these pages is true: we can't bear the fruit of godliness without God at the center of our work. When we keep on showing up, keep on practicing what his Word asks us to do, keep on letting his wisdom override our own big, bright ideas, *he will show us what's ours to do.*

I couldn't have predicted that, as a church, we'd be helping a single mom turn a side hustle into a bona fide revenue stream; or that we'd fund the final payments of dental school for a young woman with giant dreams; or that we'd connect so many would-be aborted babies with loving, adoptive parents; or that we'd be tutoring kids in English week after week. These interventions weren't part of some grand scheme; they were just the next right steps to take, based on clear-cut direction from God.

What does this have to do with you? *Everything.* Have you ever wondered what you should do about your nephew who has asked for a place to live for the summer? Or about whether you should sponsor a child in a developing country? Or about how to support your neighbor whose teenage son just got arrested for drugs?

Have you ever come upon a protest march over one issue or another and wondered how to respond?

Have you ever seen a child get slapped in the face by a parent and had no idea what to do?

Have you ever learned of a friend's job loss but had no clue what that meant for you?

These and a thousand other scenarios might vex us were it not for the presence of God.

And how near that presence is—to those in need and also to us.

He sees.

He knows.

He sympathizes.

He works.

And then he *invites us into that work*. What's more, he promises that, as we join him in his redemptive efforts, our stance will be eternally sure. "My help comes from the LORD, / the Maker of heaven and earth," the psalmist declares. "He will not let your foot slip— / he who watches over you will not slumber" (Psalm 121:2–3).

I'm telling you: we can move toward need with confidence. We can know *precisely* what's ours to do. We can live this life with great wisdom, if only we'll pause to pray. The reason we unclenched our fist before, letting every last fear fall to the ground, is so that God can take our hand and lead us wherever he sees fit.

◇◇◇

Pushing Pause: Chapter 6

Today's challenge is aimed at helping you to nurture a prophetic imagination, as you look at the corner of the world in which you live.

Read

Jesus points out a powerful truth about our ability to act on the visions he gives us for the future in John 15:1–8. There we find these words: "I am the true vine, and my Father is the gardener. He cuts off every branch in me that bears no fruit, while every branch that does bear fruit he prunes so that it will be even more fruitful. You are already clean because of the word I have spoken to you. Remain in me, as I also remain in you. No branch can bear fruit by itself; it must remain in the vine. Neither can you bear fruit unless you remain in me.

"I am the vine; you are the branches. If you remain in me and I in you,

you will bear much fruit; apart from me you can do nothing. If you do not remain in me, you are like a branch that is thrown away and withers; such branches are picked up, thrown into the fire, and burned. If you remain in me and my words remain in you, ask whatever you wish, and it will be done for you. This is to my Father's glory, that you bear much fruit, showing yourselves to be my disciples."

Reflect

- Why do you suppose our ability to bear fruit in this life is so intimately tied to our ability to stay connected to Jesus?
- When have you felt the fruitlessness of being disconnected from Jesus? What was the situation, and what unfolded as a result of your refusal to surrender the situation to him?

Respond

The challenge for this chapter is to use not your own wisdom but rather the wisdom of your heavenly Father to make a simple decision today. Sometime across the next twenty-four hours, when you find yourself facing even a seemingly inconsequential decision, instead of trusting in your own logic, pause for a moment. Whisper a few sentences of prayer. Sit still until you receive a prompting from God. Then—and only then!— act on the insight you've received.

Part Two

YOUR MONEY

7

When Mission and Money Collide

No one has ever become poor by giving.

ANNE FRANK

S I MENTIONED BEFORE, I've been paying attention to the people around New Life whom I consider "extravagant"—observing their posture and patterns, absorbing their practices, learning from their ways—and, as expected, they tell me that a big factor in their knowing what is "theirs to do" in the world has been the divine direction they've received from God. For followers of Jesus, guidance from the Holy Spirit is invaluable as we navigate daily life. I wondered where that guidance had led.

When I asked about the things they've been "divinely directed" to do, I couldn't help but notice a theme. Upon discovering that a colleague was out with the flu, one person told me she was prompted to bring dinner to that person's family. When another person learned that an elderly neighbor was unable to get to and from a series of doctor appointments happening over the span of several days, he jockeyed his schedule to be able to offer the neighbor a ride. One woman heard that our team at our women's clinic wanted to provide every woman who comes for a sonogram a handmade scarf or baby blanket and decided to carve out time one evening a month to knit and crochet with others who have that knack. Another woman found out that the mother of her kid's classmate was suffering through agonizing divorce proceedings and needed someone to watch her three preschool-age kids several afternoons a week for who knows how long.

A man I talked to opened his family's home for three weeks to a friend who was estranged from his wife and had nowhere else to go.

A mom to three teens agreed to go to Al-Anon to support a colleague whose teenage daughter was struggling with substance abuse. She'd been there before . . . she knew her associate would need a nonjudgmental friend.

An older couple has taken care of their granddaughter five days a week, every week, for *eight full years* while their son, a single dad, holds down two jobs to make ends meet.

What is the common denominator for these and countless other examples I could offer up? Time? Yes, each of these people took a significant amount of time away from other things they could have been doing to help someone else. It always costs us something to be helpful. But often that cost is not just time. We can't rightly handle our mission unless we are also able and willing to take on the financial burden of generosity.

THE COST OF HELPFULNESS

To be sure, there are helpful things that you and I can offer someone in need that cost us nothing but a moment of time. You can smile at the garbage collector. I can offer an encouraging word to the harried mom in the next bay at the gas station. We can chase down the receipt that the elderly man dropped that is now being carried off on the wind. Reflecting on Mother Teresa's observation that "we can't do great things, only small things with great love," author Margot Starbuck wrote, "Small things happen when I learn the name of my daughter's school bus driver. Small things happen when I listen to the dreams of a woman who lives in a group home on my block."[1] Of course, she's right. But at some point this list we're making of these kind, noble, and free interventions is going to exhaust itself and we're going to have to start a new list. That new list is of the not-free stuff, and entries are far more plentiful there.

Take the woman who brought a pot of homemade chili and a bag of premade salad to her colleague who was sick in bed. At first blush, it seems like such a straightforward, inconsequential act, but what did those groceries run her, twenty-five or thirty bucks?

Or how about the guy who retooled his schedule so that he could take his neighbor to her doctor appointments? The gas for those four trips wasn't that big of a deal, but workday interruptions always set a diligent worker back.

The one who gives up a few hours on the first Tuesday of every month to head over to the women's clinic . . . that's a half hour each way, which means bearing the cost of gas. Plus, each woman brings her own crafting supplies, which, according to the craftier people on my staff, can really add up.

It doesn't seem like having a friend stay with you for two weeks would introduce that many extra expenses, but houseguests are never cheap. Your utility bills may be higher, and you'll likely need to buy extra food. I know whenever Pam and I have people come to stay with us, we put added pressure on ourselves to have the house clean and neat, to prepare more thoughtful meals instead of just winging it, and to have supplies and snacks on hand that we think our guest(s) would enjoy.

The mom who went to Al-Anon as a sign of solidarity with her friend reported that most times, either before or after those meetings, the two women would grab a cup of coffee together or stop by one of their favorite restaurants to eat dinner and talk. Such commitment to being a listening ear absolutely comes with a cost.

And I probably don't have to lay out the incidental costs involved with caring for—or *raising*—kids.

If we look closely at our story of the Good Samaritan, we see the same theme at work: While the helper could *stop what he was doing* and bear no financial burden, *look at someone in need* and bear no financial burden, *come close to the man lying in the ditch* and bear no financial burden, and *feel compassion in his heart* and bear no financial burden, eventually his helpfulness would cost him something tangible, as he invested himself monetarily in the man's cause. He bandaged the man's wounds with bandages he himself possessed. He poured oil and wine on the man's body—oil and wine that belonged to him. He put the man on his donkey—a donkey he himself owned. He took the man to an inn, where he paid cash for the man's sleeping room. And he then essentially handed over his debit card, saying, "Whatever else this man may need, please put it on my account . . ."

If you've ever stepped beyond your own needs to lift a burden from someone else, then you know that what I'm saying is true: it always costs us something to be helpful, and that cost is often measured in cash. Which is why, in my humble opinion, Jesus spoke so often about money. To love well, over time, takes funding. Which begs the question: *How prepared are we to love well?*

THE STEWARDS AND THE SLACKER

Tucked between the story of the ten virgins and the story regarding end-times sheep and goats, Jesus told a parable about what "good stewardship" really means. Matthew 25:14–30 (NKJV) reads this way:

"For the kingdom of heaven is like a man traveling to a far country, who called his own servants and delivered his goods to them. And to one he gave five talents, to another two, and to another one, to each according to his own ability; and immediately he went on a journey. Then he who had received the five talents went and traded with them, and made another five talents. And likewise he who had received two gained two more also. But he who had received one went and dug in the ground, and hid his lord's money. After a long time the lord of those servants came and settled accounts with them.

"So he who had received five talents came and brought five other talents, saying, 'Lord, you delivered to me five talents; look, I have gained five more talents besides them.' His lord said to him, 'Well, good and faithful servant; you were faithful over a few things, I will make you ruler over many things. Enter into the joy of your lord.' He also who had received two talents came and said, 'Lord, you delivered to me two talents; look, I have gained two more besides them.' His lord said to him, 'Well done, good and faithful servant; you have been faithful over a few things, I will make you ruler over many things. Enter into the joy of your lord.'

"Then he who had received the one talent came and said, 'Lord, I knew you to be a hard man, reaping where you have not sown, and gathering where you have not scattered seed. And I was afraid, and went and hid your talent in the ground. Look, there you have what is yours.'

"But his lord answered and said to him, 'You wicked and lazy servant, you knew that I reap where I have not sown, and gather where I have not scattered seed. So you ought to have deposited my money with the bankers, and at my coming I would have received back my own with interest. So take the talent from him, and give it to him who has ten talents.

"For to everyone who has, more will be given, and he will have abundance; but from him who does not have, even what he has

*will be taken away. And cast the unprofitable servant into the
outer darkness. There will be weeping and gnashing of teeth.'"*

Scholars have long debated what the "talents" in this parable represent: Are they what you and I would consider true talents, distinctive capabilities or gifts that mark our lives? Or perhaps the "talents"
Jesus is referring to are evangelical propensities . . . our willingness to
share the gospel with people who are far from God. And then there is
this option: Jesus is speaking here of money—what the New International Version of the Bible refers to as literal "bags of gold."

I'll bypass the debate and simply draw our attention to three things
we can know for sure, as it relates to this story Jesus told: first, a "talent" is some unit of value; second, that value has been entrusted to
those in the master's care; and third, the master seems to be concerned with only one thing, which is that those who have been entrusted with these units of value not hoard the abundance but rather
have something profitable to show for it in the end. In heaven's economy, this "profit" we're talking about centers on people's redemptive
potential. You and I will either help convert that potential to reality or
we'll allow that potential to remain concealed. We will "turn a profit"
in this sense, or we'll settle for a loss. We'll invest wisely in the needs
around us, or we'll be driven to foolishness by fear.

I've come to think of those three servants in Jesus' story as falling into
one of two categories—categories that remain applicable to us today.
Depending on how we regard the abundance given to us by *our* Master, Jesus, we will either show ourselves to be wise stewards or else the
slackers we truly are. That abundance God has provided is intended
to further his aims. Will we cooperate with God's intentions or will we
choose instead to do our own thing? I like how Randy Alcorn frames this
idea. "When God provides more money," he says, "we often think, *This is a
blessing.* Well, yes, but it would be just as scriptural to think, *This is a test.*"[2]

Only wise stewards pass the test.

WE GET TO CHOOSE

What does it mean, then, to be a "wise steward"? I like to think of it like this: regarding the financial resources that come into our care, there are essentially four options that we can pursue. We can either view those funds as a gift from God or as the product of our own hands. Similarly, we can either view the funds as *still owned* by God, or as a possession belonging to us. The four options, then, are these:

> *Option 1:* I earned my money, and this money I earned belongs to me.
>
> *Option 2:* I earned this money, but all things, including this money, belong to God.
>
> *Option 3:* This money was a gift from God, which now belongs to me.
>
> *Option 4:* This money was a gift from God, and it should serve his purposes in the world.

As you'd guess, I'm a strong proponent for option 4, the one that says everything belonged to God to begin with, and everything belongs to him still. Yes, he may choose to entrust a human being with the care of a resource, but that resource is God's alone. To put it crassly, the first three options fall under the "slacker" column; only the fourth is where stewardship lives.

When I was a pastor at Gateway Church, we frequently held seminars for married couples to help them achieve stability in their financial lives. One of the grids that still sticks with me lays out the difference between being financially motivated by the world and being financially motivated by the Spirit of God. In our four-options paradigm, the first three options would be considered at least in part motivated by the world, which is me-centric at its core. "The world" is concerned with things like independence, autonomy, self-starting, self-sustaining, and self-aggrandizing. At Gateway we taught couples that if you're motivated by the world, then you are driven by your wants and desires; your efforts are pointed at *getting more*, even if that "more" comes to you via personal debt; you set the timing for all purchases, and your focus is on pleasure . . . now; your life is characterized by a lack of contentment (which is what all good advertising aims to do); and your value is directly connected to the income you pull down.

Admittedly, not a great place to be.

Thankfully, there is another path to walk. If you are financially motivated by the Spirit, a whole different set of things will be true. You will be compelled by God to display things like peace and patience and self-control, tabling desires and fleshly wants. You will trust God's timing implicitly, believing that if you are indeed to acquire something, that acquisition will happen in due time. You will do seemingly *crazy* things like create and stick to a budget. You will experience radical contentment even as the world seems to "pass you by." You will see your value as tied not to what you are able to get but to God, who has given much to you.

I agree that I've painted these two sets of characteristics with a broad brush, but as you scan the themes I've written, which seems to more accurately reflect your ways?

Would those who know you well say that you're a patient person when it comes to getting what you want? Or would they say you're always pushing, always driving, always getting the new and improved version of that thing?

Are you up to your eyeballs in consumer debt? Would you say that you're a *contented* person, or are you always itching for something more?

It's a real gift to be able to look at categories such as these and self-assess. In a world filled with so much confusion and chaos, astoundingly, by God's Spirit, we can know the truth about ourselves. And knowing the truth is the perfect place to start for anyone seeking transformation in life. My counsel, if you are starting to see that you're not *exactly* being motivated by the Spirit when it comes to "your" money, is to simply ask God to begin altering your motivations. Tell him you want his Spirit to lead. This petition is one that God is all too pleased to answer. "God, help!" we can say from our frustration and pain, to which he will *always* say, *I will!*

MORE, OR LESS

So, yes, being motivated by the Spirit—which is at the root of becoming a wise steward—is good for your mind, your heart, your soul, and your monthly budget. But it goes beyond that. Being motivated by God's Spirit in our finances also allows us to be a real blessing to others. Have you ever wondered why there is such financial imbalance in the world? Think of it: if you're like me, then you were born in a prosperous time in history, in a free country where dreams can be pursued, to parents who were at least able to keep you alive. In other words, you came onto the scene with resources. With capacity. With some amount of *stuff.*

Now, if this description fits you, then you're probably aware that you represent the top 5 percent of resourcefulness in the world. Your parents had jobs, most likely, that allowed them to work five days in order to feed your family for seven days. You're probably in that same situation now, working Monday through Friday to eat on those days and weekends too. Do you know what a privilege that is? When Jesus taught his disciples to pray, "Give us today our daily bread" (Matthew 6:11), he did so because most everyone in his audience had to work *every* day if they hoped to eat that day. There was no middle class. There was the ruling elite—the political and religious leaders of the day, which made up about 3 percent of the population—and there were the poor. We may have a "middle class" today, but still, we see the same numbers . . . the tiny minority with plentiful resources, and the vast majority with nothing but need.

This reality ought to trouble us. Remember, in God's Word, we read that God loves all people in all places at all times. If that's true, and if my earlier assertion is true that all resources belong to God now and have always belonged to him, then why would he choose to give some people more things and some people less things? Shouldn't he be more equitable than that?

More than a decade ago, author Mike Yankoski was left breathless by a jolting idea that came to him one day at church. *"What if I stepped out of my comfortable life with nothing but God and put my faith to the test alongside of those who live with nothing every day?"*[3]

The thought prompted Yankoski to launch a five-month experiment living like those who are homeless and hopeless live. He recruited his buddy Sam for the journey, and off they went, each taking nothing but a pack containing a pair of boxers, a pair of shorts, a pair of jeans, a T-shirt, and a sweatshirt. They would stay on the streets and in the rescue centers of Denver and D.C., of Portland and San Francisco, and of other cities, each day trying to better understand what life was like for those there. Partway through his trek, Yankoski wrote this: "Something critical is missing in places that care for the broken and needy if the only people there are also broken and needy. Without the presence of people in the rescue missions whose lives are not defined by addiction, alcoholism, crime, and mental illness, there is little positive influence. Chaplains and pastors can only spread themselves so far."[4]

Around New Life, we often talk about how the broken need those whose lives have been put back together and how those with "together" lives need the broken in their midst. From the together ones, we gather up hope and belief; from the broken, humility and the reminder to stop and give thanks.

Likewise, the young need the old, and the old need the young.

The black need the white, and the white need the black.

The educated need the uneducated, and the uneducated need the educated.

The married ones need the singles, and the singles need the married ones.

And related to our topic at hand, the rich need the poor, and the poor need the rich, because as we give and take and take and give, we practice the community God intends. Again, from Alcorn: "Why does God give some of His children more than they need and others less than they need? So that He may use his children to help one another. He doesn't want us to have too little or too much . . . When those with too much give to those with too little, two problems are solved. When they don't, two problems are perpetuated."[5]

More directly, if we say that we value "Christian community" and yet we keep all of our money for ourselves, then we don't actually value Christian community. At least, not as much as we value our stuff. "I dare say that if the innocent suffer," Scott Cairns once wrote, "they do so because one of us—you or me or some other thug—now or in the past, has set their pain in motion."[6]

We don't like this language, do we? *I* don't like it, anyway. I *hate* the thought that someone else is suffering because of something I did—or did not—do. And yet, if it's true that there are enough resources on this planet to care for each person living here, as nearly all economists agree, then we must admit that Cairns has a point. Case in point: International Monetary Fund chief Raghuram Rajan wrote in his book, *The Third Pillar: How Markets and the State Leave the Community Behind,* "We are surrounded by plenty. Humanity has never been richer as technologies of production have improved steadily over the last two hundred fifty years . . . For the first time in our lives, we have it in our power to eradicate hunger and starvation everywhere."[7]

But if this is a problem that we can solve today, then why on earth aren't we solving it? I think the answer's a straightforward one: we keep our stuff for ourselves.

And yet there stands Jesus, whom you may recall also relied on the generous gifts of others, to get his ministry objectives met (see Luke 8:1–3), whispering, "Gang, yes, 'your' stuff is a blessing. But remember, it's also a test."

Right.

There's going to be a test.

But Jesus is *telling us what will be on the test,* just as all of my favorite teachers did growing up. This test will have two questions:

1. Did you love God with all your heart, mind, soul, and strength?
2. Did you love your neighbor as yourself—even when it cost you something . . . perhaps *especially* when it cost you much?

That's it! That's the whole test. Who can't pass a two-question test? Maybe more people than we think.

THE SLACKERS

I mentioned earlier that there are four—and only four—postures we can take when it comes to the money we find in our hands. I'd like to spend the balance of this chapter looking more closely at each of them—the three "slacking-off" postures (harsh, but true) as well as the one posture that characterizes wise stewards. Then, in chapters 8 and 9, we will do a deep dive into how to progress from each of the slacking-off postures to a place of wise stewardship.

Option 1: The Scrooge

If your posture toward money tends to be "I earned it, and therefore it's mine," then you just might fall into the unfortunate category of "Scrooge." Good ol' gruff, selfish, narcissistic Scrooge. You remember the story: according to Charles Dickens's 1843 novel, *A Christmas*

Carol, Ebenezer Scrooge hated people and hated Christmas. Dickens described him as "a squeezing, wrenching, grasping, scraping, clutching, covetous old sinner! Hard and sharp as flint, from which no steel had ever struck out generous fire; secret, and self-contained, and solitary as an oyster."[8]

I'm telling you, you *don't* want to be a Scrooge. When you turn inward from the world, believing that neither people nor holidays can be trusted, you'll be in a sorry state for sure. You, too, will hold on to your money at all costs. You, too, will pridefully judge those who spend time and money on Christmas. You, too, will squander key relationships in your life . . . all because you've become a scrooge.

Contemporary history is littered with stories of people who rose to the top of whatever their individual universe was—music or venture capitalism or real estate or professional golf—only to suffer a terrible fall. They were served divorce papers. Or they were asked to resign. Or they were exposed by a scathing news report. Or, in some cases, they were jailed. Their me-first self-reliance left them wanting for more. Their strategy let them down. And there, from the pit they'd fallen into, this sobering realization set in. "A heart out of tune, out of sync with God's heart," Jim Cymbala once wrote, "will produce a life of spiritual barrenness and missed opportunities."[9]

Missed opportunities? For the onetime kings of the game? It's hard to imagine, isn't it? Just yesterday they had the world by the tail. Those missed opportunities are of a different kingdom, a kingdom where the true King reigns.

And so: What to do now?

As the adage can attest, when you've reached the bottom of anything, the only way to go is up. Which brings me to the one slice of good news in this sorry scenario: it's in that pit that some will choose to change.

What people here in Colorado refer to as "cement" I grew up calling "concrete." I'm a pastor, not a stonemason, but my dad worked in the construction business for a time. And one thing I learned by watching him work was that timing is everything when you're pouring a slab. During the hour that was slated for the pour, you've got to scrutinize the air temperature, the humidity level, the amount of sunlight hitting the designated area, and more. Because once that wet concrete comes flowing out of the mixer, you have only a certain amount of time to work with it before it dries and holds its shape. If you leverage that window correctly, then you can mold and shape and smooth out the concrete as though it were warm putty in the palm of your hand. But if you wait too long, that stuff will become utterly immovable. You'd have to take a jackhammer to it to get it to budge.

Here's something I've noticed about self-reliant people whose self-reliance is found lacking in the end: their bottom-of-the-pit predicament is not unlike wet cement. If they will see the opportunity for what it is—a chance to go in a different direction, an invitation to serve a different master, an impetus to consider *others* perhaps for the first time in their lives—then God can mold them and shape them and turn their lives into works of art. The temperature is right. The humidity is right. The sunlight—it's right too. *Now* is the time they know they must change. The path has been paved leading out of that pit.

To be sure, if they stay in there too long and refuse to leverage the opportunity they've been given, despondence and depression will set in. The jackhammers will have to come out. But in those first few moments of realization, when they see plainly that their strategy hasn't worked . . . *that* is when some choose to act. And by acting, they save their lives.

A few weeks ago, seventy miles northwest of my home, on the east–west interstate that runs from Utah to Maryland, splitting Colorado in half along the way, a truck driver lost control of his rig and barreled into a traffic jam. The truck took out four other semis and twenty-four passenger vehicles, catapulting its massive load of lumber far and wide and, in the end, killing four.[10] The inferno that erupted from the series of collisions was visible from miles away, but given the standstill traffic and the resource drain of an unrelated wreck several miles up the road, it took first responders more time than usual to arrive on the scene.

During those in-between moments, a man named Darin Barton decided to act. Darin is a forty-five-year-old panhandler who has been homeless for more than five years. He spends his days camped out on the guardrail at the intersection of I-70 and Denver West Boulevard, holding a sign that reads, "I'm hungry." The crash occurred at that same intersection, and when Darin heard the initial explosion, he dropped his sign and ran.

He ran not away from the chaos but toward it.

Darin estimates that fifteen additional explosions occurred as he was running, the fire overtaking one vehicle after another. "I was trying to stay calm and just kept pushing on until I found somebody who needed help," he later told reporters.[11]

He found someone soon enough. Darin helped a man drag a woman with a broken arm and severely lacerated face from her burning vehicle into the vehicle of another driver, who agreed to rush the woman to the hospital. As emergency personnel arrived, Darin stayed on the scene, determined to be of help. He stayed until dark, when the wreck was cleared.

So, back to the people who choose to change, who begin the transformation from being a *passerby* to one who *pauses* in the course of daily life: How, exactly, does that change unfold? Like Darin Barton, they decide to drop the figurative sign they've been carrying, the one that tells the world how hungry they are. They've been hungry for power. Or hungry for recognition. They've been hungry for promotion or money or sex. They've been hungry for the spotlight. They've been hungry for affirmation. And they've made feeding that hunger their job. Like a panhandler, they've gone through life with their arm outstretched: *What can you do for me?*

The priority has been all about *their* ideas, *their* desires, *their* needs, *their* plans . . . but, seeing where such self-absorption has led them, at last they're ready to change. As if seeing clearly for the first time in their lives, they realize their purpose is far greater than being comfortable and racking up wins. They've been called to a mission that's bigger than their self-focused plans.

Option 2: The Starter

If there is one group who is most at risk for sliding into the "Scrooge" category, it's those whom I call "Starters." Starters believe that they worked hard for and earned their money, even as they concede that "everything belongs to God." Most of the people I know in this category are believers who struggle to fully believe in the provision of God. They think highly of their contribution to the marketplace, they negotiate for a fair financial exchange, and with each new level of compensatory accomplishment they feel just a little bit better about themselves.

Unfortunately, what they're building is a house of cards.

They feel overly protective of their funds, if not completely possessive. They control their income and expenses with a level of detail that would make others' heads spin. Which is why, when something outside their control happens to them, like Scrooges they are left disillusioned if not totally wrecked.

Back in 2011, I remember meeting with several Starters following what became known as Black Monday, the day when global stock markets crashed after the United States' credit rating was downgraded. These were all finance guys who were utterly rocked by this news, and because the foundation on which they had built their worlds—the money they had made from the market—was shaking, they were shaking too. Many of these men are part of New Life, and I remember being mystified as to why they were refusing resources that were available to them in the form of the peace of God, the comfort of Christ, the direction of the Holy Spirit. They said they were "trusting God through the storm," but their actions betrayed them. Starters do as Starters believe, I suppose, and if they believe that their financial world revolves around their productivity and success, then when outside forces threaten those activities, those worlds will fall apart.

Here's a bright spot to the story: on one of those late-August days, I met a financial planner I know from the church for a cup of coffee. We'd had the get-together on the calendar for weeks, long before either of us knew what was to come in world finance. After we sat down, I asked, "How's your week going?" to which he said, "Kind of troubling."

I then asked, "How's your peace?"

"Great," he said. "Really . . . great."

What Starters can't see is that we don't serve the god of this world, and when we try, we will lose, every time. For those of us who follow Jesus, we have planted our feet on solid rock. No wind from hell, no scheme of man—no power from outside—can shake us from our sure foundation. We can be steady when the world is not. We can be generous when times are tough. We can drop the self-centered charade we've been keeping up, letting God resume his rightful place in our lives.

We can be "great; really . . . great," even when the circumstances surrounding us aren't.

Option 3: The Spendthrift

Spendthrifts believe that while the money they have came from God, it was a gift from him to them and is therefore theirs to use as they please. They spend "their" money on what *they* want, buying things when *they* want them, rarely if ever pausing to check in with God. And why would they? His job is giving, and theirs is receiving. Once the funds have changed hands, God is free to move along and tend to whatever celestial business is in the works. "I'll take it from here," the Spendthrift says. The brilliant theologian and author Richard J. Foster wrote, "Contemporary culture is plagued by the passion to possess."[12] Spendthrifts know all about this plague.

In his "money language" schema, financial psychologist Dr. Kenneth Doyle refers to Spendthrifts as "Expressives" and has this to say of their approach: To Expressives, according to Teresa Ambord on the website Senior Voice, "money is acceptance . . . Shopping, buying, and spending are the ways they gain acceptance from people. If there is a weakness in Expressives, it's that they spend to hide feelings of pain, insecurity or incompetence. They may over-rely on money to solve problems and calm fears."[13]

Dr. Doyle's assessment perfectly reflects what I've seen over the years with this type. For so many Spendthrifts, the motivation behind their spending is pure. They are often lavish with gift giving and "generous to a fault." They might see something that reminds them of someone, and, regardless of whether they can afford to purchase that thing, they go ahead and do so, overcome by the emotion of the moment as they are. This is called "pathological generosity" for a reason: this type of spending is a *disease*.

Recently, during a summertime break in my preaching calendar, I caught a documentary I'd wanted to see, on the last of the Russian czars, Nicholas II—a Spendthrift through and through. A mild, awkward young man, Nicholas would assume the throne of the Romanov Empire at the tender age of twenty-six, after his father passed away unexpectedly. This empire was massive—by some estimates ruling a full one-sixth of the globe—and Nicholas was hardly ready for this level of power. Upon learning of his new role, Nicholas famously asked his advisor, "What is going to happen to me . . . to all of Russia?"[14]

Not exactly the kind of language that engenders a nation's confidence in its leader. To the people living in his culture, the czar was just below God in terms of influence, and Nicholas was nothing like him.

Known as "the most extravagant" rulers of all the empires, the Romanovs knew how to party, and so Nicholas figured that what he lacked in leadership prowess he would make up for in opulence. Lavish six-hundred-guest dinner parties became the norm, even as the people of Russia sank deeper and deeper into poverty and destitution. Nicholas, his wife, and their children lived in a nine-hundred-room palace following his coronation in 1896, a five-hour ceremony at the Kremlin that featured a nine-pound imperial crown being placed atop his head and the beginnings of a raucous, weeklong celebration of this transfer of power.

Nothing could touch this luxurious life he had carved out for himself, Nicholas thought, as he clinked glasses with his fellow aristocrats. But his footing wasn't as sure as he believed.

Within nine years' time, by his gross mismanagement, Nicholas II toppled the three-hundred-year Romanov Empire and set things in motion for outright revolt. Factories were closing, food was scarce, and people's discontentment was at an all-time high. Early one Sunday morning in 1905, workers marched to the czar's palace to demand better treatment. What they would receive instead was death. "Bloody Sunday," it was called, and the massive loss of life—some say it was upward of 50,000 people—caused a once-loyal people to turn on their leader. Things went downhill from there.

In 1917, the Bolshevik Revolution was in full swing, led by the maniacal communist Vladimir Lenin. Nicholas was trying to return to the palace when revolutionaries blocked his train and demanded that he abdicate the throne. He eventually conceded and was put under house arrest in the immense home, forced to wear tattered trousers and shovel snow. The Bolsheviks cut water and power to the palace, causing Nicholas and his family to struggle to survive.

In 1918, Nicholas and his family were taken to a "house of special purpose" in Siberia. Three months later, at one thirty in the morning, they and their remaining extended family members were systematically murdered, burned with acid, and disposed of in an abandoned mineshaft.

It was an awful blot on Russia's history and a turn of events that ushered in the brutal communist era. Which made me wonder: What would have happened if Nicholas II had been a benevolent leader instead?

Two wrongs never make a right, and Lenin and his cronies were accountable for their dehumanizing actions that day. But Nicholas will always go down in my mind as the perfect if not tragic example of money habits reflecting relational ones. As I wrote in the introduction, the way that we regard money reflects the way that we regard people—and, ultimately, how we regard God. When we are sloppy, presumptive, and entitled with our spending, we will be sloppy, presumptive, and entitled with the people around us and with God. Christ followership demands better of us.

OPTION 4: THE STEWARDS

Well, on to a cheerier subject. The fourth option for how we may regard money is that of a *wise steward*, someone who believes that the money they have was a gift from God, and that that money belongs to him still.

Earlier I mentioned the story of the widow who gave from her scarcity and was commended by Jesus, who looked on. Let's look at the fuller story here.

Both Mark and Luke record the event, but the Mark account gives a little more to go on. In chapter 12 we read, "Jesus sat down opposite the place where the offerings were put and watched the crowd putting their money into the temple treasury. Many rich people threw in large amounts. But a poor widow came and put in two very small copper coins, worth only a few cents.

"Calling his disciples to him, Jesus said, 'Truly I tell you, this poor widow has put more into the treasury than all the others. They all gave out of their wealth; but she, out of her poverty, put in everything—all she had to live on" (v. 41–44).

Now, let me acknowledge at the outset that while we're about to laud this woman for her noble actions that day, there's something about this scene we just don't like. We don't like meekness. We don't like reminders of loss. We don't like frail humanity. We don't like poverty or scarcity or lack. We're Americans, most of us . . . bold and brash and proud. I'm an 8 on the Enneagram, for crying out loud; people *know* when I'm in a room.

And yet, still, this picture speaks to me, this scene of a devoted one holding nothing back.

The steward.

This is who you and I both want to become.

We want to be generous, thoughtful, careful, faithful, *extravagant* with our funds. Why? Because it means we've caught God's grand vision for redeeming all humankind. When we care for people the way that God cares for people, our needs take a back seat. We give everything we can give right back to God, believing *it's his stuff anyway*.

I can't say for sure, because the text doesn't give this away, but my best guess is that the Good Samaritan was also a steward, one who viewed *everything* as God's. Think about it: he gave much to a man who could give nothing in return. If that's not faithful stewardship, then what is?

The guy in the ditch wasn't a potential customer. He wasn't a "qualified lead." He wasn't part of an important network of some kind. This wasn't a you-scratch-my-back-and-I'll-scratch-yours scene. The Good Samaritan was good, in my view, because he was willing to lose money on the deal. He *did* lose money on the deal, and Jesus praised him as a result.

Just before that story about the widow's offering, Jesus had these words to say: "Watch out for the teachers of the law. They like to walk around in flowing robes and be greeted with respect in the marketplaces, and have the most important seats in the synagogues and the places of honor at banquets. They devour widows' houses and for a

show make lengthy prayers. These men will be punished most severely" (v. 38–40).

The contrast in these two passages is tough to miss. In one, the
widow is the hero; in the other, a victim at the hands of the elite. I've
said it before, but it's worth repeating: how we handle money reveals
how we treat the people in our lives. We will either return to God all
that was and is always his, or else we'll spend our lives squeezing
through loopholes, resolute that we've done nothing wrong.

Money is the currency of compassion. Wise stewardship says this
is so.

ATTITUDE, THEN ACTION

We're going to spend the next two chapters looking more closely
at how to move from those first three options—living as Scrooges,
Starters, and Spendthrifts—to the place of wise stewardship, willing
to release our grip on the money we've always thought was "ours"
and entrust it instead back to God. We are going to necessarily focus
on some actions that you can take, to begin to move toward a stewardship posture before God. But let me say at the outset that unless
your heart has been captivated by Jesus' love, those actions will do
you no good.

Well, to be fair, they'll do you a *little* good. They'll do you *limited*
good, I should say. But the extravagance our souls long for? *That* is an
inside job.

Remember that three days after Jesus rebuked the teachers of the
law for being slackers, he went to the cross and died a brutal death for
them all. He died not to redeem their actions, mind you, but rather
to redeem their hearts. Why? Because he knew that if he could cap-
ture their hearts, their actions would follow. This was something they
hadn't yet grasped. They were teachers of the law, after all. But what

does law do, apart from monitoring actions? Nothing. Nada. Zilch. Grace is what focuses on attitudes, God's lovely, lavish grace.

I'm sure you remember Jesus' parable about the sower and the seed, from Luke 8. In it, a farmer is found sowing seed. He scatters some of it along a path, which birds quickly eat up. He scatters some along rocky ground, which failed to produce hydrated crops. He scattered some among thorns, which wound up choking the plants. And then he scattered some on "good soil," (v. 8), and when that seed came up, it yielded a crop a hundred times more than was sown.

When Jesus' disciples asked him what made that soil so good, he said this: "The seed on good soil stands for those with a noble and good heart, who hear the word, retain it, and by persevering produce a crop" (v. 15).

A noble and good heart.

Jesus is speaking here of our attitude toward him, toward his teaching, toward his way. A noble and good heart, he says, leans in to hear what he says. A noble and good heart holds fast to what it learns. And a noble and good heart perseveres in that understanding, believing that God's Word is true.

If you and I are going to live extravagant lives, it will be only because we have first resolved in our hearts—our noble and good hearts—that we will live in service to God and not in service to money. We will live as the wise stewards he intends for us to be.

STARTING SMALL

When I became senior pastor of New Life, the church was $26 million in debt; and while I wasn't responsible for incurring that debt, it still became my problem. Every month, when we would make our interest payment to the bank, that verse about not being a slave to the lender came to mind and haunted me. I hated being a slave.

Soon after my arrival, the economic recession of 2008, 2009, and 2010 hit, and even as people were losing their homes, their jobs, their businesses, and their hope, those interest payments still came due. It was an awful, awful time.

To add insult to injury, the cries of our city were growing louder and louder. People needed help. *Now.*

Early one morning, I came across Proverbs 19:17, which says, "Whoever is kind to the poor lends to the LORD, / and he will reward them for what they have done." In a word, I was wrecked. I called the elders and together we made a decision. We would devote ourselves as a church to paying off the debt that was an albatross around our neck, but simultaneously we would help those in need.

From that day forward, we began to set aside a few dollars here, a few dollars there. Just a little bit of money, just to keep our hearts soft to others' need. One day I looked at a spreadsheet from our finance head and realized we had real money sitting there.

We bought a run-down apartment building on the south side of town that was full of asbestos and in grave need of repair, but we had no money to tend to those things. We were just thrilled that it was ours.

We kept saving, little by little, dollar by dollar, a bit here, a bit there, week by week. Soon enough, I looked up, and we had *more* real money there.

We renovated the complex and opened Mary's Home.

Today, that debt is down to $11 million. And during the same span of time that we cut that debt by more than half, we did more to serve our city than in our previous three decades as a church.

Think of it: if you will commit yourself to the extravagance God intends for you, then you will leap over your financial hurdles *while being a blessing to a world in need.* As you read on, keep this image in mind: a little here, a little there, fewer indulgences, fewer treats. Pennies will become dollars, and dollars will begin to add up. Regardless of how burdensome your beginning was, you'll be gaining momentum at last. Yes, you'll keep serving others with smiles and encouraging words, but you'll be equipped to help differently now. When God taps you on the shoulder and points you toward a need that can only be met with *cash*, you'll light up and say, "I've been waiting for you. Let's do it. I'm ready to go."

◇◇◇◇◇◇◇◇◇◇◇◇◇◇◇◇◇◇◇◇◇◇◇◇◇◇◇◇◇◇◇◇◇◇◇◇◇◇◇

Pushing Pause: Chapter 7

People who study the subjects of time management, habit formation, efficiency, and the like will tell you that, despite our desperate insistence to the contrary, there really is no such thing as multitasking. What is happening when we *think* we're multitasking is actually a rapid back-and-forth version of "mono-tasking" but with severely compromised results. It turns out that you and I can focus on only one thing at a time. Our attention can be aimed in one direction only. Our "top priority" is singular, not plural. We can't chase two objectives at once.

Read
On this subject, in Luke 16:13, we read, "No one can serve two masters. Either you will hate the one and love the other, or you will be devoted to the one and despise the other. You cannot serve both God and money."

Reflect
- The Message version of the verse above reads this way: "No worker can serve two bosses: / He'll either hate the first and love the second / Or adore the first and despise the second. / You can't serve both God and the Bank." What do you suppose it means to "serve the Bank"?

- Think back on a time when serving God actually cost you something. What did that cost involve? How did it make you feel, to
show up and cover that cost?

Respond

The challenge for this chapter is to try on a little "option 4 living" for a
day. You remember that option 4 is believing that all money is a gift from
God and that, even if it is in your bank account, *it still belongs to God*.
Before you make a single purchase today, check in with God. What does
he have to say regarding how his money is about to be spent? Which
expenses get cleared right away? Which ones get denied? What do you
learn about God based on how he vets expenses you try to push through?

8

The Beauty of a Boring Budget

We must consult our means, rather than our wishes...

GEORGE WASHINGTON

PAM AND I HAVE been married for thirty years, which means we've racked up a fair amount of memories across those thousands and thousands of days. On this issue of money, I refer to our early married life as characterized by "financial cancer." We had no clue how money worked. We had no idea what God's Word said about stewardship. We were oblivious to the ravaging effects of being stupid with dollars and cents. About ten years into our marriage, we looked up and were thousands of dollars in debt. We were living at more than 100 percent of our paltry income. I made next to nothing, and Pam was still in school with a part-time job at a dry-cleaning shop in the evenings. We had zero savings, and the outlook was bleak. It wasn't that we were living lavishly—in fact, we were pretty much subsisting on mac and cheese.

It's just that we had no idea how to manage the small amount we were making. The stress on our marriage was beginning to show.

Yes, we were tithing. And, yes, we were giving. But I liken our reality to that "pathological generosity" category I mentioned before. We had no business giving money to others when our finances were in such disarray.

I remember being in this desperate state when a friend of ours pointed us toward a church that taught sound biblical principles, including about finances. I still get choked up when I think about the pastor who stood before us and had the courage to tell us the truth about money and about debt and about what would become of Pam and me if we kept insisting on blowing everything we made on the junk of this world instead of choosing to live beyond ourselves. Slowly but surely, we began to tweak our practices. We caught a vision for the freedom that awaited us, and we were determined to get to that place. Finally, we understood that if we would simply prove faithful in the little things, God would entrust to us with so much more.

Before we dive into the one thing that saved our finances—and maybe our marriage—let me say something to you, heart to heart. If you are in the same desperate state today that Pam and I were in during those early years of our marriage—if you feel like you know next to nothing about how to manage money and you're overwhelmed by disillusionment and debt—hope is on the horizon. Stick with me through this chapter, and together we'll begin to turn things around.

THE B-WORD

The title of this chapter already cued you to the solution Pam and I eventually found. Despite our initial disdain for the idea, once we began crafting and sticking to a budget each month, our financial reality took a long-awaited turn.

I'm curious: What do you think of when you hear the word "budget"? Based on hundreds of conversations with people over the years, I've found that people generally fall into one of two categories on the matter. They either view a budget as a straitjacket, something to coerce them, confine them, and keep them from having any fun. Or else they view it as what personal-finance authority Rachel Cruze calls "permission to spend." They see it as a certain *emancipation* from the chaos, confusion, and grief that is inherent in money mismanagement. They understand that if God cares about what we do with the first 10 percent of our income—and he does—he probably also cares about how we manage the remaining 90 percent.

What I'd like to work through in this chapter are the three big ideas of why we (all) need a budget; how to craft a budget, which will be especially useful if the practice is new for you; and the one thing that's better than even the best budget. More on that last one in a moment.

The point of all this money talk is to train our minds and hearts to leverage this key resource we've been given for the good of people in need. It's to ensure, as did the Good Samaritan, that when a pain point presents itself, we have available funds to dip into in working to meet that need. The world says to use people, love things, and serve money, but God's Word turns those ideas on their head. He says to use *things*. To *love* people. And to serve *him* all our days.

When we learn to care for the money God has entrusted to us, we necessarily learn to care for the people God died to save. We become "helpful" to the world around us, in the truest sense of the word. We become *extravagant* people. We become who we were meant to be.

SPARKLY! SHINY! MINE!

Several winters ago I caught a news story online out of Eugene, Oregon, featuring a mule deer and a string of Christmas lights. The buck, entranced by the blinking lights on the shrubs outside someone's home, came close for a better look. Which is when those lights became utterly irresistible to him. He tugged at the lights until one strand broke free, he thrashed about until those lights were wound around his antlers, and then he bolted into the night. Success! The lights he'd longed for were his.

Locals spotted the buck over the next couple of days and snapped countless pictures with their cell phones. A Christmas buck! A reindeer! How adorable! That is, until those lights almost took the deer's life. The wildlife biologist who was interviewed for the story said that if the lights had stayed loosely entangled on the deer's antlers, all would have been fine. The bucks shed their antlers in late winter anyway; those lights would have been shed too. But the lights didn't stay put, instead falling around the deer's neck and tightening as the animal moved about town. Department of Wildlife officials knew what they had to do: tranquilize the deer, remove the Christmas lights, and set the animal free.

Sparkly! that deer had thought, upon seeing the flashing Christmas lights. *Shiny!*

Mine.

Does this progression ring a bell?

Left to our own devices, we're as driven to acquire as was that deer. We see the sparkly bigger house and we think, *I've got to make that mine.*

We see the shiny new truck, and we think, *Mine. Must. Be.* Mine.

We see the super-cute pet Halloween costume and are standing in line to pay for it before it ever crosses our minds what we're doing. (Of the $70 billion spent on pets annually in this country, $440 million is spent on these costumes. Just sayin'.)[1]

Those of us with little ones see the latest and greatest baby this and baby that and are instantaneously convinced that if we don't buy it *now*, we will be setting our children up for a lifetime of hardship and distress. "I, for one, want my money back," wrote wised-up parent and author Brett Graff. "For all the stupid things I bought for my daughter because I was afraid *not* buying them would mean she wouldn't be as smart, as athletic, as healthy as she could be."[2] In his book, *Not Buying It*, Graff reports that in the United States in 2013 "we bought about $5.8 billion worth of baby stuff online" and "about $11.9 billion in stores that same year, according to research from IBISWorld.[3]

We could keep going down through the litany of all the things we overspend on, but if you're anything like me, a quick look at your recent Amazon orders will prove the point just fine. "Using money you haven't earned to buy things you don't need to impress people you don't like," wrote syndicated humorist Robert Quillen in a 1928 column.

The term he was defining? "Americanism."[4]

GOING NOWHERE FAST

On July 15, 1979, then president Jimmy Carter delivered an address to the America people, interrupting broadcasting on all three of the major TV stations. He had planned to talk about the energy crisis our nation had been facing, but upon further reflection he decided to dig deeper into why it was that a country full of smart, capable, ambitious people couldn't come together to solve the problems facing it, the energy crisis included. Partway through his talk, he said, "In a nation that was proud of hard work, strong families, close-knit communities, and our faith in God, too many of us now tend to worship self-indulgence and consumption. Human identity is no longer defined by what one does, but by what one owns. But we've discovered that owning things and consuming things does not satisfy our longing for meaning. We've learned that piling up material goods cannot fill the emptiness of lives which have no confidence or purpose.

"The symptoms of this crisis of the American spirit are all around us," he continued. "For the first time in the history of our country a majority of our people believe that the next five years will be worse than the past five years. Two-thirds of our people do not even vote. The productivity of American workers is actually dropping, and the willingness of Americans to save for the future has fallen below that of all other people in the Western world."

President Carter then spoke of the two paths available to our country: we could either follow the path of self-interest or the path of others-centeredness. We could continue to fragment or we could come together as one. We could continue amassing individual fortunes or we could follow the Golden Rule. Only one path would lead to our ultimate success, and with pale, pleading eyes, the president asked us to carefully consider following that path. "Little by little," he said in closing, "we can and we must rebuild our confidence. We can spend until we empty our treasuries, and we may summon all the wonders of science. But we can succeed only if we tap our greatest resources—America's people, America's values, and America's confidence."[5]

I look back on those words today and see both truth and untruth in the president's words. Yes, we *were* worshippers of self-indulgence and consumption. Yes, our identity *was* wrapped up in what we owned. And, yes, our refusal as a nation to live beyond ourselves *did* cause every aspect of life to plummet instead of thrive.

True, true, true.

The untruth? That we "discovered that owning things and consuming things does not satisfy our longing for meaning" and "learned that piling up material goods cannot fill the emptiness of lives which have no confidence or purpose."

Had the sentiment been true, we would not, as a country, have entered mere seconds after Carter's speech into the conspicuous consumption–laden "Decade of Materialism."

Still today, our nation's health is measured in large part by how much money is flowing through the system—in short, by *how much we spend.* On stuff. On all that stuff we don't need, purchased with money we don't have, to impress people we don't always like.

If there's one thought that captivates my mind whenever I pray for my congregation, it's that during these prosperous years economically we wouldn't lose our way. When the market is down, times are tough; but when the market is up, times are tougher still. Why? Because the temptation is all the greater to worship money instead of God. The prophet Malachi spoke along these lines when he said to the Israelites, "Ever since the time of your ancestors you have turned away from my decrees and have not kept them" (Malachi 3:7).

When the Israelite priests pushed back, asking what they'd done wrong, Malachi said that they had been robbing God "in tithes and offerings" (v. 8). And then that beautiful phrase from Scripture appears: "Bring the whole tithe into the storehouse," God said through the prophet, "that there may be food in my house. Test me in this . . . and see if I will not throw open the floodgates of heaven and pour out so much blessing that there will not be room enough to store it" (v. 10).

THE BIG DEAL

Malachi wanted the nation of Israel to remember that God longed to be near to them but that he couldn't come close to sin. And remember: if Israel was being negligent with money, they were also being negligent with the people God adored. He wanted them to course correct. He wanted their full and unadulterated worship. He wants the same from us.

See, the reason this subject of budgeting is such a big deal is that when we are faithful to steward well every penny in our care, it tells God something about how we'll treat the people he puts in our path. It tells him that we haven't drifted from his redemptive mission of being helpful to those in need, of putting others' concerns above our own, of living beyond ourselves. It tells him that he can trust us to *see*, and *go near*, to *serve*.

It tells him that we're not sitting there sidelined with Christmas lights wrapped around our neck.

So, where to begin? "Return to me," God said to the nation Israel through his prophet Malachi, "and I will return to you" (Malachi 3:7).

We, too, can return.

We can begin where God asked all his followers to begin, by giving the first fruits of their labor to him. We read in Proverbs 3:9–10: "Honor the LORD with your wealth, / with the firstfruits of all your crops; / then your barns will be filled to overflowing, / and your vats will brim over with new wine."

TITHING 101

Whenever I mention the word "tithe"—literally, "one tenth"—most people think of an Old Testament practice that may or may not have any relevance to their lives today. They vaguely remember pastors in various churches compelling them to tithe along the way, but they're not sure what it's all about, what they think of the whole deal, and whether it's necessary for them to thrive.

To be fair, the practice was first spoken of in the Old Testament—in Genesis 14. Abraham, the father of our faith, had a nephew named Lot who forever seemed to be getting into trouble. Most families have a troublemaker; for Abraham, Lot was that guy.

In this story, Lot has been captured by a group of evil kings. This band of terrorists also took all of Lot's money and family and livestock. To help free Lot, Uncle Abraham rallies three hundred men and, astoundingly, the hastily assembled team prevails. As Abraham is walking back to his village, Lot's loot in his arms and at his side, the priest Melchizedek meets him with bread and wine. "Blessed be

Abram [Abraham] by God Most High, / Creator of heaven and earth," the priest cheers. "And praise be to God Most High, who delivered your enemies into your hand" (v. 19–20).

Abraham was stopped short. The priest had reminded him that while Abraham was the acting agent in this story, it was God who had accomplished the work. In response to this realization, Abraham gave Melchizedek a "tenth of everything" (v. 20).

Even earlier than that, in Genesis 4, we see God reject a "leftover" offering from Cain while accepting the "firstfruits" offering from his brother, Abel.

While references to tithing are far less prevalent in the New Testament, mention is in fact made. When Jesus cautions the Pharisees against hypocrisy in Matthew 23:23–24, he says, "Woe to you, teachers of the law and Pharisees, you hypocrites! You give a tenth of your spices—mint, dill and cumin. But you have neglected the more important matters of the law—justice, mercy and faithfulness. You should have practiced the latter, without neglecting the former. You blind guides! You strain out a gnat but swallow a camel."

Jesus didn't exactly mince words.

"Well," way too many people have said to me, "he didn't *specifically* say we have to tithe," as if the concept of tithing is minimized in the New Testament—as if the practice were relegated to the ancient world. Here is what I say in reply: "The idea of spiritual giving is not minimized in the New Testament; it is *radicalized*. No longer were fully devoted followers of God focused on parsing their first 10 percent. Now they were focused on *giving it all* so that the work of Jesus could unfold."

To those who want to haggle over whether to tithe today, I say: Listen, if you don't want to give 10 percent, that's fine; *you can give it all*. The decision is up to you. Either way, the moment you choose to be faithful in returning to God what has always been his, you will experience *wild, transformative growth*.

"I know of nothing that will transform someone's spiritual life more abruptly than beginning to tithe," wrote Lauren Winner. I'm with her on that one: no greater catalyst exists.

But if so much freedom and growth await those who tithe—not to mention give it all!—then why aren't more of us giving generously back to God? According to Nonprofits Source's 2018 report, only 10 to 25 percent of any congregation tithes, and if we were to average the total percent given by *all* givers in a church, full tithers included, that number hovers around 2.5 percent of one's income.[6]

Despite my persistent enthusiasm for the subject, around New Life roughly 70 percent of our congregation gives absolutely nothing to the work of God in and through our church. Granted, some of us are unemployed and have fallen on extremely hard times and need a little grace as we get back on our feet. But that is not the case for *70 percent* of us.

When only 30 percent of us give—and that giving is far from a full tithe, I should mention—we are confined to doing only 30 percent of the ministry God has for us. We can build only 30 percent of the shelters we long to build. We can help take only 30 percent of those who are homeless off the streets that we'd otherwise be able to help. We can feed only 30 percent of the hungry men, women, and children we'd otherwise be able to feed.

A few weeks ago a single mom in our community who had never been to New Life reached out to one of our pastors on staff to tell of her experience at our Friday night service the previous evening. She explained that she had been down on her luck and hadn't really wanted to come, but that her four-year-old son had been begging to go to church. "I had $1.32 in my bank account," she wrote in her email, "so if the few drops of gas that remained in my tank couldn't get us from our place on the southeast side to New Life, we were going to be stranded on the side of the road. Lucky for us, we made it there."

What she didn't know was that several people on our ministry team had been burdened by recent layoffs in our community, in sectors that employ vast numbers of people. Those staffers had taken it upon themselves to go to our local grocery stores, purchase bags and bags of groceries and gift cards, and have everything assembled and ready to hand out to anyone in need, at both our Friday night and Sunday morning worship services. At the end of that Friday night gathering, a pastor stood up and told the people gathered there, "If you and your family need a helping hand . . . if you need *food* . . . if you need *gas* . . . if you need basic supplies to get through this week, then please come take these resources. These things are here for you."

Tears streamed down the mom's face as she took in this announcement. "Unreal," she said to herself. "Just absolutely unreal . . ."

"I left your church last night with $150 in gift cards," she wrote, "a trunk full of groceries for me and my kid . . . and hope."

When we give to God, God gives to people in need. Are you catching this idea? We are stronger together than we are apart. As was the impetus for the Old Testament law of gleaning, where farmers would leave the corners of their crops unharvested so that people suffering grave hunger could come eat from that abundance, we are to remember that there is plenty to go around if we will open our hearts and hands.

(By the way, the story of this single mom is hardly anecdotal. The fact is, there are almost no problems that money cannot help fix. If only we as lovers of God would release our grip on those funds . . .)

AN INSATIABLE APPETITE TO GIVE

Someone from that "70 percent" group of non-tithers came to see me recently. She'd asked for the meeting because she was due to receive a large inheritance soon and didn't want to make any big mistakes. "I'm worth millions," she said, "but I'm embarrassed to tell you that

I've never once tithed to this church. I know I'm supposed to . . . but it feels so . . . *beyond my control.* This inheritance will be a game changer. I want to get it right."

I exhaled and said, "All right. I'll tell you what I think you should do, but you're going to have to trust my motivations here, deal? I don't need your money. New Life doesn't need your money. God does not need your money. There is no obligation here. There is only an invitation to growth."

She agreed to hear me out.

I told the woman that we could walk through every verse exhorting believers to be generous with their funds, but that at the end of the discussion only one lesson remained. It was the same lesson Pam and I had had to learn all those years ago, which is that if we are unwilling to surrender our finances to God, we will be unable to experience the freedom he has in store for us.

I don't know what that woman decided to do following our meeting. But the light in her eye and the anticipation in her gait as she left told me she indeed heard what I'd said. After she was gone and I returned to my office, I sat down and said a quick prayer: "Father, help her catch a vision for the extravagance you've embedded in each of your followers' hearts. Help her become a *giver*, not just a taker. Help her to join you— radically, expensively, sacrificially—in your work. Amen."

It's my prayer for you and me as well: that we would be quick to worship God not merely with plentiful words and noble intentions but with *real financial action* too. If you join me in this desire, read on. Things are about to get really interesting.

ALLOCATING DOLLARS AND CENTS

Earlier this summer, before my daughter, Callie, moved into her own place with her brother, I had a truly euphoric moment. I was home alone on a Saturday when the UPS driver rang our doorbell. I thanked him for the package, shut the door behind me, and then glanced at the address label. "Miss Callie Boyd," the label said. The return address was from the sportswear store Under Armor's subscription service. *Callie had purchased her own clothes.* Pam and I had graduated to some other level as parents; I could feel it. We were about to be financially free in ways we hadn't known ... ever.

When Callie got home, I motioned to the box there on the island in the kitchen and said, "I see you're buying your own clothes now." I couldn't help but grin.

"Yeah. Yeah ... ," she said, with equal parts long-awaited independence and abject fear.

"Everything okay?" I asked, to which she said, "I just want to make sure I get this budgeting thing right before I move out."

Callie has been running a video camera at New Life for several months, her first real job as an adult. She puts in wild hours—eleven or twelve at a time, depending on which ministries need her help—and makes maybe twelve bucks for each one of them logged. Ever since she got the job, she's become distinctly more capitalistic in her perspective. "Where'd my burgeoning socialist go?" I asked her once. She just looked at me and said, "Just trying to hang on to the money I earn, Dad."

Happens to us all, Callie. Happens to us all.

Back in the kitchen, Callie sat down. "Okay, so I think I made $130 working yesterday," she said, cataloguing in real life the breakdown we'd covered in theory a thousand times before, "which means I give $13 to the church and $13 to savings ..."

"Right," I said, "but then that would mean you didn't really make $130 yesterday. Start thinking of 'what you made' as the amount after you take that 20 percent off the top. You didn't make $130; you made $104."

"Ri-i-ight," she said.

"And then," I continued, "you'll eventually need to accommodate taxes, too, which can be anywhere from 10 to 30 percent or more, depending on your income."

Her cheery expression started to fade.

"Ri-i-ight," she said again, quieter this time.

"Once you and Abram move out, what will your rent be?" I asked. "How much do you guys need for groceries?" (*And what about dog food?* I thought about adding, knowing how much her giant husky, Fia, tends to eat.)

"What will your utilities run you?" I continued. "And how about gas for your car?"

My daughter blew her hair out of her face and slumped down into her chair, and all I could think was *I have been exactly where you are.*

The conversation that ensued between my kid and me is the same one I'd like to have with you now. It's the one I wish I could have with every person alive—especially those on the younger side who haven't yet racked up heart-crushing financial failures. If we learn what to do when the paycheck is $130, we will know what to do when it's $1,300 and when it's $13,000 and when it's $130,000 and more. Truly, the way we spend a single dollar is the way we'll spend a million. The principles—they are the same. This is why so many lottery winners blow their money and are forced to declare bankruptcy within five years' time.[7] Or why 78 percent of NFL players are broke within twenty-four months of leaving the league. They play an average of three years and make roughly $700,000 a year. But regardless of their having earned $2.1 million, they have nothing to show for themselves.

How can this happen? The reason is simple: we can't apply what we never learned.

Principles. It comes down to that.

In advance of our first principle, let's get the lay of the land. Callie may not be the only one whose eyes glaze over when asked how much it costs to live. Here's a little quiz for *you* to try:

Without consulting your spouse, partner, checkbook registers, credit card statements, or online accounts, how many of these questions can you answer reflexively?

- Exactly what percent of your annual income are you spending on housing right now, including utilities?
- How much money is in your savings account(s)? Can you get within $10 of the total?
- Based on your run rate these last six months, what percent of your monthly income are you spending on food, including both groceries and takeout?
- What percent of your monthly income are you spending on insurance, both for your family's health coverage and for your car(s)?
- What percent have you been spending on clothes and dry cleaning?
- Pets?
- Your tithe to your local church?
- What about education?
- Travel?
- Entertainment?
- Home improvement?
- Hobbies?
- Gym memberships?
- This one will hurt, I know: Starbucks?
- This one may hurt worse: Amazon?

How much is it costing you (and your family, if applicable) to live, month by month? How much money do you make month by month? Does the current ratio of your income to your expenses leave you ahead of or behind the game?

Knowledge is power, and power is change, it has been said. How's your knowledge on these themes?

So that's one question: How much is it costing you to live?

A second question is this: How much *should* it cost?

Richard J. Foster wrote, "Few of us would buy into the naive notion that the accumulation of bigger and better things will give us joy or purpose. Yet neither are we comfortable with the rigid ascetic who thunders down denunciations on the evil of possessions. We don't want to be materialists, ever acquiring and ever hoarding. And yet John the Baptist, with his skins and wild honey, doesn't quite seem the model either. How can we put material things in a proper perspective in a world of dental bills and piano lessons?"[8]

I may disagree with Foster about how "few of us" have bought into the idea that bigger and better will satisfy us in the end, given how many of us literally buy into this idea, but I concede his overall point: *we crave a clearer understanding of how much life is supposed to cost.*

I want to offer up three principles that you can begin implementing today that will help you formulate *your perspective* on this. I emphasize "your perspective" because nowhere in Scripture are we handed percentages on how much things are to cost us as we navigate earthly life. Jesus never lays out in specific detail how big or small our houses are to be, what model SUV we're supposed to drive, or how many pairs of jeans we are to own. So, in working to make this part of the chapter as granular as possible, I'm admittedly freewheeling a bit. And then I'm asking you to take your findings to God. As we discussed previously, he is the bearer of all wisdom, and he loves to respond favorably when our prayer is "Give me more!"

Principle 1: Spend Less Than You Make

Recently the U.S. Bureau of Labor Statistics reported that the median income for a full-time salaried American worker is $900 per week, which equates to $46,800. Adjusted for seasonal fluctuations, the total is a little less: $46,644.[9] For our purposes here, and to keep things as simple as possible, let's round up to a clean $50,000 and assume this is our working income before taxes.

To be painfully clear, this first principle states that if our income is $50,000, our expenses—tithe and housing and food and clothing and all the rest—simply cannot exceed $50,000. If they're over by even a penny, we're in that hellish place called debt. We don't want to be in debt.

I often tell newlyweds that the key to leaving a laudable financial legacy is to spend less than they make for a really long time. That's it! Straightforward, right?

This line of thinking dramatically shifts your view on dropping five bucks for a cup of coffee; on splurging on one more piece of Ernest Shackleton–worthy clothing for you to wear while you're running errands around town; on buying a brand-new car; on upgrading to the bigger, nicer house.

Spend a little less.
   Than the money you make.
      Over a really long period of time.

Now, to how we get that done.

If you were to search "personal finance" on Google, you would be inundated with 2 billion search results (literally), and while the various gurus out there have various slants on how to rightly accomplish this thing called money management, one thing they all agree on is the usefulness of a zero-sum budget in which each of the categories you spend money on has its own line item, its own designated percent of the pie. The "zero-sum" part just means that if you were to add up all of those various percentage points, you would wind up at 100 percent— not one percentage point less, not one percentage point more.

The nice thing about crafting a solid budget is that as long as you stick to it, you never have to worry about spending more than you make. Stick to your budget each month, and voilà, you've nailed principle 1.

The not-so-nice thing about crafting a solid budget is that you then *feel obligated to stick to it*, which in at least a portion of the population incites some combination of fear/frustration/ annoyance/outright rage—

what author Ann Wilson calls Money Management Avoidance Behavior.[10] If this characterizes you, take heart: as you persist in budget keeping, it gets easier. It may not get more *fun* initially, but easier? That it does.

Now to those percentages. I'm going to give you round numbers to play with in your budget, but please know that your success in long-term budgeting will come from trial and error, from misjudging and tweaking, from carving things in stone and then breaking those very stones.

For discussion purposes, let's return to our income of $50,000. Based on the "round numbers" I referred to, what follows is how a decent budget might play out. You'll likely need to make some adjustments to make this fit your circumstances: the cost of living may be higher or lower where you live, your health insurance or child care may cost more, or you may use public transportation and not own a car. But this will give you a place to start.

STARTER BUDGET for $50,000 Annual Income			
Expense Category	Percent of Income	Annual Total	Est. Monthly Total
Tithe to Local Church	10	$5,000	$417
Taxes	25	$12,500	$1,041
Savings	10	$5,000	$417
Debt	10	$5,000	$417
Housing & Utilities	20	$10,000	$833
Food	12	$6,000	$500
Car/Auto Insurance	3	$1,500	$125
Medical/Dental	2.5	$1,250	$104
School/Child Care	2.5	$1,250	$104
Clothing	2.5	$1,250	$104
Life	2.5	$1,250	$104
Generosity	0	$0	$0
Total	100	$50,000	$4,166

Before we move on, let me draw your attention to seven distinctions about the starter budget we've laid out:

1. On savings. Proverbs 13:11 promises us that "whoever gathers money little by little makes it grow," and if my own experience is any indication, even a *very* little at a time will one day form a heap. Do not skimp on your long-term savings unless you simply must. Which brings us to note two . . .

2. On debt. If you are carrying consumer debt, then pay that off before you put money into investments. While you earn some interest on a savings account and investments can increase in value over time, the profit is typically a lot less than the interest you pay on a credit card over the same period, which can be anywhere from 8 to 25 percent.[11] Do not use your retirement fund, such as a 401(k) plan, to pay off your debt, as there are heavy penalties for withdrawing funds early. But, just as importantly, do not *continue* to invest until those debts are paid. If you're heavily indebted, you might consider reducing your savings to 2 or 3 percent (instead of 10 percent, as noted above) until your debts are paid.

3. On life and how it happens. The "Life" category in the grid above intends to set money aside for the inevitabilities of . . . life. Stuff is going to break. Things are going to wear out. Something's going to need a little extra love, right when you have no extra love to give. Hence the "Life" category. Putting a few percentage points toward this emergency fund each month will provide the safety net you will invariably need when the baseball flies through the window, the furnace flares up, the struts go out, and the kids have the audacity to outgrow every last pair of pants they own. You'll thank me for the "Life" line item, I assure you, because life will always scream for more.

4. On cars. I know it's *so fun* to have a super-new, super-fast, super-cool car. But until you have a superhigh income, consider in-

jecting a little practicality into your automobile-acquisition equation. You can make up *a lot* of percentage points by opting for functional over fun. And as we've already discussed, when you free funds before God, he will make things more fun for you than you could ever hope to make for yourself.

5. On kids' activities. If you are a parent of an active child, then you know how quickly kids' activities can add up. At least until your debts (except perhaps your home mortgage) are paid, investigate free opportunities at local libraries, eateries, museums, parks, rec centers, and more.

6. On what else is missing. You may have noticed that our starter budget has no line items for gym memberships, vacations and travel-related expenses, pet-care expenses (gasp!), haircuts, hobbies, lunch with friends, gifts for loved ones, Amazon purchases, and more. You will have to adjust your budget according to your reality, but remember: when you add a category (and thus further expenses), another category must pay. In the end, the pie must equal 100 percent, no matter how you choose to slice it.

7. On generosity. Ah, generosity. Did you catch it there, in the budget's flow? If you did, then you probably also noticed the zero by its name. The zero is there to remind us that to make room for strategic generosity—generosity that we budget for; giving that is above and beyond our tithe to our local church—something else has to give. The bigger house might have to go, or the heftier car payment. The expectation for a monthly clothing allowance, or else an additional dinner out. As with the "savings" category, remember that even a small amount, when increased diligently, will grow to a handsome sum over time.

It makes no difference to me if you start with the budget I've laid out or if you craft your own from the ground up. What I care about is that you start. Start somewhere. Start anywhere. But start. Quit letting your money fly out of your pocket without telling you where it's headed. *You* start telling *it* where to go. Tinker and give it a try. Tinker some more and try again. Fail miserably. Fail better. Keep going until it works for you. If you keep overshooting your budget—you keep impulse buying at the grocery store, for example, or you keep forgetting to budget extra gas money for the frequent road trips your family takes—consider opting for cash instead of a credit or debit card. When it's out, it's out, end of story. Also, watch the incidentals: reflexively reloading your Starbucks app, ordering soda instead of water at a restaurant, grabbing overpriced goods at the convenience store, making impulse buys at the cash register. Take every dollar captive, and you will start to get set free.

Principle 2: Give Your Best to God

All right. On to principle 2, which is this: Give your best to God. At the risk of belaboring this issue of tithing the first 10 percent to your local church, let me simply say that as you refine and relaunch your budget, *do not tinker with the tithe.* "Giving" in both the Hebrew and Greek testaments in Scripture is always connected to a local congregation, and so we, too, are to bring this particular 10 percent "into the house of the Lord."

Give your first monies to God via a local church. (Yes, I know that the withholding of taxes might be the "first" thing that happens to each paycheck you receive, but in terms of volitional actions you take, let your first one be returning your best to God.)

Give *the full 10 percent* to God via a local church.

Give that first 10 percent no matter what else unfolds.

Test God in this: You prove faithful in giving your tithe, and see if God doesn't bless you as a result.

Principle 3: Watch for Opportunities to Be Generous

In his letters to the believers gathered in the city of Corinth, the apostle Paul exhorted them to set aside a bit of their income each week so that when Paul arrived, they could help cover his expenses while he stayed in town to minister to them. Those believers were under extreme persecution and pressure by the Roman government and needed all the help they could get. Paul understood that if his living expenses were covered, he could stay long enough to make a real difference with them. And so his injunction that, "on the first day of every week, each one of you should set aside a sum of money in keeping with your income, saving it up, so that when I come no collections will have to be made" (1 Corinthians 16:2).

Likewise, I believe God is saying to us here and now, "If you will set aside a portion of your funds under the banner of *generosity*, you can be part of the ministry that is coming for those in need still today." Of this much, I am sure: as you emerge from indebtedness and realize the benefits of budgeting money to be of help to those in need, you will actually *delight* in searching out these ministry opportunities God is sending your way.

Whenever my family goes out to eat, we try to keep our eyes open for people whose meal we might buy. Just last week we spotted a woman eating alone who looked like she was in a tough season of life. We called over our server, discreetly asked him to put her meal on our check without her knowing who had covered her bill, and smiled at each other over the anticipation of making someone's day.

As you continue to set aside a few dollars here, a few dollars there—asking God each day, "Is this money for him? For her? For them?"—you will be astounded by how many lives you're able to bless. Further, as that "generosity" budget line item begins to accumulate real funds each month, you can even look to systematize some of your giving, such as my family does with Compassion International.

Each month, the Boyd family sponsors two children living in El Salvador, Kevin and Nancy. We receive letters from them about once a month and love to write them back. Over the years we've watched them grow into spirited, Christ-following preteens who for their first time in their lives believe that they have a bright future in store for themselves.

The point is, don't quit tweaking your budget until you achieve total debt freedom, robustness in your savings account (having six months' worth of living expenses is best), wise recurring-expense management, and faithfulness in adding to your "generosity" line item. Watch for ways God wishes to use the funds in your care to bless the people in need where you live. And see if this newfound simplicity doesn't revolutionize your life.

RAIN IN THE STORM

I have worked with enough people along the way to shore up their finances to know that there is a good chance this pointed discussion regarding money is making you feel less than great. CareerBuilder conducted a survey two years ago that reported 78 percent of American workers are living paycheck to paycheck.[12] If true, then nearly eight out of ten people who are reading this sentence are struggling to make ends meet—a truly terrifying place to be.

If you will abide by the three straightforward principles in this chapter, you will begin to experience relief. You will make over your financial practices. You will know what it is to *live free*. You will see that there was necessary and nourishing rain in the financial storm you weathered—that you actually *grew through that season of pain*. Even now, you might spend a few minutes reflecting on the journey you've been on relating to your finances. What inner vows have been influencing you? If mismanagement has been your approach for some time, when did that begin? When did you start believing that your worth was tied to your "stuff"?

Understanding where you've been and anticipating where you're headed will go a long way in helping you appreciate the rain that has been in your storm. Yes, I know you and I both could do without the dramatic thunder and damaging hail, but sometimes we must accept the hydrating rain however we can get it. Brighter days will dawn, I assure you, as we learn . . . and apply what we've learned.

◇◇◇◇◇◇◇◇◇◇◇◇◇◇◇◇◇◇◇◇◇◇◇◇◇◇◇◇◇◇◇◇◇◇◇

Pushing Pause: Chapter 8

The fulfillment we long for comes only through generous living, and generosity at some point will hit us financially. It is no stretch to say that it is only by practicing financial freedom that we will live this life fulfilled. Where to begin in pursuit of such freedom? That's where this chapter's challenge comes in.

Read

God invites us to test him in one and only one aspect of life, and it is on the issue of our finances. In Malachi 3:10–12 we read, "'Bring the whole tithe into the storehouse, that there may be food in my house. Test me in this,' says the LORD Almighty, 'and see if I will not throw open the floodgates of heaven and pour out so much blessing that there will not be room enough to store it. I will prevent pests from devouring your crops, and the vines in your fields will not drop their fruit before it is ripe,' says the Lord Almighty. 'Then all the nations will call you blessed, for yours will be a delightful land,' says the LORD Almighty.'"

Reflect

- If God is so sure that when we surrender our finances to him, we will receive "so much blessing that there will not be room enough to store it," then why are we so *unsure* that this outcome will occur?

■ When have you surrendered something to God financially and experienced blessing as a result?

Respond

This chapter's challenge is coming to you in three parts. First, take the "Callie quiz" on page 197. This time, feel free to consult financial records, bank accounts, and any other resource that may prove helpful. The goal here is to get your arms around your expenses, not to prove how self-sufficient you are. The starter set of questions follow, but feel free to add to the list.

1. Exactly what percent of your annual income are you spending on housing right now, including utilities?
2. How much money is in your savings account(s)? Can you get within ten dollars of the total?
3. Based on your run rate these last six months, what percent of your monthly income are you spending on food, including both groceries and takeout?
4. What percent of your monthly income are you spending on insurance, both for your family's bodies and for your car(s)?
5. What percent have you been spending on clothes and dry cleaning?
6. Pets?
7. Your tithe?
8. What about education?
9. Travel?
10. Entertainment?
11. Home improvement?
12. Hobbies?
13. Gym memberships?
14. Amazon?
15. Starbucks?

Next, please complete a budget for the coming month. Take a peek at page 200 for an example of a simple starter budget, and adjust things from there. It is said that you'll never hit a target you don't take aim at, and those words are true. Tell your money where it will be going these next thirty days. Decide now whom you will serve.

And finally, as part of that budgeting exercise, commit to giving your first 10 percent to God. Test him in this. I dare you!

9

Enough Is Enough

We are not living in a world where all roads are radii
of a circle and where all, if followed long enough, will
therefore draw gradually nearer and finally meet at the
centre: rather in a world where every road, after a few
miles, forks into two, and each of those into two again,
and at each fork, you must make a decision.

C. S. LEWIS

BUDGETING IS LIKE EXERCISING a muscle: with each rep, each iteration, each revision you perform faithfully, you will be amazed by how strong you will get. The process of mapping out your monthly spending plan and then living as though that plan is law will become as much of a habit as brushing your teeth every morning, clicking your seat belt into place each time you climb into your car, or saying, "Bless you" when you hear someone sneeze. But that's not all that might change. Because once the budgeting process is *this predictable* in your life, an emotional shift can also take place. Now that you're careful with every dollar, every cent, you'll start seeing how much money is necessary in life and how much you were just *blowing* before. You'll prove to yourself how efficient and effective you can be . . . how trustworthy you've become with cash. You'll discover, perhaps for the first time, that for so long you were just plain *duped.* You were duped into craving it all. You were duped into getting it all. You were duped into believing that *having it all* would fill the void that existed in your life.

HAPPINESS AWAITS AT THE STUFF MART

My kids were in elementary school when *VeggieTales* debuted, and instantly they were enthralled with the antics of Bob the Tomato and Larry the Cucumber, both talking vegetables who bounced instead of walked, because what vegetable has arms and legs? The show's theme song was as sticky as "It's a Small World," and soon enough Pam and I were inundated with all things *VeggieTales*: DVDs and T-shirts, posters and plush toys, and more.

Despite the annoying voices and songs, we had to admit that the show's themes were spot-on. How to love people who are different from us, how to manage peer pressure, how to stand up for biblical values—these and hundreds of other important lessons were depicted by those talking vegetables in a way that my kids enjoyed.

One episode opens with Larry the Cucumber zooming around on his new Susie Action Jeep, a toy he'd been wanting "just forever." Bob the Tomato oohs and aahs over the jeep, telling Larry that it must make him *so happy* to have such a cool toy, to which Larry says, "Yeah, well . . . *almost.*"

But what else does he need to make him happy when he has this amazing new jeep? Bob wonders. "There's just one more thing I need to be really happy," Larry explains: the Susie Action Camper.

Oh, and the Susie Action Dirt Bike.

And the Susie Action Jet Ski.

And the Hang Glider.

Then . . . *then*, Larry will be happy.

A trio of French peas hops onto the scene, telling Bob and Larry that in France, where they're from, there's a woman named Madame Blueberry who faced this very same dilemma. Madame Blueberry was very blue, we come to find out—so blue, in fact, that she doesn't know what to do. What's making her feel blue? Well, there in her expansive tree house, her plates are chipped. Her knives don't cut like they used to. Her sofa is tattered and worn.

Her two butlers try to console her—"You have so much food!" they tell her. "And this beautiful home!"—but it's no use. She's just plain blue.

That is, until she peeks out her window and sees a construction project underway. Just below her treehouse, a Stuff Mart is being built. *This will solve all of my problems!* she thinks.

On cue, two representatives from Stuff Mart appear, touting the store's tagline: "Happiness awaits at the Stuff Mart. All you need is more stuff."

Soon enough, Madame Blueberry is headed to Stuff Mart, where she'll fill cart after cart with new dishes, new knives, a new couch . . . new *anything* to make her not blue.

En route to the store, she passes two kids who each sing a song about a "thankful heart" being a happy heart as one receives a modest gift and the other nothing at all. Madame Blueberry passes by, perplexed.

Soon shopping carts overflowing with new stuff are being delivered to Madame Blueberry's tree house, and the madame has a revelation. "Maybe what I need to make me happy isn't in those shopping carts," she thinks, "but rather in a heart of gratitude."

But it's too late. The treehouse is so filled with stuff that it begins to buckle, toppling from the sheer weight of all those goods. The house sways dramatically from one side to another before falling over entirely, causing all of Madame Blueberry's new stuff to pour from the house into the river. Once the house is empty, the tree springs back upright, flinging the house off its branches and into the parking lot of Stuff Mart, where it lands in a heap of slats and dust.

Since those *VeggieTales* days, that image of Madame Blueberry's tree house toppling from the weight of her myriad acquisitions has haunted me every time Pam and I have moved from one house to another. Invariably I have stood amid hundreds of moving boxes, each one filled to overflowing with mounds of plenty, and thought, *Where did we get all this stuff?*

According to people who study such things, I am told that you and I receive upward of 1,500 advertising images each day, which means that on 1,500 occasions throughout a given twenty-four-hour period we are bombarded with someone somewhere telling us that we just won't be happy until we get this new-and-improved, can't-live-without-it, why-would-you-deny-yourself-this? super-cool thing.

I was in advertising before I went into ministry, which is how I know firsthand that advertisers' primary objective is to stir up discontent. They know you're sitting there with your old iPhone, watching your old TV while wearing last year's clothes and shoes. "New and improved!" they rave about their product. "Look what *this* one can do!"

You were content with your stuff five minutes ago, but now? Well, that's all changed.

"Oh, yes, you should!" advertisers persuade us. "This can be yours. *Today.*"

So, we say yes.

Just this once.

But then "once" turns into "twice," which turns into "occasionally," which leads to "as a matter of course," until the day dawns when we find ourselves standing there surrounded by boxes and boxes, each filled with useless stuff.

Talk to people who have mastered the budgetary process, and to a person they'll have this to say: "It's a losing game."

By "it" they mean the entire system: marketing, advertising, merchandising, sales—the whole bit. It's a game. A losing game. More stuff only stuffs us full. It's miserable to feel stuffed full.

Listen, we can have stuff. Even these people who declare the stuff-acquisition process a losing game have stuff. The distinction here? While they have stuff, that stuff does not have them.

FLIPPING THE LIST

There are only five things you can do with money. You can spend it. You can save it. You can invest it. You can loan it. You can give it away. That's it: spend, save, invest, loan, or give. Now, I've noticed a trend among those who have had this revelation regarding the pointlessness of incessantly accumulating more and more stuff, which is that they start to *flip the list*. Whereas their priority used to be spending money, spending is now at the bottom of their list. What has taken top spot? Giving money away.

Why do they do this? Why do they work hard to earn money that they then just . . . *give away*?

They do this because they spend their time and energy not pining for all the material possessions advertisers have told them they need but rather thinking about *people*—people God loves, people who are in need, people who would benefit from a helping hand. They have flipped their *thinking*, which in turn has flipped their list. And guess what else gets flipped, once your list is flipped? Your budget.

That's right: instead of crafting a zero-sum budget, in which every dollar gets spent every month however you see fit, these people craft a monthly financial freedom plan in which, upon meeting their basic needs, astoundingly, they give their money away.

Just after the American Civil War, William Worrall Mayo began a medical practice, making house calls to ailing folks living in southeastern Minnesota. Even on the snowiest of nights, upon getting word that a nearby resident was ill or injured, he would load his black doctor's bag into his buggy, whip his horses into a frenzied gallop, and head off to try to fix whatever was ailing them. Dr. Mayo was not only a fantastic physician; he also *cared deeply* for the patients he served. People couldn't help noticing this, and so his practice grew and grew.

Eventually, Dr. Mayo's two sons, Will and Charlie, joined his practice, and the effort grew three times as fast.

Nearby was a Franciscan convent, where fifty or so sisters lived. Dr. Mayo often approached Mother Mary Alfred Moes with the request for her to open additional beds to him so that his patients would have a place where they could safely rest and heal. On one such occasion Mother Alfred told Dr. Mayo that she'd had a vision from God. The two were to partner in opening a world-class medical facility there in Rochester, Minnesota. According to the nun, people would come from all over the planet to receive care at this facility. It would be the first of its kind in terms of innovation and patient care. This was supposed to happen, she told the doctor. He simply *had* to say yes.

Eventually Dr. Mayo would see things her way. The agreement was struck with a handshake, and the building of this new state-of-the-art hospital was underway.

Now, to some extent, the rest of the story is history—history you and I both know well. That hospital went on to become the Mayo Clinic, today home to 63,000 employees—including 4,800 physicians—and the chosen treatment facility each year for 1.3 million patients from all 50 states and 138 countries around the globe. Expansions over time have made Mayo appear as an outright city there in Rochester, and eventually locations in Florida and Arizona would be added, yielding what is today a $12 billion nonprofit.

But you know that. You know it's big. You know it's impressive.

You know its reputation is good. What you may not know is that, beginning in 1919, thirty-one years into the clinic's existence, the Mayo brothers, Will and Charlie, who took over the operations of the clinic after their father passed away, decided to cap their salary just above what they needed to maintain a reasonable lifestyle and funnel the rest of their earnings back into the business, declaring by their actions that enough was, in fact, enough. Adjusted for inflation, the amount they gave away? *Thirty-seven million dollars.*

The Mayo brothers enacted what is known in personal-finance circles as a financial-freedom plan. In such a plan, you determine how much money you need to be "okay" and then you give 100 percent of the rest of your earnings away. You determine how much is enough for you and then you part—voluntarily—with all that remains.

I put this idea in your mind for one simple reason: while you can work your fingers to the bone fine-tuning a budget in which you yourself spend every last dollar you make, you will never experience the level of full and complete surrender that you reach when you courageously *choose to send money back.*

While reading of the senior Dr. Mayo, I was struck by a practice he adhered to back in his horse-and-buggy days. If he got wind of a patient of his selling off part of his farm to cover his medical bills, Dr. Mayo would send the farmer's payment back. If he learned that a patient had taken on extra work—work that drew him away from his family for an extended period—to pay his medical bills, Dr. Mayo would send that worker's payment back. If he discovered that a family had had to go without food to cover the wife's medical bills, he would send that family's payment back. It's no wonder Dr. Mayo's sons caught the spirit of sending money back, isn't it? They'd seen their father do it for years.

Similarly, when those of us who bear the name and image of God, the One who *couldn't not be extravagant* if he tried, wonder how best to reflect our Father's goodness and grace in the world, we could do worse than *sending cash back.*

For weeks now I've been meditating on a passage of Scripture from Proverbs, chapter 30. It says: "Two things I ask of you, LORD; / do not refuse me before I die: / Keep falsehood and lies far from me; / give me neither poverty nor riches, / but give me only my daily bread" (v. 7–8). To ask to be kept from poverty is one thing; who in their right mind wants to be poor?

But to ask to also be kept from riches, from wealth? What a bold, bright prayer to pray. Jonathan Edwards once wrote, "Let him that glorieth, glory in the Lord."

Not glory in our bank account.

Not glory in our snazzy possessions.

Not glory in our custom home or of-the-moment car or Instagram-worthy vacations.

Not even glory in our polished and perfected budget.

If we are to glory, may we glory only in God.

I say whatever gets us to *that* aim quickly, that is the thing we should be about.

And yet in the same breath I acknowledge that to "be about" this aim will take some serious, reflective work. For starters, the endeavor will require that we define "enough."

HOW MUCH IS ENOUGH

When I was a younger man, a loving pastor who knew I was struggling financially agreed to meet with me, and during that meeting he taught me something I remember to this day. "Brady," he said, "if you will spend some time with your wife sorting out what your 'circle of contentment' is, God will break through this wall you think you're up against and will begin to use you in profound ways."

The "circle of contentment," he explained, was the boundary around what Pam and I needed financially to survive. It would be great if there were a nice, tidy formula I could hand you that would take the guesswork out of this exercise, but, really, that approach would only hamstring your awareness and growth.

To calculate your own circle of contentment, you'll need to ask yourself what's necessary from a financial standpoint for every key aspect of life. Engaging in conversation with loved ones—especially those who live under the same roof as you—is a priceless part of this process and of vital importance to getting the measure of your circle's diameter right. As your categories flow and become more nuanced, they'll surely be different from mine; but because the first few are ones most all of us share, let's tackle them here. First up: *the place you call home.*

How Much House Do You Need?

How big a place do you need? That's the question here. When attempting to answer that question, you'll need to consider a few things:

- The number of people in your family
- How often you host overnight guests
- Whether you or your spouse works from home
- What types of gatherings/activities you host in a given year
- Which spaces you have in your *current* living situation that go unused? A sitting room of some sort? A spare bedroom? Half of an unfinished basement? Those are real square feet—square feet your next place does not need.
- How much house can you afford? Remember that, in our starter budget, we designated no more than 25 percent of your take-home pay on housing.

At the risk of sounding like a killjoy, it's worth mentioning that the criteria for how much house to buy should *not* be equivalent to the note the bank is willing to approve. Bank managers aren't nearly as concerned about your financial, spiritual, and emotional well-being as they are closing a deal that's profitable for them.

How much house you *actually* need takes some thought. Some reflection. Some candor among your family and you.

"We need about 1,200 square feet."

"We need 3,000 square feet."

"We need somewhere between 1,500 and 2,000 square feet."

"We could totally live in a tiny house."

How much space do you need? This question deserves an answer, and that answer must come from you. Keep mulling until you and any other interested parties land on an actual figure, an actual measurement of your housing circle of contentment.

Note it and then move on.

How Much Car Do You Need?

The next nearly universal category of expenses is *transportation*. In some parts of the country, car ownership just doesn't make sense, given how ubiquitous public transportation is. For the rest of us, it's worth it to have a car.

During those cancerous financial days that Pam and I endured early on, I kind of had a "car problem." Which is perhaps what brought on the cancer.

At the time, I was working at a job in television, making pretty good money, when I felt prompted to go pastor a church in West Texas where their membership boasted a whopping fifty folks. My pay cut would be substantial—about $30,000, as I recall. But I truly felt like God was in this decision, and so I said yes.

I did okay swallowing the idea that I'd be making far less money going forward, given that this was "God's plan," "God's idea," "God's work." The sole trouble spot for me had nothing to do with the future but rather with a decision I'd made in the past. The very recent past, as it turns out . . . in the form of a shiny sports car.

Will you sell that car and live below your means?

I don't know if the question came from God or from the evil forces at work in this world, but it haunted me for months.

My car.

My beautiful red sports car.

Who in a right mind would sell a red sports car for God?

If my memory serves me correctly, I paid $1,200 cash for a very used GMC S15 pickup that possessed such a wild multitude of smells that it made my stomach turn every time I climbed in. Regardless of how delicately I clutched, the second gear always, always ground. And it was neither shiny nor red. "Lord," I remember praying with great frequency, "I want to be a giver, not a taker. This truck gets me where I need to go. Thank you for this truck."

I don't think I ever verbalized the last part of that standard prayer— "And would you give me back my shiny red sports car someday?"—but I meant it all the same.

I think of that old GMC truck every time I counsel people at New Life to forego the new-car purchase and drop a hundred bucks on having their trusty minivan detailed instead. Once the Cheerios smell is banished, I tell them, the thing will ride like a dream. The fact is, somewhere around 100 percent of all new-car purchases are made on an emotional high. Think about it: nobody in a rational state of mind walks into a dealership and says, "I'd like the newest model you've got, complete with every bell and whistle known to humankind."

No: if you're that person, you've been sold a bill of goods. You've bought into the hype that this vehicle really will make you a debonair adventure-seeking first-class flyer who never has to follow the rules. Come on, now. Nobody *really* lives that way. Or if they do, they've probably sold their soul to get there. Think prudently about how many people need access to the vehicle you're considering and how far from home they need to go. Any road trips on your annual docket? Any lifestyle concerns to factor in, such as helping with a carpool, needing to lug massive supplies of some sort, dealing with frequent wintertime snowstorms, or driving a ride share on the side?

If you were coaching a friend with your exact transportation needs on the type of vehicle to acquire, what would you point him or her to?

Most likely, that's your answer. That's the car for you as well.

What About Household Repairs?

One of the joys of homeownership is the frequency at which things bust and break, and home warranties, while useful, don't cover everything. Toilets. The hot-water heater. Dishwashers. Sprinklers. The AC. If you've been in the same home for more than ten years, you would be wise to set aside funds to cover this kind of thing. Home repairs aren't "if" but "when."

And Eating Out?

Quick question: Have you ever tracked how much money you pass through your driver-side window? Or log with your Uber Eats account? Or flow through DoorDash?

What's that you say? You're *above* drive-through restaurants? My point is the same. You mean to tell me that eating out—even at the best restaurants in town—is better than a home-cooked meal at home? You'll never convince me of that.

Ever.

And Vacations?

In the same way that most toddlers are far more fascinated with reusable plastic food containers than even the most expensive, elaborate baby toys on the market, what most kids truly long for in a family vacation is time with you . . . with no device in hand. My family and I have made some of our best memories free of charge—at parks, on streams, even at home. If you set the bar at "Disney World," you'll do both your children and you a disservice. Head out for a big trip for your child's graduation from high school, maybe. Until then? Low-key might just scratch the itch.

On this issue of recreation, also consider your values when sorting out where to go, when to go, how to get there, and so forth. I learned this lesson all over again a few years ago when Pam and I considered buying a camper. We'd taken the kids camping for a few days, and they loved it. I thought, *This is incredible! Camping is relatively inexpensive, and, living in Colorado, we have dozens of places to camp. Perfect. Vacation solved, for years and years to come.*

Pam and I began scouring Craigslist for campers, because while our kids can sleep with no problem in a tent on the ground, there comes an age in life when it just doesn't work for adults. Pam and I have reached, and passed, that age.

We thought we'd found the right camper for us, when it occurred to me that really the only day we could camp was Saturday. During the school year, the kids were occupied Monday through Friday, and during the summer they had activities those days. Sundays were out because of church. Saturday, then, was it.

We'd have to leave late on Friday, which meant we'd go through the hassle of gathering all the gear and prepping all the food for an overnight trip. To add insult to injury, we'd be returning late Saturday night totally wiped out—which, for a pastor who is expected to preach a couple of times on Sunday morning, isn't exactly wise.

It's not just pastors who ought to run recreational considerations through this grid, though. I know of a family who built a massive custom home with a six-car garage. This family happens to have four members in it: a husband, a wife, and two school-age children. Six cars? Why would they need space for *six* cars?

"We have a lot of . . . toys," the wife told a ministry partner of mine. "The boat to take to the lake, the snowmobiles to take up to the mountains, a couple of quads, and my husband's Jeep for going off-roading . . ."

The thing is, if I had that husband's income, I'd love those toys too!

Who wouldn't? But, practically speaking, when does a family such as this one have time to use such things? You guessed it: on Saturday.

They will need to play all day most Saturdays with those toys, to justify the ownership and six-car-garage storage of those toys. Which means they'll be fried most Saturday nights.

Which means that, some percent of the time, they'll have no energy to come to church on Sunday morning, let alone volunteer in service of other families who are investigating the claims of Christ.

I know, I know: *killjoy*. Again. But the reality is that, at least here in Colorado, we will lose families for *months* at a time as they relish ski season, club sports, summertime excursions, and more. They love New Life but they can't make it to New Life because these other things have pulled them away. Which would be fine except that if they are looking for some of the lowest-hanging fruit around in terms of how to serve people in need, church is *it*. We have people in need show up every Sunday desperate for someone to care. And if too many of those caring someones are still sleeping in the camper they just had to have . . . well, those needs will go unmet.

A few months ago, on a Sunday morning, I looked up during worship from my front-row seat and spotted my son singing in the choir and my daughter running the video camera that was trained on the main stage, both having a ball. Yeah, we could have bought that camper, and, yeah, I guess some awesome memories would have been made. But in terms of what Pam and I hope to form in our children as they enter the independence of adulthood, it's service to the bride of Christ. In terms of real *re-creation*, it doesn't get better than that.

ENOUGH IS ENOUGH

We could keep going with this list of gotta-bes, drawing our circles of contentment, determining needs versus wants, but I think you get the point. *How much is enough?* That is the question waiting to be addressed.

How much do you need just to live?

Not *How much do you want?*

Not *How much does everyone else have?*

But *How much do you need?*

Before we move ahead, let me acknowledge that in this day of social media saturation, it's all too easy to fall into the trap of comparison, which tells us we'll never have enough. Take a sixty-second scroll-break on Instagram and you'll see that someone is always wearing trendier clothes, eating a more beautiful meal, and vacationing in a more exotic locale. Allow that sixty seconds to turn into sixty minutes and you'll be borderline depressed.

When I was a kid, I had exactly two pairs of shoes: a pair for church on Sunday and a pair for everything else. I remember wearing my Sunday shoes down to the creek one time and promptly sinking into the mud. The minute I walked back into the house, I thought my mom's head just might explode. I can't remember if my mom or my dad spanked me that time, but I do remember being outraged that they wouldn't listen to my excuse. The fact was the canvas tennis shoes I was *supposed* to be wearing were so old and ratty that my big toes stuck out through the fronts. Still, I had no idea this equated to poverty until I noticed my classmates' abundance of shoes.

That's generally how it goes, right? We don't know how much we're doing without until we see what others have. This dynamic has risen to near-epic proportions, causing us to one-up each other for sport.

Comedian Brian Regan, reflecting on this human-nature tendency to constantly trump those around us, said in one of his bits that he has a recurring social fantasy involving his being one of the twelve astronauts who has walked on the moon. "He can sit back quietly at a dinner party while some other Me Monster is doing his thing and let him go," Regan reasons. The other guy can wax on about his frequent trips to Aspen on his private jet, the global enterprise he's running, how amazing the Autobahn is to drive on, and more. Then, at just the right time, after the guy has worn himself out beating his chest in a prideful show of exuberance, that astronaut can calmly take a sip of water, sit back in his chair, and say with smug subtlety, "I walked on the moon."

And then quietly take another bite.

It's what we're all after, right? That mic-drop moment of ultimate toppage; the line that nobody else can beat.

We want the house that nobody can top.

The car that nobody can top.

The wardrobe that nobody can top.

The vacations that nobody can top.

We want to be on top. We want to *be* the top, even as it's an impossible goal to reach. And to center a life on that mission is to live completely in vain. It's the *last* who are first, Jesus promised. It's the *meek* who inherit the earth. No, we do much better to take those things we think will give us status and simply lay them down.

A while back I challenged our church to do this very thing—and in a practical, tangible way. One Sunday morning, after exhorting our people to really consider this message of extravagant living, I told them that for the next two weekends we were going to have huge tractor trailers parked outside the auditorium and that I wanted those rigs to be *completely full* by the time they left our lot. "Together," I told our congregation, "we're going to fill them."

I explained that our local rescue mission downtown was low on many things—nonperishable food stores, small appliances, summertime clothing, baby gear, furniture, medical equipment, and more— and that we as a church were going to help solve that problem. "Now, don't be bringing your cast-off stuff," I said to them. "I want us to give from our abundance. I want us to give our *best*."

Our finance guy estimated that in the end we collected more than half a million dollars' worth of goods those two weekends, and these were *quality* things. Once everything was collected and sorted, we laid out the donations and invited those who were served by the rescue mission and also those served by relief agencies in town to come "shop" our parking lot. Volunteers loaded each person's vehicle with the goods they'd selected, and in the end more than three hundred families were served. It was one of the best offerings our church has ever made to our community, not just because of the donations themselves, but because of the sacrifice involved in handing them over.

As I watched one New Lifer after another drive up with one more excellent donation, a donation that *cost them something to give*, I thought back to when my daughter, Callie, was a little girl. She used to love a toy called Webkinz, which was a plush animal that came with a unique code to unlock a game featuring a virtual version of the animal on the Internet. When Callie logged onto the Webkinz site, she could "care for" her little animal, virtually feeding and clothing the thing as often as she pleased.

My mom and Pam's parents knew how much Callie loved Webkinz, and so, every birthday, they'd add to Callie's collection until the things were stacked in a corner of her room two feet high. She adored those toys and played with them all the time.

One night I was reading the Bible to Callie and came across a verse about giving generously to those in need. Noticing all those Webkinz in the corner, on a whim I said, "Hey, Callie, how many Webkinz do you think you really need?"

Panic flashed across her eyes as she considered what I was asking.

"I'm not asking you to give them away," I said to my daughter. "I'm just wondering if you'd be willing to ask God what he would have you do. If he tells you to keep them, fine. But if he prompts you to part with some of them, I'm wondering if that's something you'd be willing to do . . ."

Callie eyed me somberly and said, "Yes, sir. I'll do that."

I told Callie that if she would ask God about her Webkinz, then I'd ask God about my prized 1958 shotgun that my dad bought brand-new when he turned sixteen years old. He had passed it down to me, and she knew it was my favorite possession, one I hoped to keep forever.

"Okay, Dad!" Callie said, freshly energized by my having some skin in the game now too.

The fact is, regardless of what your "Webkinz" or your "prized shotgun" is, at the end of the day *it's just stuff.* It's okay to get some stuff. It's even okay to like the stuff you get. But when the choice is between valuing our stuff—either by fiercely protecting our current possessions or by striving to acquire still more—and valuing people, well, I think you know what must win. For the record, Callie kept her Webkinz and I kept my gun. The point wasn't what happened in the end but rather what we were *willing* to let happen in the end.

Here's an experiment for you to try: Just for today, whenever you catch yourself thinking about stuff—say, reaching for your phone to place an Amazon purchase, or scrolling some store's online site for the couch you and your spouse have been eyeing, or else amping up over your kid dropping his ice cream cone on one of your car's beautiful leather seats—practice thinking a different thought. Think about that colleague who had to file for bankruptcy. Think about your neighbor whose spouse just passed away unexpectedly. Think about your sister-in-law whose son's life is still ravaged by drugs.

Yes, assuming your budget allows for it, you can still get what you need on Amazon.

Same goes for the couch.

You can also teach your kid how to be more careful with sticky food.

I'm just asking you to do these things from a place of gratitude and servanthood and peace instead of from a place of entitlement and consumerism and greed. Let people take top spot in your thought life, and that stuff will lose its grip.

THE CONTENTMENT OF THOMAS

I had a translator named Thomas during a talk I was giving in Nairobi not long ago, and within sixty seconds of meeting this guy I was his number one fan. He had a huge smile, a fantastic energy about him, and an endearing way with audiences. To this day I joke with him that whatever he was saying in Swahili was ten times better than what I had said in English, because it was the best reception in *any* culture that my preaching has ever received.

I was in Africa with three other ministry leaders, and on our last day there, when we were all exhausted and ready to get to the airport so that we could get on the plane and sleep, Thomas said, "I have a house now! I'd love for you to see it."

We had time before we needed to leave for the airport, so we agreed to go. Thomas phoned his wife, said, "I'm bringing over my American friends!" and then led us along winding paths to a three-story cinder-block apartment complex that had just been built.

Thomas and his wife have four children, and I couldn't help but start counting rooms the moment I entered Thomas's space. It didn't take me long, because there were only two: a living area and a sleeping area. Where *all six* would live and sleep. The sleeping area was maybe half the size of my office at New Life. Translation: *not big*.

After a few minutes I asked Thomas if I might use the facilities. He grinned and said, "Of course! Of course!"

He then pointed outside.

I grinned back as I headed out the door, down the cement steps, and into the blazing African heat.

Several hours later, after my colleagues and I had made it to the airport and were settled at the gate, waiting to board our flight, I thought about Thomas and his wife and how elated they'd been over our visit to their new home. I thought about the simplicity of that dwelling—

a safe place with a room to eat in, a room to sleep in, protection from the elements, somewhere to call their own.

I thought about how grateful I was for flush toilets.

And for the fact that Abram and Callie didn't share a bedroom with Pam and me.

And for the thousands other modern conveniences I enjoy.

Even so, experiencing Thomas's contentment had shifted something deep inside of me. It had reset somehow what I define as *enough*. It had reminded me that, regardless of the specifics of our circumstances—whether our homes have two rooms or ten, whether our bathroom breaks happen inside or outside of our house, whether we have completely empty pantries or a six-month supply sitting there—there is a way to put people first. There is a way to have our possessions—however plentiful they are or are not—without those possessions having *us*.

There is a way to live contented, having declared that enough is enough.

◇◇◇◇◇◇◇◇◇◇◇◇◇◇◇◇◇◇◇◇◇◇◇◇◇◇◇◇◇◇◇◇◇◇◇◇◇◇◇

Pushing Pause: Chapter 9

To whom much is given, much really is required. But how are we supposed to know when enough is enough? In this chapter's challenge, you'll be invited to draw some bold lines around your sense of "enoughness" and work from there.

Read

In his letter to his protégé Timothy, the apostle Paul reminds him of the need to teach those with resources how to be good stewards of the resources they have. "Command those who are rich in this present world not to be arrogant nor to put their hope in wealth, which is so uncertain, but to put their hope in God, who richly provides us with everything for our enjoyment," he wrote. "Command them to do good, to be rich in good deeds, and to be generous and willing to share. In this way they will lay up treasure for themselves as a firm foundation for the coming age, so that they may take hold of the life that is truly life" (1 Timothy 6:17–19).

Reflect

- To Paul's exhortation to Timothy that those with resources are to be "willing to share," how would you rate yourself? How willing to share are you? What resource are you *good* about sharing? What types of things do you tend to hold back?
- What do you expect the "firm foundation for the coming age" Paul speaks of to include?

Respond

For this chapter's challenge, I'd like you to designate ten categories of expenses that you'd like to assess. In this chapter, I offered up five for scrutiny: your house, your car(s), your household repairs, your pattern of eating out, and the vacations you choose to take. Feel free to start with those and add on, or else craft ten fresh categories of your own.

Next, draw your "circles of contentment" around each of these categories. How much of each do you need? (Notice that I didn't use the word "want.") Feel free to solicit input from friends and loved ones who know your heart and share your passion for surrendering all things to the lordship of Jesus Christ.

Finally, consider coming before God in prayer to present the circles of contentment you've drawn. Does he agree with your assessment? Any adjustments you believe he'd make? Ask for his input and be patient as you listen for his reply.

10

Spending Well

*It is through the mediation of human beings, fallen and
fallible, but also seeking to be a community of vicarious
love in the world, that reconciliation becomes a reality.*[1]

JOHN W. DE GRUCY

CAME ACROSS SOME INTERESTING research findings recently that
captured my imagination for two reasons. The study, published
by the Brookings Institution, a Washington, D.C.–based public policy
nonprofit that researches and reports on societal trends around the
globe, reported that in the United States, of adults who followed three
straightforward principles, only "2 percent are in poverty and nearly
75 percent have joined the middle class," which Brookings defines as
earning $55,000 or more per year. (For context, at this writing the pov-
erty line in America sits just below an annual income of $13,000.)

The three principles are these: (1) finish high school; (2) get a full-time job—or have a partner who is employed full-time; and (3) wait until age twenty-one to marry and to have children if children are desired.[2]

Researchers readily acknowledge that other factors are always at play in the equation of impoverishment, but still, the statistics stand: if you graduate from high school, if you find full-time employment, and if you wait until you are twenty-one before marrying and having children, you have a 98 percent chance of steering clear of poverty. And a three-in-four chance of making better than fifty grand a year.

The content of this research is intriguing, but the facts weren't the only thing of interest to me. I was also drawn to the if/then approach.

CONSEQUENTIALLY SPEAKING

What are you sure of? I mean *absolutely, positively* sure of? If pressed, what would you say? Along the way, people have been "sure of" a spouse's love, a child's devotion, a job's security, a house's existence, only to have those assurances dashed by infidelity, irresponsibility, a down market, a fire. We were so sure! And then . . . *poof.* All we were sure of vanished, just like that.

From the earliest days of my relationship with Jesus, I have been captivated by passages of Scripture that lay out things we can know *for sure*. In a world of ambiguity and uncertainty, it is comforting to feel assured. Consider this claim of Jesus that we looked at briefly before: "Truly I tell you, if you have faith as small as a mustard seed, you can say to this mountain, 'Move from here to there,' and it will move. Nothing will be impossible for you" (Matthew 17:20).

If you have faith as small as a mustard seed, *then* you can literally move mountains.

Or how about this one, which I have leaned into during many a vitriolic political season: "If my people, who are called by my name, will humble themselves and pray and seek my face and turn from their wicked ways, then I will hear from heaven, and I will forgive their sin and will heal their land" (2 Chronicles 7:14).

If we will humble ourselves, pray, seek God, and repent, *then* our sin will be forgiven and our land will be healed.

Jesus said this as well in Mark 8:38: "If anyone is ashamed of me and my words in this adulterous and sinful generation, the Son of Man will be ashamed of them when he comes in his Father's glory with the holy angels."

If we are ashamed of Jesus, *then* he will be ashamed of us.

On a brighter note, these two assurances appear: "*If* we confess our sins, [*then*] he is faithful and just and will forgive us our sins and purify us from all unrighteousness" (1 John 1:9, emphasis mine). "[*If*] anyone . . . loves me [and obeys] my teaching . . . [*then*] my Father will love them, and we will come to them and make our home with them" (John 14:23, emphasis mine).

Our relationship with Jesus is far from formulaic, but that doesn't mean that aspects of it can't be anticipated, apprehended, *known*. Our attitudes and actions carry predictable consequences—the if/thens, if you will, of our faith. And as it relates to our topic at hand—becoming *extravagant* as followers of Christ—there is an if/then that ought to stop us in our tracks and make us more thoughtfully consider our days. Here is what Isaiah 58:10 says:

> *If you do away with the yoke of oppression,*
> *with the pointing finger and malicious talk,*
> *and if you spend yourselves in behalf of the hungry*
> *and satisfy the needs of the oppressed,*
> *then your light will rise in the darkness,*
> *and your night will become like the noonday.*

If . . .

If we will do away with oppression and with the blame game and with senseless speech, if we will spend ourselves not on ourselves but on those who are hungry and in pain . . .

. . . *then* . . .

. . . then our light, the light of Christ that lives in us and shines through us, will rise in the darkness, quite literally transforming the bleakest night into high noon.

Staggering, isn't it?

This claim from the prophet Isaiah, spoken on behalf of our great God, is an important one, because hasn't every human ever to walk this big blue planet wondered when the darkness would stop? Enter the power of the if/then. The beauty of the if/then is this: it is when the "if" of our reality starts to become too tough to take that the "then" stands firm, reminding us that our labor is not in vain.

WHEN DARKNESS DESCENDS

For most people, the economic collapse of 2008 was not a fun time. The situation was so devastating that it led to what has been dubbed the Great Recession—to date, the worst financial crisis on record since the Great Depression of the late 1920s. During this decidedly not-great Great Recession, we saw housing prices fall more than 30 percent and an unemployment rate hovering around a staggering 10 percent. The Treasury Department blew a cool $440 billion buying bank and car stocks, more than $180 billion on bailing out global insurance giant AIG, and its reputation guaranteeing more than 27 million high-risk home loans, and yet *still* they couldn't stop what was an absolute freight train intent on barreling down the tracks.

On several occasions that season, I thought back on my childhood in the early 1980s, when another recession had hit. My dad owned his own construction business, and when that economic crisis rolled through our neck of the woods in 1982, he lost everything. Interest rates in his industry climbed toward 20 percent, and Dad could no longer compete.

As I said, my family wasn't exactly rolling in dough before that crisis; when Dad was forced to declare bankruptcy, daily life grew grimmer still. Jobs were scarce. Money was scarce. Household goods were scarce. The only thing we had in abundance was anxiety—anxiety, fear, and despair.

This is how darkness feels: like a life sentence, like a shroud.

This is why the world tells you to rack up as much as you can while you're here, to "make hay while the sun shines," to look out for number one, so that you'll never fall prey to the natural ups and downs of life. "Get while the gettin' is good" is a deeply embedded practice in our society for the simple reason that most people *can conceive of no other approach.* And so we head out there into the world's economy, determined to negotiate our way to the top, buying, selling, trading, producing, working ourselves until we burn out.

The only problem here is that when we reach the top, we realize it's a trash heap we've dutifully climbed.

Which is why, back in 2008, as the financial rug was being yanked from underneath our collective feet, I stood in front of New Life's congregation week after week and compelled them to engage, to serve, to *give.* Spiritual rookies in our midst must have thought I'd lost my mind. "You want us to hand over what little cash we have left? *Now*?"

Yes, that was exactly what I wanted.

And I said so.

Why? Because I knew about that powerful *if/then.*

What was going through my mind then is what races through my mind as I write to you now: extravagance will sometimes be painful, but there is purpose in its pain. What's more, the productive pain of extravagance will *never* rival the unproductive pain of the self-focused life. When we give of ourselves even during dark days of our time and abilities and cash, we declare to the spiritual forces surrounding us that we are in the world's system but not of it. We remind our own feeble hearts and the pressing darkness surrounding us that we worship God—and God, alone. More powerful still, we cast bright beams of light onto that darkness, rendering it impotent, insignificant, incapable of killing our hope.

If we will give toward the eradication of oppression, if we will spend ourselves on behalf of the hungry, if we will satisfy the needs of those who have been marginalized and ostracized and kept down, then our light will rise in the darkness.

Our night will become like noonday, when all is awake, alive, and bright.

> *If we will give.*
> *When it is dark.*
> *To help others step into the light.*
> *Then the darkness surrounding us will dissipate.*
> *Then our hope will come back to life.*

Nice, right? Very poetic, down to my rhyming conclusion. But how do we get it done? Practically speaking, what am I asking for us to do?

STAYING THE COURSE

I'd like to spend the balance of this chapter working through three ultra-practical ways to stay the course of financial extravagance even when darkness descends. Because if your life is anything like mine, darkness *always* descends.

1. Stay Thankful

When I think of the personification of staying thankful, what comes to mind is the face of a single mom in our church, a woman who over the past year has endured loss after agonizing loss. And yet still she praises God. In a staggeringly short period of time, her husband left her, her car died in an unrecoverable sort of way, and her home was found to be infested with black mold. Everything had to go: the furniture, the window coverings, the bedding—everything.

She had no money for replacement goods, let alone the rental to put them in, and so one afternoon recently an army of volunteers from our church descended on her with piles and piles of donated furniture, sheets, blankets, dishes, clothes, the whole works. That team funded six months' worth of an apartment, enough to give her time to get back on her feet. They painted her new place. They helped her assemble and arrange her furniture. And they stocked her refrigerator full.

When one of the other pastors on staff told me about this little get-together, I was moved by the team's generosity. Of course I was. They had given much to help this woman begin to put her life back together again, and I knew that her life had been changed that day. More moving still? The woman who had been helped was sincerely and soulishly joyful *long before that assistance arrived.*

As our pastoral team worked to assess her situation and get their arms around the magnitude of all she'd been through, they were struck by how genuinely *happy* she was, by the delighted expression on her face.

Delighted?

When everything was going wrong?

Madame Blueberry from *VeggieTales* had it right: "A thankful heart is a happy heart," and this woman was living proof.

Yet I got called on this principle on a cold winter's day last year.

It was Thursday afternoon, and I'd just put the finishing touches on my sermon for the weekend. I was ahead of schedule, so I was feeling pretty good about myself. I was going to *nail* this message.

Clouds rolled in just then, which prompted me to check the afternoon forecast; and when I got to the weather app, I noticed a storm alert. On the little box with Sunday's expected weather, there was a line of red text: "Blizzard warning," it read.

By way of context, whenever there is a blizzard warning in Colorado Springs, people heed it. They heed it because it's usually correct. I know that weather people get a bad rap for never accurately predicting the weather, but here in the mountains they're right. When people heed a blizzard warning on Sunday morning, this translates to their *not coming to church.* And when they don't come to church, our giving is down by half. Yes, those stay-homers could give online, but most forget to do so.

Also, by way of context, we were in a bit of a budget crunch— nothing serious, but a trend I was paying attention to. We needed each week's giving to keep the (rather large) commitments we'd made.

As I took in the warning, a sense of entitlement filled my thoughts. A blizzard was fine. A Monday blizzard, a Tuesday blizzard, a Wednesday blizzard . . . heck, even a Saturday blizzard I could deal with. But a blizzard on Sunday morning? Couldn't God do something about that?

As ridiculous as it now seems, I prayed this prayer to God: "Lord, please make it not snow on Sunday. Please have this warning canceled."

I stood there in my office for a few beats, wondering if God had heard what I said. Then, in a wave, this thought came and settled on my mind: *Brady, I'm curious: Where is the gratitude for the ways I've shown up for you this week? You've had a busy week, and I have sustained you. You were tangled up in your thoughts regarding your sermon, and I gave you clarity of mind. You were struggling in a few relationships, and I showed you creative ways forward in them all. You're wondering if I heard what you said? I'm wondering if you saw that I did!*

Humbled, I sat down, reached for my phone, and pulled up Philippians chapter 4. "Rejoice in the LORD always," I read. "I will say it again: Rejoice! Let your gentleness be evident to all. The LORD is near. Do not be anxious about anything, but in every situation, by prayer and petition, with thanksgiving, present your requests to God. And the peace of God, which transcends all understanding, will guard your hearts and minds in Christ Jesus" (v. 4–7).

Rejoice in the Lord always.

Even when the storm clouds are gathering.

Even when the warnings are posted.

Even when the blizzard howls, as it did that Sunday at dawn.

Rejoice in the Lord always.

When life is running smoothly and also when bumps abound.

When everyone's getting along and when misunderstandings hurt hearts.

When all is as it should be and when nothing at all makes sense.

That single mom I mentioned had caught this vision. Rejoice! *No matter what.*

Rejoice! Why? Because it is by rejoicing in God that we give him entry into our minds and hearts. It is that posture of worship that protects the essence of who we are. The word "guard" at the end of the passage in Philippians means to referee. When we rejoice always, when we stay thankful, we essentially place a divine ref at the door of our heart and tell him, "Only peace may come in."

Of all the things the enemy has been able to counterfeit, happiness and fulfillment and joy, he has come up with no counterfeit for peace. There is no substitution for peace; it is found nowhere but in God alone.

The peace of God, which transcends all understanding, comes to us by way of our choice to rejoice.

Rejoice. Always. Rejoice in the Lord and you will find peace. The darkness will not overtake you, because you've rooted yourself in the light.

That Sunday morning, when the wind was blowing five feet of fallen snow all over the place and the temperature strained to get above two below, I lay in bed, thinking, *Lord, I'm so thankful this morning. I'm thankful for your grace, that's as pure as all this snow. I'm thankful to you*

for New Life and for the fact that later this morning I will get to worship
you with that congregation of people who are just wildly devoted to you.
I trust that you will work in and through all of us today, and for that I am
thankful. I love you, Father. Amen.

As it relates to our finances, we will benefit greatly from choosing gratitude instead of despair. If you're like me, then financial security has come and gone and come again along the way. A job layoff, a loved one's illness, needing to fund a kid's education—everyone has a few seasons when money is more than tight. The question isn't whether we'll face them; the question is how we'll respond.

My encouragement to you and me both is to come to these seasons with thanks on our lips for the faithfulness of God to that point. We can trust him today because we know he was faithful yesterday and because we know that God does not change. "He who did not spare his own Son, but gave him up for us all—how will he not also, along with him [Jesus], graciously give us all things?" Romans 8:32 says.

We thank God even during dark times because he is the giver of all good things. We thank him because a grateful heart really is a happy heart, and only happy hearts are prompted to serve. Have you ever stopped to consider that truth? When you are stuck in despair's awful cycle, how likely are *you* to serve? No, nine times out of ten, the person who joyfully gives, joyfully serves, joyfully pauses to assess someone's need, is a person with a happy heart. Gratitude will get you to happiness. Stay thankful—that's the first practice.

2. Stick Together

When I was a kid, my family lived across the street from where my dad's brother and his wife lived. This was common where I grew up, family all living in the same zip code, and as far as I was concerned, Aunt Sybil was about as good as life got. I'm sure she had many fine qualities, but the one that was most relevant to me—a growing boy with a massive appetite—was her expertise in the kitchen. That woman could make some *mean* chicken and dumplings, and whenever I heard through the screen doors dividing their house and ours the sound of pots and pans banging around, I was over there in a flash. There was nothing better than the sound of Aunt Sybil saying, "You hungry, hon?" and the smell of salty roasted chicken and pie crust turning golden brown.

I would tug a chair from underneath Aunt Sybil's wooden kitchen table, sit down, and reflexively lick my lips. From the moment that first scoop of peas and hot-water corn bread reached my plate, it was never empty again. I would get to the last few bites of a serving, and here would come Aunt Sybil again. " 'Nothah spoonful, hon?" she'd ask, even as the next serving had already made its way to my plate. I would eat and eat and eat until I could not eat a single bite more.

Aunt Sybil is gone now, but the legacy she left lives on. Anyone's hunger was her own hunger, and she was determined to feed you full.

When you read the accounts of the early church, this same spirit was at work. Anyone's need was everyone's need, and they didn't quit until those needs were met. If you had been watching New Life following the tragic murders we endured in December 2007 by an armed gunman who walked through our children's wing following a Sunday morning worship service, you would have assumed our destiny was to become a used-car lot at best. Who would want to stay at a church where people got killed for worshipping God?

But we didn't become a used-car lot. Far from it. Our best days were on the other side of that shooting. And the reason we were able to experience them is because enough of us came together, sharing our resources and also our hope, and chose to stay and serve. It was dark. It was hard. It was exhausting. But the results of those particular labors are some of the sweetest fruit we've known.

When the darkness of self-interest or self-importance or rampant materialism or stinginess or greed or fear shows up, one of the surest ways to dispel it is to refuse to go it alone. We are better together, especially when skies turn gray. My weakness needs your sturdy strength as much as your weakness sometimes needs mine.

My poverty may be crying out for your resources today, as yours cried out for mine last week.

We need each other—that's my point here. We're brighter together than we are apart.

3. Trust the Flow

A third practice, on days when you need an injection of hope: *Trust abundance's flow.*

I came across a secular book on money not long ago that was written for an undoubtedly secular audience. The author had been on Oprah's show and had sold more than a million copies seemingly overnight. I thought I'd have a look. In the book, the author asserted some pretty profound ideas about how abundance tends to flow back to people who give what they have away—about how givers actually *attract* abundance into their lives.

I kept reading this book, thinking, *Yes! The world is catching on to what God has been promoting all along.*

Here's how God says it, in his Word: "Give away your life; you'll find life given back, but not merely given back—given back with bonus and blessing. Giving, not getting, is the way. Generosity begets generosity" (Luke 6:38 [MSG]).

Generosity begets generosity.

Abundance begets abundance.

Blessing begets blessing.

This is the flow that we can trust.

Now, we should be quick to acknowledge that we don't always attract the exact "abundance" we're after. If we give only to get, we will be disappointed every time. Yes, as we saw before, God promises through his prophet Malachi that when we give, he (God) will "throw open the floodgates of heaven and pour out so much blessing that there will not be room enough to store it" (Malachi 3:10). But how might that "blessing" show up?

Would you count it a blessing if your heart were more devoted to God?

Would you count it a blessing if someone had a need you were able to meet?

Would you count it a blessing if you were handed a bonus at work and then a divine prompting to give it away?

You see, when we broaden our understanding of God's blessings and how they come to us, we see clearly that we are indeed *blessed.* And then when we faithfully give of *all we have,* God passes more and more things our way.

There is a reason we incorporate the giving of tithes and offerings into the worship portion of our services at New Life, and it's this: giving *is* worship. When we return to God the finances he has entrusted to us, we are saying, in essence, "God, I know that you are searching the earth for generous people and that, as I'm faithful to be generous, you will be faithful to bless me. However that blessing shows up, I am grateful. I treasure *all* of your blessings, God."

One of the most liberating moments in the life of a believer is the moment when he or she says, "God, I trust you with everything, for everything, and in spite of everything. You hold all of life together, and so I trust you with all my life."

In his letter to the believers at Corinth, the apostle Paul exhorted them to finish strong as it related to their financial giving. He wrote:

> And now, brothers and sisters, we want you to know about the grace that God has given the Macedonian churches. In the midst of a very severe trial, their overflowing joy and their extreme poverty welled up in rich generosity. For I testify that they gave as much as they were able, and even beyond their ability. Entirely on their own, they urgently pleaded with us for the privilege of

sharing in this service to the Lord's people. And they exceeded our expectations:

They gave themselves first of all to the Lord, and then by the will of God also to us.

So we urged Titus, just as he had earlier made a beginning, to bring also to completion this act of grace on your part. But since you excel in everything—in faith, in speech, in knowledge, in complete earnestness and in the love we have kindled in you—see that you also excel in this grace of giving.

I am not commanding you, but I want to test the sincerity of your love by comparing it with the earnestness of others. For you know the grace of our Lord Jesus Christ, that though he was rich, yet for your sake became poor, so that you through his poverty might become rich.

And here is my judgment about what is best for you in this matter. Last year you were the first not only to give but also to have the desire to do so. Now finish the work, so that your eager willingness to do it may be matched by your completion of it, according to your means. For if the willingness is there, the gift is acceptable according to what one has, not according to what one does not have.

Our desire is not that others might be relieved while you are hard pressed, but that there might be equality. At the present time your plenty will supply what they need, so that in turn their plenty will supply what you need. The goal is equality, as it is written: "The one who gathered much did not have too much, and the one who gathered little did not have too little" (2 Corinthians 8:1–15).

Did you catch that? Those Paul esteems count it a *privilege* to share in service to God's people! Why? Because they had caught the idea of community, the idea that our plenty can supply each other's need, if we'll let it . . . that impoverishment does not need to have its way.

"Since you excel in everything . . . see that you also excel in this grace of giving," Paul wrote (v. 7).

Man, do I ever want that to be said about me.

No matter what else I excel at in this earthly existence, I pray I'm a *giver* at heart.

I wonder if that's true for you too.

You might be an *excellent* salesperson.

Or an *excellent* writer.

Or an *excellent* doctor.

Or an *excellent* parent.

An *excellent* artist or teacher.

An *excellent* fund-raiser or personal trainer.

Excellent at *a million and one* different things.

But if you're not excellent in this grace of giving, are you excellent at anything at all?

In another of his epistles, Paul prayed for a local church—and also for us—that they would know "the riches of his [God's] glorious inheritance in his holy people, and his incomparably great power for us who believe. That power is the same as the mighty strength he exerted when he raised Christ from the dead and seated him at his right hand in the heavenly realms, far above all rule and authority, power and dominion, and every name that is invoked, not only in the present age but also in the one to come" (Ephesians 1:18–21).

The riches we crave in our heart of hearts? They can't be measured in dollars and cents. We give—extravagantly so—because we understand that the most powerful among us are those who have surrendered to Christ.

We spend ourselves fully on this mission of God's because we know there's no better use for a life.

We offer ourselves to those in need because we are compelled to be light and love.

We stand strong despite the enemy's fiercest attacks because that battle? It's already been won.

◇◇

Pushing Pause: Chapter 10

Peace. If there is one thing we're after, it's that. We long for peace in our heart. We long for peace in our relationships. We long for peace in our finances. We long for peace in our world. But where is true peace found? According to the apostle Paul, it is found only in the context of our walk with God.

Read

The peace we crave, the peace that is *beyond* us, can be ours. In Philippians chapter 4, Paul reminds us how to obtain such peace. "Rejoice in the Lord always. I will say it again: Rejoice! Let your gentleness be evident to all. The Lord is near. Do not be anxious about anything, but in every situation, by prayer and petition, with thanksgiving, present your requests to God. And the peace of God, which transcends all understanding, will guard your hearts and minds in Christ Jesus" (v. 4–7).

Reflect

- Which of the five predecessors to experiencing the peace of God do you find most challenging to uphold: rejoicing, practicing gentleness, refusing to be anxious, maintaining a spirit of gratitude, or presenting your requests to God in prayer? Why?
- How does your answer to the previous question impact your willingness to practice extravagant—even *dangerous*—generosity?

Respond

The challenge for this chapter: *Pursue peace.* When anything else threatens to enter your mind or heart today, tell the divine referee inside of you to shut the door. Employ those Philippians 4 traits you read about above with great intention and intensity.

Be gentle with those you come across.

Be grateful for the blessings in your life.

Pray before fretting.

Pray before speaking.

Pray before doing *anything* else.

Make your requests known to God, and let the first one be "Come, Holy Spirit. Empower me to serve you today."

Conclusion

Resolutions of the Extravagant Life

The cautious faith that never saws off a limb on which it is sitting, never learns that unattached limbs may find strange unaccountable ways of not falling.

DALLAS WILLARD

A T THE OUTSET I told you that my inspiration for writing this book came from noticing and then studying a portion of our church's congregation marked by a spirit of generosity, service, and love—the *extravagant* in our midst. And what I've tried to do in the preceding chapters is lay out what they do, why they do it, how they do it, and the results they experience from practicing this sort of extravagance not just from time to time but *habitually* throughout the course of their days.

As I sit here with these people in mind, their impressive legacies of goodness and others-centeredness in plain view, I am reminded that before all the noble gestures were offered, before all the acts of selfless service were taken, before all the sizable checks were written, there was this: a simple decision to live like God asks for his people to live.

That's it.

They surveyed the state of our world today and said, "I can't fix every problem, but by God's grace I can fix the selfishness that threatens to rule my heart."

They decided—willfully—that no matter what it took, if nothing else was said of them when their earthly existence was all said and done, they would be known as generous people . . . as extravagant . . . as no-holds-barred lovers of God.

"I just decided . . .": that's the language they've used with me. "I put a stake in the ground and said, 'This is who I'm going to be . . .'"

A decision.

A stake in the ground.

A choice.

That's where this journey began for each one of them. And it's where it can begin for you.

When I started poking around the "decision" these women and men had made, something of a progression began to emerge—and it was essentially the same progression every time. First was declaring a specific posture of the heart; next came the decision to act on that posture; and finally the installment of a sustainability plan, a means for loving and serving well over the long haul.

I began referring to these three elements as "resolutions," three conscious and deliberate choices these extravagant people made. As our time together draws to a close, I'd like to share them with you.

RESOLUTION 1: "I CHOOSE HUMILITY"

Is there a more challenging character trait to pin down than humility? The moment you try to become a bit humbler, you're probably puffed up with striving again!

During a visit with Eugene H. Peterson, author of *The Message: The Bible in Contemporary Language*, in Kalispell, Montana, my colleague Daniel and I tried in vain to get him to talk about a recent trip he'd had to spend a few days with the rock legend Bono. We'd heard through the grapevine that Bono had sent his private jet to pick up Eugene and that the red-carpet treatment only grew from there. Eugene suggested that Daniel and I join him at a little café in town for lunch. I remember looking across the table and seeing—really seeing—Eugene, who was quietly and slowly taking spoonful after spoonful from his bowl of potato soup.

Such brilliance in that man's mind. Such prowess. Such expertise. Add to this his mounting star-studded experiences, and his celebrity soared higher still. And yet there he was, eating a bowl of plain potato soup in a no-frills diner on the outskirts of a tiny Montana town. And *enjoying* it nonetheless.

That image of Eugene was seared in my mind as humility personified. He wasn't *trying* to be humble. Humble is just who he was. Humble, gentle, steady, grateful . . . these words easily come to mind. "Took me sixty-five years to be an overnight success," he always said of himself. Made me grin every time.

Now contrast that picture with the person who swears that nobody "gets" how great they are. They plow through life utterly stunned by the fact that people don't appreciate their genius, that the world has yet to see just how special they truly are. "Vain conceit," Paul calls it in the book of Philippians.[1] It's humility, stripped of itself.

It's foolhardy, to say the least.

The extravagant ones I've known? They prefer that God, alone, gets the glory, for anything good in their life.

Let that sink in for a moment.

They don't merely tolerate God getting the glory; they *long* for that state of affairs. They long to hide themselves under their Father's strong wing, invisible to the watching world.

This concept of hiding ourselves intentionally is so foreign to us today that our brains can barely make sense of it. Stay hidden? Stay obscured? For how long?

Forever.

For always.

Every day.

Glory to God.

Later in that same chapter of Philippians where Paul talks about vain conceit, he paints a vivid and quite shocking picture of the kind of humility we're to offer those around us in the world, and if you're anything like me, his words leave you sobered and undone. "In your relationships with one another," he wrote, "have the same mindset as Christ Jesus:

> *who, being in very nature God,*
>> *did not consider equality with God something to*
>> *be used to his own advantage;*
> *rather, he made himself nothing*
>> *by taking the very nature of a servant,*
>> *being made in human likeness.*
> *And being found in appearance as a man,*
>> *he humbled himself*
>> *by becoming obedient to death—*
>> *even death on a cross!*
>
> *Therefore God exalted him to the highest place*
>> *and gave him the name that is above every name,*
> *that at the name of Jesus every knee should bow,*
>> *in heaven and on earth and under the earth,*
> *and every tongue acknowledge that Jesus Christ is Lord,*
>> *to the glory of God the Father (v. 5–11).*

The "quite shocking" thing about this passage isn't that Jesus behaved well, even when the stakes were high. He's Jesus. He always behaves well. He always chooses wisely. He always does the right thing.

No, the shocking thing here is that Paul—and, by extension, God, who inspired Paul to write the letter—thinks that you and I can "have the same mindset" as Jesus did . . . that we can be humble, just like him.

Think of it: no more striving to be "in." No more straining for recognition. No more fixating on number of likes. Can you imagine such a reality? Can you see yourself in it? The extravagant ones I know surely can.

"I choose humility," they say. And with that singular resolution made, the most useful of courses is set.

RESOLUTION 2: "I CHOOSE GENEROSITY"

My daughter, Callie, and I spent a few days alone in the mountains this summer, just an eighteen-year-old and her dad. She and her brother were about to move into an apartment together, their first time living outside of our house, and I thought it would be wise to have a few unhurried conversations before she got too far down the road of adulthood. This getaway would afford us that time.

Callie has always been frugal and responsible in terms of her spending habits, and yet, as I alluded to earlier, she's still getting her arms around all that a generous life entails. During a leisurely hike one afternoon, Callie explained that she had saved several thousand dollars from her paychecks over the past couple of years and was "feeling pretty good" about things. I complimented her on her financial win and then shifted gears to ask her if she understood the power that money possessed.

"I think so," she said. "I mean, I know that it's a critical part of life . . ."

Callie had been working on her budget for several months and was starting to catch her stride. "I'm definitely going to keep giving 10 percent to the church," she said, reflecting on the habits she'd forged, "and

I'm only putting 10 percent into savings right now, but I'm planning to bump that up to 20 . . ."

I said, "Callie, if you can live on 70 percent of your income for the rest of your life, you will be one wealthy woman."

Then I asked her this question: "Callie, what will you do with all that wealth you've accumulated? How will you spend those funds?"

Given the pervasiveness of this line of thinking among Callie's generation, what she said next should have come as no surprise to me. "Dad," she said, "I want to live my best life."

I wasn't sure what that meant, so I asked.

Callie wasn't entirely sure how to respond. She tried out some possibilities: "Adventure, maybe? Or freedom? Happiness? I like to travel . . ."

Nothing wrong with those things, I suppose, except that the center of them all was *self.* "Let me come at it from this angle," I said to my daughter. "If we were focused on 'winning' in the kingdom of earth, then those strategies would work just fine. But remember, the reality we inhabit is the kingdom of heaven . . . and there things are upside down."

Callie and I talked about how, from God's perspective, the "best life" we can live is the life that's surrendered to him. "Living our best life," for believers, means completely laying that life down for God—loving the people he says to love, serving the people he says to serve, caring for the people he says need care, and doing it all for his glory, not ours.

I put an arm around my kid and said, "Callie, I know it seems like those things will add up to your 'best life,' but at some point you're going to realize that you'll never be able to take enough trips to fill the void in your heart."

I reminded Callie that her mom and I have been to dozens of countries, enjoyed lavish vacations, and invested significant money and time in seeing some of the most incredible parts of this world, and yet those experiences—as terrific as they were—could not ground our marriage or give us as a couple the fulfillment that we craved.

Callie nodded. She knew I was telling the truth.

Likewise, even though it's so ridiculously hard to admit it, that new car we're eyeing can't fill the void. The dream house we're building can't fill the void. The promotion at work, as amazing as it would be, cannot fill the void. The void only gets filled by surrendering to God all that he has entrusted to us.

"This approach to life has killed my idea of what's 'mine'"—that's how one extravagant friend of mine described it. We can be generous with *all* that we find in our hands, knowing that they've been placed there to bless others' lives.

RESOLUTION 3: "I CHOOSE TO BE SUSTAINED BY GOD"

"I choose humility."

"I choose generosity."

And then there is resolution number three: "I choose to be sustained by God."

When I was twenty-seven years old, still stuffed full with ambition and hard-core people-pleasing tendencies, a mentor-friend of mine named Garvin invited me to breakfast. I can still envision the sticky vinyl-covered booth where we were sitting, in the corner of one of Amarillo's two IHOP restaurants, the smell of maple syrup clouding my thoughts.

By way of context, I'll mention that at that point in my life I had taken my college patterns of overachievement and overwork (in addition to carrying a full class load, I also worked three part-time jobs) right into adulthood. I said yes to more opportunities than was prudent, I insisted on excellence in all that I did, and I measured my success in terms of busyness. It was a dangerous way to live. "You can't keep doing all that!" Pam would declare, night after night. (She tells me that still, today.)

As we ate our meal, Garvin and I spent several minutes catching up on each other's lives. Then Garvin looked at me with characteristic compassion and said, "Brady, I see how hard you're working, how hard you are pushing yourself..."

I nodded, pleased that he'd noticed.

"And there's something I feel compelled to tell you. *You don't have to earn your way.*"

Suddenly my neck felt hot. I wasn't sure I liked where this conversation was going. My strategy *centered* on earning my way.

"Brady," Garvin continued, "self-appointed people have to be self-sustaining people. And self-sustaining people have zero use for God."

In a flash, the restaurant around us disappeared. The people at nearby tables disappeared. The stack of pancakes in front of me disappeared. All that existed was the sentiment Garvin had courageously conveyed.

Self-appointed people have to be self-sustaining people, and self-sustaining people have zero use for God.

I was trapped by the truth of those words. Somewhere along the way, I'd abandoned my need for God. The One for whom I was doing all this work, the One for whom I'd been exerting all this tireless effort— that same One I'd sidelined with an apathetic shrug. *Thanks, God, but I'll take it from here.*

I drove away from that meeting with Garvin with the words of Philippians 1:4–6 flooding my mind: "In all my prayers for all of you," the apostle Paul wrote to the believers at Philippi, "I always pray with joy because of your partnership in the gospel from the first day until now, being confident of this, that he who began a good work in you will carry it on to completion until the day of Christ Jesus."

As well as the words of Romans 8:32: "He who did not spare his own Son, but gave him up for us all—how will he not also, along with him, graciously give us all things?"

And also Philippians 4:19: "And my God will meet all your needs according to the riches of his glory in Christ Jesus."

I hadn't meant to refuse God's provision, but it was clear to me that I had.

The memory of that breakfast meeting more than two decades ago is as sharp in my mind as memories of last week. And the clarity of Garvin's statement helps me choose wisely still today. I can either barrel through this earthly existence, forcing outcomes and demanding my way, or I can slow down and pay close attention to where God has asked me to be.

Where has God appointed me?

What assignments has he given me to do?

Where are people flourishing, simply because I am there?

Where he has placed me, he will sustain me. His provision for me there will abound.

Those who live lives of extravagance have caught the truth of this idea. They don't push or force or insist or demand. They pause. They look. They think. They pray. They patiently wait on God.

Then, when God says go, they go in full confidence that they're right where they're supposed to be.

I think of Jesus' reminder to his disciples just before he ascended back to his heavenly home. Those disciples, you'll recall, craved Jesus' bodily presence, but Jesus had something better in mind. He told them that his gift to them wasn't merely his *person* but rather his unparalleled supernatural *power*. He then laid his hands on them and commissioned them to go and do important work on his behalf. The effects of those labors would be significant, we learn from Mark's gospel: "In my name," Jesus said, "they will drive out demons; they will speak in new tongues; they will pick up snakes with their hands; and when they drink deadly poison, it will not hurt them at all; they will place their hands on sick people, and they will get well" (Mark 16:17–18).

Did you catch the confidence in those verbs?

They *will* . . .

They *will* . . .

They *will* . . .

When you and I look to God for our provision, we *will* see the needs around us. We *will* long to be of help. We *will* find strength to offer our service. We *will* accomplish noble work. If there were a fourth resolution, that would be it:

"I will be humble."

"I will be generous."

"I will be sustained by God."

And by my heavenly Father's power and faithful provision, *I will accomplish good work.*

THE PARABLE TOLD ABOUT YOU

Have you ever wondered what Jesus would say if he told a parable about you? What would the moral of *your* story be? What might people learn from *your* plot?

You're climbing into your car to leave church one Sunday morning, perhaps, when you see a man writhing in pain on the side of the road. *Does anyone else see that guy?* you wonder. *Hasn't anyone thought to call 911?*

You look around the parking lot and see streams of cars heading various ways. On all sides people pass the man, who is clearly in pain. Don't they see him? Don't they care?

You've got one leg in your car already, and you really need to get going. Tomorrow's going to be a bear if you don't tend to some things today. You're hungry. You're antsy. The big game will be on in an hour. So many reasons to just carry on. But that guy . . . he's still there, in pain.

"That guy" is your neighbor who needs a ride to work.

"That guy" is the single mom who asks you to cover her shift.

"That guy" is the little girl living on your street whose dad has fled the scene.

"That guy" is the longtime friend who is battling clinical depression.

"That guy" is the business associate who always drinks a little too much.

"That guy" is the acquaintance you bump into who is quick to explain away the bruises on her face.

"That guy" is *any* of the nearly 8 billion people alive today, who need help—perhaps from you . . . perhaps from me. The question isn't whether there are needs to meet but rather if we'll be found available to meet them.

Will we pause?

Or will we pass by?

Will we lean in or look away?

I've resolved in my heart to look after the ones God places along my life's path. In humility I will see them as the prized creations they truly are. In generosity I will serve them the best that I know how. By faith I will give of the resources I have, trusting God's promise of abundance for me. I will accomplish good work, each and every day, not for my sake but for God's sake—and God's sake, alone.

I will follow the path of extravagance wherever it leads me, whatever it takes.

Now it's your turn.

What will you do?

Acknowledgments

THIS BOOK TOOK A lifetime to write. I am so thankful for the generous people who have marked my life.

Pam, you are the most generous person I know. You challenge me daily to be a better man. You are my best friend.

Abram and Callie, you are remarkable in every way. You are both strong, fearless, and generous. My love for you knows no limits.

Ashley, thanks for your hard work on this project. You are relentless, kind, and a joy to work alongside.

New Life Church, you serve selflessly and love joyously. I love being your pastor and serving our city by your side.

Notes

NOTE: All Scriptures are from the New International Version (NIV) unless otherwise noted.

Book Epigraph
1. Hebrews 10:23–25.

Introduction: Give and Take
1. The United Nations Food and Agriculture Organization (FAO) estimates that about 815 million people of the 7.6 billion people in the world, or 10.7 percent, were suffering from chronic undernourishment in 2016. Almost all the hungry people live in lower-middle-income countries. There are 11 million people undernourished in developed countries. See https://www.worldhunger.org/world-hunger-and-poverty-facts-and-statistics/ for more information.
2. Craig L. Blomberg, *Interpreting the Parables*, Second Edition (Downers Grove, IL: InterVarsity, 1990), 36.
3. Ibid., 43.
4. Kris Vallotton, *Poverty, Riches & Wealth: Moving from a Life of Lack into True Kingdom Abundance* (Bloomington, MN: Chosen Books, 2018), 42.
5. Alicia Britt Chole, *Anonymous: Jesus' Hidden Years . . . and Yours* (Nashville: Thomas Nelson, 2006), 61.
6. Christian Smith and Hilary Davidson, *The Paradox of Generosity: By Giving We Receive, by Grasping We Lose* (New York: Oxford University Press, 2014), 1.
7. Warren W. Wiersbe, "Mid-life Crisis? Bah, Humbug!," *Christianity Today*, May 21, 1982, https://www.christianitytoday.com/ct/1982/may-21/mid-life-crisis-bah-humbug.html.

8. A. W. Tozer, *The Wisdom of God: Letting His Truth and Goodness Guide Your Steps* (Grand Rapids, MI: Bethany House Publishers, 2017), 57.

9. "Volunteering in the U.S.—2015," Bureau of Labor Statistics news release, February 25, 2016, https://www.bls.gov/news.release/pdf/volun.pdf.

10. Jayson D. Bradley, "Church Giving Statistics, 2019 Edition," Pushpay, July 18, 2018, https://pushpay.com/blog/church-giving-statistics/.

11. Barna Group, "By the Numbers: Growth & Decline of the Church," National Black Robe Regiment, April 9, 2015, http://nationalblackrobe regiment.com/shocking-statistics-church-decline/.

12. Michelle Castillo, "Americans Will Spend More Than $60 Billion on Their Pets This Year," NBC News, July 12, 2015, https://www.nbcnews.com /business/consumer/americans-will-spend-more-60-billion-their-pets -year-n390181.

13. "Hunger a Harsh Reality for 14 Million Children Nationwide," Anne E. Casey Foundation, April 2, 2018, https://www.aecf.org/blog/hunger -a-harsh-reality-for-14-million-children-nationwide/?msclkid=9daed7fa9 fa618df176f8b07cef05133&utm_source=bing&utm_medium=cpc&utm _campaign=AECF%20Site&utm_term=children%20go%20to%20bed %20hungry&utm_content=Child%20Hunger/.

14. Maurie Backman, "Here's What the Average American Spends on Restaurants and Takeout," *Motley Fool*, January 1, 1017 (updated October 3, 2018), https://www.fool.com/retirement/2017/01/01/heres-what-the-average -american-spends-on-restaura.aspx.

15. "State of Homelessness," National Alliance to End Homelessness, n.d., https://endhomelessness.org/homelessness-in-america/homelessness -statistics/state-of-homelessness-report/.

16. Laura Entis, "Chronic Loneliness Is a Modern-Day Epidemic," *Fortune*, June 22, 2016, http://fortune.com/2016/06/22/loneliness-is-a-modern -day-epidemic/.

17. Chole, *Anonymous*, 135.

18. Depending on who you talk to, you will get a different total. Parables can be full-blown stories or else short, pithy quotes. One scholar counts as many as forty-six parables in all. I use forty as a decent estimate.

19. Dietrich Bonhoeffer, *The Cost of Discipleship* (New York: Touchstone, 1995), 116.

20. Archimandrite Sergius (Bowyer), *Acquiring the Mind of Christ: Embracing the Vision of the Orthodox Church* (Waymart, PA: St. Tikhon's Monastery Press, 2015), 7.

PART ONE: YOUR MISSION

Chapter 1: Life, and Where It's Found

1. Randy Alcorn, *The Treasure Principle: Unlocking the Secret of Joyful Giving* (Colorado Springs, CO: Multnomah Books, 2001), 45.
2. Amended from the chapter titled "Nothing Stays in Vegas" in Gretchen Rubin's fantastic book *Better Than Before: Mastering the Habit of Our Everyday Lives* (New York: Crown, 2015).
3. "Ian Maclaren: Quotes: Quotable Quote," Goodreads, n.d., https://www .goodreads.com/quotes/436360-be-kind-for-everyone-you-meet-is -fighting-a-hard.
4. For the full story, see Joshua 13 to 19.
5. See Proverbs 23:10–11.

Chapter 2: On Interruptibility

1. Robby Dawkins, *Do What Jesus Did: A Real-Life Field Guide to Healing the Sick, Routing Demons and Changing Lives Forever* (Bloomington, MN: Chosen Books, 2013), 27.
2. Robert Morris, *The Blessed Life: Unlocking the Rewards of Generous Living* (Bloomington, MN: Bethany House, 2016), Kindle edition, location 156.
3. Ken Blanchard and S. Truett Cathy, *The Generosity Factor: Discover the Joy of Giving Your Time, Talent, and Treasures* (Grand Rapids, MI: Zondervan, 2002), 60.
4. Gretchen Rubin, *Better Than Before: What I Learned About Making and Breaking Habits—to Sleep More, Quit Sugar, Procrastinate Less, and Generally Build a Happier Life* (New York: Crown/Archetype, 2015), 6.
5. Abhijit Banerjee and Esther Duflo, *Poor Economics: A Radical Rethinking of the Way to Fight Global Poverty* (New York: PublicAffairs, 2011), 194.
6. Emphasis mine.
7. See Malachi 3:10.
8. See Acts 20:35.
9. See Proverbs 21:26.
10. See Proverbs 22:9; Luke 6:38.
11. See Matthew 5:37.
12. Genesis 22:1.

Chapter 3: The Five Fears

1. Steve Allocca, "The Age of Convenience: It's More Than We Can Afford," *Forbes*, March 12, 2018, https://www.forbes.com/sites/forbesfinance council/2018/03/12/the-age-of-convenience-its-more-than-we-can -afford/#537532a0735e.
2. Melanie Curtin, "Are You on Your Phone Too Much? The Average Person Spends This Many Hours on It Every Day," *Inc.*, October 30, 2018, https:// www.inc.com/melanie-curtin/are-you-on-your-phone-too-much -average-person-spends-this-many-hours-on-it-every-day.html.
3. Scriptures from Luke 10:33–35, The Message (MSG).
4. Luke 10:36 (MSG).
5. Luke 10:37 (MSG).
6. Robert J. Brown, *You Can't Go Wrong Doing Right: How a Child of Poverty Rose to the White House and Helped Change the World* (New York: Convergent Books, 2019), 11.
7. D'Vera Cohn and Rich Morin, "Who Moves? Who Stays Put? Where's Home?," Pew Research Center, December 17, 2008 (updated December 29, 2008), https://www.pewsocialtrends.org/2008/12/17/who-moves -who-stays-put-wheres-home/.
8. Sally Kohn, *The Opposite of Hate: A Field Guide for Repairing Our Humanity* (Chapel Hill, NC: Algonquin Books, 2018), 85.
9. Hope Schreiber, "Young Man Asks Widow Eating Alone to Join Him: 'This Woman Changed My Outlook on Life,'" Yahoo! Lifestyle, April 23, 2019, https://www.yahoo.com/lifestyle/men-ask-widow-to-share-a-meal-and -the-internet-believes-it-shows-true-compassion-132549254.html.
10. Lidia Yuknavitch, *The Misfit's Manifesto* (New York: TED Books, 2017), 4.
11. Greg Paul, *The Twenty-Piece Shuffle: Why the Poor and Rich Need Each Other* (Colorado Springs, CO: David C. Cook, 2008), 41.
12. Ibid., 43.
13. Ibid., 44.

Chapter 4: Unclenching the Fist

1. Henri J. M. Nouwen. *Here and Now* (New York: Crossroad Publishing, 1994).
2. Michelle Swenson and Crystal Starkey, "Taking Care of Each Other at Pikes Peak Atheists and Pikes Peak Atheist Families," Foundation Be-

yond Belief, March 20, 2015, https://foundationbeyondbelief.org/news /taking-care-pikes-peak-atheists-pikes-peak-atheist-families/.

3. Jon Egan, "Here in Your Presence" (release date December 26, 2006), New Life Worship, n.d., https://genius.com/New-life-worship-here-in -your-presence-lyrics.

4. Phakchok Rinpoche and Erric Solomon, *Radically Happy: A User's Guide to the Mind* (Boulder, CO: Shambhala, 2018), 47.

Chapter 5: What We Mean When We Say "All"

1. John Owen, *Communion with God* (n.p.: Bibliotech Press, 2020), 110.

2. Acts 2:3.

3. Jen Pollack Michel, *Teach Us to Want: Longing, Ambition, and the Life of Faith* (Downers Grove, IL: InterVarsity, 2014), 29.

4. Alcorn, p. 57.

5. James Orbinski, *An Imperfect Offering: Humanitarian Action for the Twenty-First Century* (New York: Walker Publishing, 2008), 7.

6. Michelle Schmidt, *Carried: How One Mother's Trust in God Helped Her Through the Unthinkable* (Salt Lake City: Deseret, 2018), 9.

7. Alicia Britt Chole, *Anonymous: Jesus' Hidden Years . . . and Yours* (Nashville: Thomas Nelson, 2006), 150.

8. Access the fuller story here: https://www.washingtonpost.com /local/social-issues/were-human-beings-the-homeless-woman-yelled -acknowledge-us-then-people-did-in-a-way-she-didnt-expect/2019 /03/28/64131000-50b5-11e9-8d28-f5149e5a2fda_story.html.

9. Michel, *Teach Us to Want*, 198.

10. Scott Cairnes, *The End of Suffering: Finding Purpose in Pain* (Brewster, MA: Paraclete, 2009), 13.

Chapter 6: What's Yours, and Mine, to Do

1. Gordon MacDonald, *Secrets of the Generous Life: Reflections to Awaken the Spirit and Enrich the Soul* (Carol Stream, II: Tyndale House, 2002), 111.

2. www.worldhunger.org.

3. Water for Life, November 24, 2014.

4. Jordan Wilkerson, "Future Widespread Water Shortage Likely in U.S.," Harvard University, March 20, 2019, http://sitn.hms.harvard.edu/flash /2019/widespread-water-shortage-likely-in-u-s-caused-by-population -growth-and-climate-change/.

5. Annea Harstedt, "Here's Why More Americans Are Struggling with Water Scarcity," Metro.us, October 25, 2018, https://www.metro.us /news/water-scarcity-in-united-states.

6. Neil Howe, "Millennials and the Loneliness Epidemic," *Forbes*, May 3, 2019, https://www.forbes.com/sites/neilhowe/2019/05/03/millennials -and-the-loneliness-epidemic/#1bd36b507676.

7. Ibid.

8. Hara Estroff Marano, "The Dangers of Loneliness," *Psychology Today*, July 1, 2003, https://www.psychologytoday.com/us/articles/200307 /the-dangers-loneliness.

9. "State of Homelessness," National Alliance to End Homelessness, n.d., https://endhomelessness.org/homelessness-in-america/homelessness -statistics/state-of-homelessness-report/.

10. "World Prison Populations," BBC News, n.d., http://news.bbc.co.uk/2 /shared/spl/hi/uk/06/prisons/html/nn2page1.stm.

11. Bryan Stevenson, *Just Mercy: A Story of Justice and Redemption* (New York: Spiegel and Grau, 2014), 15.

12. Ibid.

13. Heart Gallery Colorado, https://www.coheartgallery.org/.

14. Jennifer Brown, "Breakdown: Mental Health in Colorado," *Denver Post*, n.d., https://extras.denverpost.com/mentalillness/index.html.

15. Proverbs 15:33 (MSG).

16. Walter Brueggemann, *The Prophetic Imagination* (Minneapolis: Augsburg Fortress, 2001), xiv.

17. A. W. Tozer, *The Wisdom of God: Letting His Truth and Goodness Direct Your Steps* (Minneapolis: Bethany House 2017), 91.

18. Archimandrite Sergius (Bowyer), *Acquiring the Mind of Christ: Embracing the Vision of the Orthodox Church* (Waymart, PA: St. Tikhon's Monastery Press, 2015), 18.

19. Alec Penix, *Seven Sundays: A Faith, Fitness, and Food Plan for Lasting Spiritual and Physical Change* (Brentwood, TN: Howard, 2018), 63.

20. Andy Crouch, *Playing God: Redeeming the Gift of Power* (Downers Grove, IL: InterVarsity, 2013), 13.

PART TWO: YOUR MONEY

Chapter 7: When Mission and Money Collide

1. Margot Starbuck, *Small Things with Great Love: Adventures in Loving Your Neighbor* (Downers Grove, IL: InterVarsity, 2011), 15.
2. Randy Alcorn, *The Treasure Principle: Unlocking the Secret of Joyful Giving* (Colorado Springs, CO: Multnomah, 2001), 72.
3. Mike Yankoski, *Under the Overpass: A Journey of Faith on the Streets of America* (Colorado Springs, CO: Multnomah, 2005), 15.
4. Ibid., 46.
5. Alcorn, *The Treasure Principle*, 75.
6. Scott Cairns, *End of Suffering: Finding Purpose in Pain* (Brewster, MA: Paraclete Press, 2009).
7. Raghuram Rajan, *The Third Pillar: How Markets and the State Leave the Community Behind* (London: Penguin Press, 2019), xi.
8. Charles Dickens, *A Christmas Carol*, (London: Global Classics, 2020), 8.
9. Jim Cymbala, *The Life God Blesses: The Secret of Enjoying God's Favor* (Grand Rapids, MI: Zondervan, 2001), 11.
10. Lance Hernandez, "I-70 Crash Victim Praises Good Samaritans, Says She's 'Lucky to Be Alive,'" Denver Channel.com, April 26, 2019 (updated April 27, 2019), https://www.thedenverchannel.com/news/local-news/i-70-crash-victim-praises-good-samaritans-says-shes-lucky-to-be-alive.
11. Christy Steadman, "I-70 Crash Was 'Like a Scene out of a Movie,'" *Lakewood Sentinel*, April 26, 2019, https://lakewoodsentinel.com/stories/i-70-crash-was-like-a-scene-out-of-a-movie,279861.
12. Richard J. Foster, *Freedom of Simplicity: Finding Harmony in a Complex World* (New York: HarperCollins, 1981), 3.
13. Teresa Ambord, "Miscellaneous Information About Your Money," Senior Voice, July 1, 2014, https://www.seniorvoicealaska.com/story/2014/07/01/finance-and-legal/miscellaneous-information-about-your-money/500.html. For more on money types, check out Dr. Kenneth Doyle's book, *The Social Meanings of Money and Property: In Search of a Talisman* (Thousand Oaks, CA: Sage Publications, 1999).
14. Erik Blakemore, "Why Czar Nicholas II and the Romanovs were Mur-

dered," March 29, 2019, accessed 3/22/20. https://www.history.com /news/romanov-family-murder-execution-reasons.

Chapter 8: The Beauty of a Boring Budget

1. Sandra Woien, "The $70 Billion Americans Spend on Pets Could Do More Good," Salon, October 16, 2018, https://www.salon.com/2018 /10/15/the-70-billions-americans-spend-on-pets-could-do-more-good _partner/.
2. Brett Graff, *Not Buying It: Stop Overspending and Start Raising Happier, Healthier, More Successful Kids* (Berkeley, CA: Seal, 2016), 6.
3. Ibid., 15.
4. "Using Money You Haven't Earned to Buy Things You Don't Need to Impress People You Don't Like," *Quote Investigator*, n.d., https://quoteinves tigator.com/2016/04/21/impress/.
5. Jimmy Carter, "Energy and the National Goals—A Crisis in Confidence" (delivered July 15, 1979), American Rhetoric, n.d., https://www.american rhetoric.com/speeches/jimmycartercrisisofconfidence.htm.
6. Jayson D. Bradley, "Church Giving Statistics, 2019 Edition," *Pushpay*, July 18, 2018, https://pushpay.com/blog/church-giving-statistics/.
7. Abigail Hess, "Here's Why Lottery Winners Go Broke," Make It, August 25, 2017, https://www.cnbc.com/2017/08/25/heres-why-lottery-winners -go-broke.html.
8. Richard Foster, *Freedom of Simplicity: Finding Harmony in a Complex World* (New York: HarperCollins 1981), 17.
9. Steve Fiorillo, "What Is the Average Income in the U.S.?," *TheStreet*, February 3, 2019 (updated February 11, 2020), https://www.thestreet.com /personal-finance/average-income-in-us-14852178.
10. Ann Wilson, *The Wealth Chef: Recipes to Make Your Money Work Hard, So You Don't Have To* (Carlsbad, CA: Hay House, 2014), 8.
11. Melissa, Lambarena, "What Is a Good APR for a Credit Card?," *NerdWallet*, January 30, 2020, https://www.nerdwallet.com/blog/credit-cards /what-is-a-good-apr-for-a-credit-card/.
12. Emmie Martin, "The Government Shutdown Spotlights a Bigger Issue: 78% of U.S. Workers Live Paycheck to Paycheck," Make It, January 9, 2019 (updated January 10, 2019), https://www.cnbc.com/2019/01/09/shutdown -highlights-that-4-in-5-us-workers-live-paycheck-to-paycheck.html.